Cooking with MARILYN

Cooking with MARILYN

By Marilyn Harris

PELICAN PUBLISHING COMPANY
Gretna 1995

First published by Paxton Press, 1988
Published by arrangement with the author by
   Pelican Publishing Company, Inc., 1995
First Pelican edition, January 1995

The word "Pelican" and the depiction of a pelican are trademarks
of Pelican Publishing Company, Inc.,
and are registered in the U.S. Patent and Trademark Office.

Library of Congress Cataloging-in-Publication Data

Harris, Marilyn M. (Marilyn Marion)
    Cooking with Marilyn / by Marilyn Harris. — 1st Pelican ed.
        p.   cm.
    Includes index.
    ISBN 1-56554-075-1
    1. Cookery, American. 2. Cookery, American—Southern style.
I. Title.
TX715.H2998 1995
641.5973—dc20   94-15962
                                                                       CIP

Manufactured in the United States of America

Published by Pelican Publishing Company, Inc.
1101 Monroe Street, Gretna, Louisiana 70053

Contents

Foreword 7

Acknowledgments.................................9

Bountiful Breakfasts 13

Buffet Brunch..21

Be a Guest at Your Own Party 31

Fun and Fancy Menus............................69

Light and Lovely....................................99

Southern Comfort Suppers....................113

Dinner in a Dish 131

One-Fork Buffets....................................147

Make-Ahead Meals 161

Students' Favorites 189

Marilyn's Favorites................................219

Index..249

Foreword

Every circle of friends has one or two good cooks. You know, the ones who get the calls for help in the kitchen.

How fortunate that the people of Greater Cincinnati have Marilyn Harris with her cooking talents, her cooking classes, her newspaper column, and her regular radio show on WCKY. To all of Cincinnati, she is that special friend who knows cooking. You can call her during her broadcasts, ask questions, and get answers on the spot. But what of people outside the Cincinnati area? This book is especially for them.

Marilyn Harris is one of many cooks I know. What makes her unique is that she has you in for dinner. And she does it so effortlessly . . . even after working all day.

I'm another of Marilyn's many fans who felt this book just had to be written. And I guarantee you can trust her recipes.

Her talent as a cooking teacher comes across in this book. It's full of tips and ideas for simplifying, varying, or otherwise altering many of the recipes—like her advice about not washing berries until just before serving . . . and wash them in white wine to enhance the flavor. Her stuffed mushrooms are anything but a cliché; she uses pecans and tender pork!

Marilyn stresses the importance of breakfast, reminding us that it's the meal we run on all day long. While the recipe selections in this book take you all over the culinary map, her brunch—today's popular mode of entertaining—has a decidedly Southern touch. Many of her recipes reflect her Southern roots: Piquant Pecans, Angel Biscuits, Spicy Sweet-Potato Petite Pancakes, French-Fried Sweet Potatoes, Golden Peach Strudel, Praline Cheesecake Squares, Zesty Red Beans and Rice, Shrimp and Chicken Creole Supreme. I salivate!

I even note an idea from my youth in New England—grilling fish with a light coating of mayo—as with her Salad Niçoise with Fresh Tuna Filet. And there are lots of one-dish and make-ahead meals.

As you go through this book, pay special note to the "steaming spoon" symbols. They flag tips and ideas as only Marilyn can offer them . . . from her years of cooking, teaching, and interchanges with her audiences. They make this more than a cookbook. They make it an annotated text, excellent for beginners and seasoned cooks alike.

In her teaching, Marilyn likes to tell her students that cooking is a creative art that is fun to do. This book proves it.

CORNELIUS O'DONNELL

Acknowledgments

My thanks to:

My loving, patient, and persuasive husband, who gave me the courage to write a cookbook and guided me through every step. My students, who over the years have encouraged me and cheered me on, with extra thanks to those who contributed recipes to this book. Gene Archbold, my ferocious friend, for all of the effort and energy expended in making this book a reality. Cynthia Hardie for her professional and inspirational guidance. Carol Lloyd and Jay Bachemin for their creative contributions. Bert Greene, whose friendship was an inspiration and whose spirit is an enduring legacy. Phillip Stephen Schulz for his help and encouragement. My friends and colleagues—including Jan Mikelson—from WCKY and WCET. With love and appreciation to the following friends who helped in more ways than they can imagine: Mary Sue Morris, John Chesteen, Neal O'Donnell, Bette Sherman, Marj and Bob Valvano, Lee Harper, Sharon Shipley, Carmen Jones, Amy Hoffman, Jill Bentgen, Yen Hsieh, Glenn Rinksy, Carol and Rex Stockwell, Carol Fuerst, Nancy and John Whitehurst, Jane Miller, Dorothy Wartenberg . . . and others, many of whom are named in this book.

This book is dedicated to the memory of Rose Marie Palazzolo.

Cooking with MARILYN

Bountiful Breakfasts

Pecan Bran Muffins

Individual Pan Omelet
with Mushroom and Smoked
Turkey Filling

**Ham and Eggs in Easy
Pastry Cups**

Breakfast Burritos

Breakfast Muffins Deluxe

Pecan-Glazed Bacon

Perhaps because of my Southern background, breakfasts are central to my notion of good food. In the rural South where I grew up, people put away a substantial morning meal before proceeding to do serious hard work. They needed that kind of start to their day.

Beyond its importance from a nutritional standpoint, however, breakfast can be a wonderful social occasion. It's those bountiful breakfasts that I remember . . . the meals, usually on the weekends, when the entire family could be together. Whether outside on the terrace or in the dining room with the morning sun streaming through the lace curtains, they were fun and they were filled with good flavors. They were breakfasts with a capital *B*.

Some of my recipes in this chapter are drawn from those I have inherited from my mother and grandmothers. I have made very definite changes in those recipes, however. I no longer use lard in biscuits and some dishes have been made lighter.

Upon hearing that I was writing a cookbook, one of my students exclaimed, "I certainly hope you're going to include Mexican." I had to laugh, considering that although I have no Spanish blood or formal training in Mexican cooking, my palate certainly has a decided affinity for Mexican food. It was hard to come by authentic Mexican food when I first moved to the Cincinnati area in the 1970s, and I quickly determined that if I was to have any kind of real Mexican food, I'd have to cook it myself. Back then, it was a challenge just to assemble all the needed ingredients. Little by little, what I had taught myself about Mexican cooking began to seep into my classes. I've been in the terrifying position of teaching a Mexican cooking class to my friend Pedro Fontova, who produces fine Mexican food in our area. I was tremendously flattered when he told me after one such class that it was the best food he'd had since sitting in his mama's kitchen. Anyway, that may or may not explain the presence of breakfast burritos in this chapter.

Pecan Bran Muffins

To toast pecans for the muffins: spread the pecans in a baking pan and place in a pre-heated 375-degree oven for 6-8 minutes, depending on how coarsely they are chopped. Let cool.

Bran muffins were always a favorite at our house. Note that these contain no raisins; the true nutty flavor of the bran comes through better without them. Pecans, my favorite nut, enhance the sweet and elegant taste. The recipe calls for allspice, which lends a more subtle hint than the traditional cinnamon. Not too sweet, the muffins are great au naturel, or with fresh blackberry or raspberry jam.

2 cups natural wheat bran
1¾ cups self-rising flour
1½ tsp. baking soda
½ tsp. salt
1 tsp. allspice
⅓ cup vegetable oil
1 cup dark brown sugar
1½ cups plain yogurt*
2 large eggs
1 cup coarsely chopped toasted pecans

- In food processor with steel blade, process together the bran, flour, baking soda, salt, and allspice. Process by pulsing on and off 5 or 6 times. Remove and set aside in a mixing bowl.
- Put the oil, sugar, yogurt, and eggs in the processor bowl. Process just to blend.
- Pour over dry ingredients and add the pecans. Stir with a few quick stirs just to blend.
- Spoon into a generously greased muffin pan.
- Bake in a preheated 400-degree oven for 20-25 minutes or till golden brown. Remove from pan and cool on racks.
- Serve warm or room temperature with butter and jam.
- Makes about 18 regular-sized muffins.

This recipe may also be mixed completely by hand or made in the mixer. I simply find the food processor the most convenient. However, as with *all* muffins, it is important to complete the process of mixing together the liquid and dry ingredients by hand with a gentle folding motion. For a light, properly textured muffin, it is very important not to overmix.

*Sour cream may be substituted for the yogurt.

Individual Pan Omelet
with Mushroom and Smoked Turkey Filling

This omelet is based on the way I was originally taught to make an omelet while learning French cooking in New Orleans. For the calorie or cholesterol conscious, the omelet can be made with only one egg. The mushroom and smoked turkey filling is delicious and not terribly sinful. Well-drained, crisp bacon that has been coarsely crumbled can be added or used in lieu of the turkey.

Filling

3 large mushrooms
1 tbsp. butter or margarine
2 tbsp. chopped onion
Salt and pepper, to taste
1 tbsp. chopped parsley
3 oz. smoked turkey, cut into small strips

- Clean and trim the mushrooms. Slice thinly.
- Melt the butter in a small skillet over high heat. Add the onion and cook for 1-2 minutes, stirring constantly.
- Add the mushrooms and sauté, stirring, for 2-3 minutes over high heat.
- Season lightly with salt and pepper and add the chopped parsley. Reserve the turkey (see below).

Omelet

1 or 2 large eggs
Dash salt, to taste
Freshly ground black pepper, to taste
1 tbsp. butter or margarine
Extra chopped parsley

- Using a table fork, beat together the eggs, salt, and pepper just until frothy.
- Melt butter over medium-high heat in a small (7-8 inches), well-seasoned omelet pan.
- The butter will foam as it melts. When the bubbles subside, and before it has a chance to turn brown, quickly pour in the egg mixture. Stir rapidly with the tines of the fork at right angles to the

How to season an omelet pan: wash the new pan in warm, sudsy water, rinse, and dry well. Pour approximately one-half inch of vegetable oil in the pan and brush oil onto the sides. Place over medium heat and heat until the oil is very hot. Do not allow to smoke. (Should not go above 400 degrees.) Remove from heat and let sit until oil reaches room temperature. Pour out oil. Wipe out pan with a paper towel. It is ready to make an omelet. Try not to scrub the inside with detergent. Use a small handful of table salt to clean out any stubborn foods, like cheese, and just rinse quickly with clear water. You know that your pan is properly seasoned if the omelet moves about readily when the pan is gently rotated.

Mushrooms should always be sautéed at a high temperature. Dry them well before adding them to the skillet. For whole caps, do not overcrowd the skillet, so that they do not touch and can be rolled around to lightly brown on all sides. Initially the mushrooms will absorb the fat in the pan. When the fat is released, it is a sign that they are done. If cooked much beyond this point, they release their own juices and become overcooked and less tasty.

pan, for about 10 stirs. Shake the pan, moving the egg mixture back and forth until mixture is puffy and set on the bottom.

- Quickly spoon in the mushroom mixture across the middle, at right angles to the pan handle. Sprinkle the turkey over the mixture.
- Fold one side of the egg mixture over the filling.
- With a firm grip on the handle, slide the omelet forward and out of the pan directly onto the warmed serving plate, allowing the other side to fold under the filling so that the omelet is then folded into thirds.
- Sprinkle with extra chopped parsley and serve immediately.

How to clean mushrooms: if you have purchased mushrooms with very little dirt on them, it is probably possible to get them clean by scrubbing lightly with a damp paper towel. Or, your favorite kitchen-gadget store will provide you with a brush designed for the purpose of cleaning mushrooms without exposing them to a lot of water. These are both ideal methods because mushrooms will absorb water readily, making them less firm when cooked. (Also difficult to brown when they are being sautéed.) If, however, the mushrooms are quite dirty with a lot of soil packed around the stem, I find that the best method is to hold them, one at a time, under a running stream of lukewarm water. Use your fingertips as a "sponge" to clean thoroughly. Never soak in water. Always trim off the end of the stem after washing so that it is less absorbent. Always allow mushrooms to dry completely before cooking. If they are cleaned longer than a few minutes before they are to be cooked, acidulate them to prevent darkening by tossing lightly in lemon or lime juice.

Ham and Eggs in Easy Pastry Cups

Several of my students have told me that Ham and Eggs in Easy Pastry Cups have become a family favorite for weekend breakfasts. It is one of those recipes that looks as if it requires much more effort than is actually necessary. Add some fresh fruit and you've got all you need for an attractive and tasty meal.

Using the phyllo pastry from the freezer at the grocery store is the secret to this elegant but easy breakfast made in a muffin tin. Thaw the frozen package of phyllo overnight in the refrigerator. Remove the number of leaves needed, wrap any remaining pastry tightly in plastic, and refreeze for later use.

> **6 sheets phyllo pastry**
> **1 stick unsalted butter or margarine, melted**
> **6 oz. grated Swiss or Cheddar cheese**
> **4 oz. lean cooked ham, cut into a small dice**
> **6 large eggs**
> **Freshly ground pepper and salt, to taste**
> **Parsley sprigs (optional)**

- Using a soft-bristle pastry brush, brush a sheet of phyllo with some of the melted butter or margarine.
- Place a second sheet on top and smooth it with your hands.
- Repeat until you have a stack of all six sheets. Brush the top with butter.
- Place on a cutting board. Using a sharp knife, cut the stacked sheet into 6 squares (approximately 5 inches).
- Lightly brush butter into a muffin tin with 6 cups.
- Push the squares into the muffin cups, buttered side up. Mold them to fit smoothly into the cups with the corners sticking up around the edge.
- Distribute the cheese evenly in the bottom of the pastry cups.
- Sprinkle the ham over the cheese.
- Carefully break an egg into each cup.
- Season with freshly ground pepper and salt.
- Place in the center of a preheated 350-degree oven.
- Bake for 12 minutes for soft eggs and 15 minutes for hard eggs.
- Serve hot. Top each with a small sprig of parsley.
- Makes 6.

Notes: crisp bacon may be substituted for the ham. Allow one strip of crumbled bacon for each cup. For a simpler dish, the cheese can be omitted.

For a reduced-fat phyllo recipe, spray the pastry with an olive-oil spray.

Breakfast Burritos

The thin flour tortilla is a delightful bread, perfect for wrapping up every type of filling. So why not wrap up a breakfast mixture? This recipe can be varied for eating later in the day by adding some spicy tomato salsa along with the dollop of sour cream.

1 stick unsalted butter
1 medium onion, chopped
16 large eggs
¼ cup milk
1½ tsp. salt
¼ tsp. hot pepper sauce
8 large flour tortillas
3 cups (¾ lb.) shredded mild Cheddar cheese
½ cup thinly sliced scallions
Sour cream
Chopped cilantro

- Melt the butter in a large, heavy skillet. Sauté the chopped onion for 3-4 minutes, stirring.
- Whisk together the eggs, milk, salt, and hot pepper sauce. Pour into skillet and scramble to a soft set.
- Spoon egg filling into center of the tortillas. Sprinkle with cheese and scallions and roll up "burrito style."
- Place in a lightly greased baking dish. Cover dish with heavy foil and place in a 350-degree oven for about 15 minutes.
- Serve with sour cream spooned over the top. Sprinkle with chopped cilantro.
- Serve immediately with a fresh fruit garnish.
- Serves 8.

Notes: for a "burrito-style" fold, leave a margin of 2 inches on the side edges when the egg mixture is spooned into the burrito. Fold the sides over the filling, roll, and place seam side down into the lightly greased baking dish.

The burritos may be made as far ahead as the night before and refrigerated. The heating time will increase by at least 10 minutes, depending on how cold they are when placed in the oven.

My first choices for a fruit garnish are fresh pineapple spears, sliced papaya or mango, and sliced avocado.

Breakfast Muffins Deluxe

4 large English muffins, split, buttered, and toasted
1 recipe Pecan-Glazed Bacon (recipe follows)
8 slices sharp Cheddar cheese

• Cover toasted sides of muffins with bacon slices. Top with cheese.
• At serving time, broil just to heat and melt cheese.
• Serves 8.

Pecan-Glazed Bacon

1 lb. bacon
¼ cup brown sugar
1 tsp. flour
⅓ cup finely chopped pecans

• Arrange bacon on a rack over a baking pan.
• Stir together sugar, flour, and nuts. Sprinkle evenly over bacon.
• Bake in a 350-degree oven until crisp—about 25 minutes.
• Drain on paper towels.

Buffet Brunch

My Favorite Country Ham

Angel Biscuits or Deep South Sticky Biscuits

Homemade Spicy Sausage

Baked Cheese Grits

Melon-Berry Compote or Orange-Pineapple Compote

Mimosas or Strawberry Mimosas

Summer Egg Mousse

Cinnamon Coffee

In many ways brunch has replaced the more formal dinner party with damask napkins and candlelight. My classes on this more casual, relaxed meal have always filled very quickly.

My definition of a good brunch is one in which most of the work can be done ahead of time. The host and/or hostess can then set out the food, much of which may be served at room temperature, and let the guests serve themselves.

Certainly a brunch should be tasty, but it should also be fairly hearty, as most people will not have eaten anything substantial beforehand. Brunch then becomes a chance to let your guests have a real splurge, and you can assure them they have the rest of the day to work it off.

The following is my favorite brunch menu. It reflects, as much of my food does, Southern overtones. Country ham has been regaining popularity and is becoming easier to find throughout the country. Its preparation is time consuming, requiring that you start in the middle of the week for a Sunday brunch, but the flavor is well worth the effort. This particular recipe adapts a technique I learned from the late Bert Greene, one of my all-time favorite cooks. We taught a class together at the Cincinnati Playhouse in the Park years ago, and he used this flavorful glaze on a fully cooked ham. I think you'll love the results with a cured country ham.

Baked cheese grits may help some folks who live outside of the South overcome their prejudice against grits. They usually have the mistaken conception of grits as some pasty concoction that coagulates on the plate and stares back at them. Not so with this recipe, which assumes a very elegant, soufflé-like consistency.

For the fruit dish, which is essential for rounding out the brunch meal and adding lovely color to the buffet, the season will dictate which recipe to use. In spring and summer, the Melon-Berry Compote is my favorite, while the Orange-Pineapple Compote is the choice for winter.

The accompanying drink should be elegant and refreshing. Your choice also depends on the season, with the Strawberry Mimosa an excellent summer drink and the plain Mimosa the winter choice.

Orange juice is best when freshly squeezed. Many grocery stores have it in bottles now should you not wish to squeeze the oranges yourself.

My Favorite Country Ham

1 10-12-lb. dry cured whole ham
Whole cloves
¾ cup apricot preserves
4 tbsp. good spicy Dijon mustard
Splash of bourbon whiskey
1 cup light brown sugar

- Scrub the outside of the ham with a vegetable brush to remove any mold (a normal occurrence). Rinse well with lukewarm water and dry with paper towels.
- Place in a large pot. Cover with cold water and let sit overnight to soak. (The soaking process is to remove the excessive salt, which is necessary in the curing process. Depending on the saltiness you desire, you may want to change the water after the first 24 hours and repeat for a second day.)
- Pour clean water into the pot, bring to a boil, partially cover, and simmer 25-30 minutes per pound—or until tender when pierced with a fork. Let cool in the water.
- Remove and cut away as much of the outside fat as possible, leaving a smooth and attractive outside surface.
- Using a sharp knife, score the ham by first making diagonal slices, cutting in about ⅛ inch, crosswise and then repeating lengthwise. (This will create diamond shapes that are about 1 inch in size.) Stud each corner of the "diamonds" with a whole clove.
- Place the ham on a sturdy rack in a shallow baking pan.
- Stir together the preserves, mustard, and bourbon. Spread evenly over the entire surface of the ham. Pat the brown sugar over the preserve mixture, making sure it adheres well.
- Pour 1 cup of water in the baking pan under the rack.
- Bake the ham in the center of a 300-degree oven for 2 hours. Let sit for 20 minutes before slicing.
- Slice small slices on the diagonal against the bone. A 10-pound ham will easily serve 24 people for a brunch.

Notes: when you have finished eating the ham, save the bone for Zesty Red Beans and Rice (see index) or bean soup.

A large roaster or a stockpot will be needed to boil this whole ham. If finding one large enough is a problem in your kitchen, ask your butcher to saw off the shank bone to make it smaller.

Angel Biscuits

Angel biscuits are a new slant on an old tradition. So called because they are fluffy and angelically light, they are even better if the dough is made the night before and covered tightly with a double layer of plastic wrap. In the morning, after you cut them out, they can sit for another hour or so before you pop them in the oven. They are a perfect brunch item, not requiring you to be messing about with flour as your guests arrive.

> **6 cups self-rising flour**
> **⅓ cup sugar**
> **¼ tsp. salt**
> **1 tsp. baking soda**
> **1 stick (4 oz.) unsalted butter**
> **½ cup vegetable shortening**
> **2 pkg. dry yeast**
> **¼ cup warm (110 degrees) water**
> **2 cups buttermilk**

- Sift together the flour, sugar, salt, and soda.
- Place in large bowl and cut in the butter and shortening until mixture resembles coarse meal.
- Dissolve the yeast in the water.
- Add yeast mixture and buttermilk. Mix.
- Turn out onto a floured board.
- Knead for 3-4 minutes, kneading in more flour if necessary to make a smooth dough.
- Roll out to ¾-inch thickness and cut with biscuit cutter.
- Place on an ungreased baking sheet. Allow to sit at room temperature for 30 minutes.
- Bake in a preheated 450-degree oven for 12-15 minutes.
- Makes about 32 medium biscuits.

Note: these biscuits may be made in a food processor using the steel blade.

Deep South Sticky Biscuits

½ recipe Angel Biscuits
1 cup light brown sugar
1 tsp. cinnamon
1 stick + 2 tbsp. butter (10 tbsp.), melted
1 cup finely chopped pecans

- Make biscuits according to Angel Biscuit recipe, but do not bake.
- Stir together the sugar and cinnamon to mix well.
- Spread butter evenly in the bottom of two 9-inch round cake pans.
- Sprinkle over the sugar-cinnamon mixture evenly. Sprinkle in the pecans.
- Place the raw biscuits directly over the topping.
- Bake in the center of a preheated 450-degree oven for 12-15 minutes or until golden brown on top. Remove from pans immediately. Serve warm.

Note: this recipe may be made ahead and baked just before serving. Cover the pans well and refrigerate. Bake directly from the refrigerator. Baking time may increase by 3-4 minutes.

When rolling out biscuits, use just enough flour to prevent the biscuit dough from sticking to the board. Try not to roll the dough out more than twice. Too much manipulation of the dough will cause the biscuits to be tough. By cutting square biscuits, you can cut all of the dough in one rolling.

Homemade Spicy Sausage

1½ lb. lean pork
½ lb. pork fat
2 tsp. dried sage
½-1 tsp. crushed red pepper
Pinch thyme
1 tsp. fennel seeds (optional)
1 tbsp. salt
1 tbsp. freshly ground black pepper

- Cut pork and pork fat into 1-inch cubes. Chill for 20 minutes in freezer.
- Chop the pork and pork fat in food processor with the steel blade to make a medium-fine ground mixture.
- Remove the pork mixture from processor and toss in the seasonings until they are thoroughly mixed.

Making your own sausage allows you to use high-quality meats for good flavors, as well as to control the fat content. Please note, however, that there must be at least 20 percent fat content in any good sausage. Otherwise the cooked sausage will be dry and tough.

- Cook a small amount in a skillet to taste and correct seasonings.
- Form into patties. Chill, well covered, overnight.
- Cook in a heavy skillet or in broiler until completely done through.
- Makes about 2 pounds of sausage.
- Serves 8-10.

Baked Cheese Grits

6 cups water
1½ cups grits, uncooked
3 large eggs
2 tsp. salt
1 stick butter
2 cloves garlic, minced
1 tsp. paprika
¼ tsp. hot pepper sauce, or to taste
1 lb. sharp Cheddar cheese, shredded

- Bring water to boil in a large saucepan.
- Stir in grits. Cook, stirring until thickened.
- Beat the eggs with the salt just until fluffy.
- Stir a bit of the hot grits into the eggs and mix the egg mixture into the grits.
- Cut the butter into pieces and add to grits.
- Stir in the garlic, paprika, hot pepper sauce, and ¾ of the cheese.
- Pour into a well-buttered 2-quart casserole and top with remaining cheese.
- Bake in a preheated 350-degree oven for 50 minutes to 1 hour.
- Serve hot.
- Serves 10-12.

Notes: this recipe may be made ahead and baked just before serving. Cover the pan well and refrigerate. Bake directly from the refrigerator, adding 10-15 minutes to the baking time.

Or, the whole dish may be baked the night before and rewarmed in a 325-degree oven or in the microwave oven.

Ordinary white grits are fine to use for Cheese Grits. Use the *quick* version, but never the *instant* type. For a special grits dish, look for yellow grits in a health-food store or in the health-food section of the grocery store. They have a milder taste and a pretty yellow color. Serve them in the traditional style with salt, pepper, and butter as well as for "Cheese Grits."

Melon-Berry Compote

1 ripe cantaloupe
1 pt. fresh blueberries, washed and drained
½ cup heavy cream
½ cup sour cream
2 tsp. honey
Sliced fresh lime
Fresh mint sprigs

- Peel cantaloupe and cut into wide wedges.
- Stir together gently the well-drained berries with the two creams and honey.
- Spoon into the cantaloupe wedges at serving time.
- Garnish with lime and fresh mint sprigs.
- Serves 6-8.

Orange-Pineapple Compote

4 large navel oranges
1 fresh pineapple
1 cup shredded coconut
¼ cup orange liqueur
Mint leaves (optional)

- Peel the oranges, removing all pith.
- Slice crosswise into thin slices.
- Cut the pineapple into small wedges. Stir together with oranges and coconut.
- At serving time pour over the orange liqueur.
- Garnish with mint leaves, if desired.

To remove both pith and peel from an orange: use a knife with a thin, flexible blade. Place the orange on a cutting board with the stem end up. Hold firmly with one hand and start the knife at the stem end; curve downward and under the orange to the opposite end, removing a curved strip of peel that includes the pith. Repeat, revolving the orange to slice off all peel. Slice, crosswise, into thin attractive slices.

Mimosas

2 cups orange juice, chilled
1 bottle chilled champagne

- Pour champagne glasses ⅓ full of orange juice.
- Fill with champagne.

Strawberry Mimosas

2 tbsp. confectioners' sugar
1 pt. strawberries, washed, hulled, and sliced
1 qt. orange juice, chilled
1 bottle chilled champagne

- Add the sugar to the sliced strawberries and let marinate for at least an hour.
- Remove half of the strawberries and crush; add back and stir into sliced strawberries.
- At serving time, put a large spoonful of the strawberries into a wine or champagne glass. Pour the glass half-full with orange juice. Fill with champagne. Serve immediately.
- Serves 8-10.

  Note: fresh orange juice tastes best in both of these recipes.

Store all berries in the refrigerator unwashed. Wash quickly in lukewarm water shortly before serving. Drain well.

To avoid diluting their fresh flavor, wash raspberries and strawberries in wine (red or white). Place a pint of berries in a mixing bowl. Pour over a cup of inexpensive table wine. Gently toss the berries with your fingertips. Remove berries to a colander to drain. Discard the wine.

Summer Egg Mousse

2 cups Béchamel Sauce (see below)
12 hard-cooked eggs
1¼ cups mayonnaise (regular or reduced fat)
2 envelopes unflavored gelatin
½ cup chicken stock
½ cup dry white wine
¼ tsp. hot pepper sauce
½ tsp. Worcestershire sauce
1 tsp. salt, or to taste
1 cup heavy cream, whipped
Parsley sprigs, for garnish

- Prepare Béchamel Sauce and cover with parchment paper to prevent a skin from forming on top; let cool.
- Chop eggs in food processor and stir into mayonnaise.
- Soften gelatin in stock, then heat until gelatin is dissolved. Stir in wine and fold into egg mixture along with cooled Béchamel.
- Season with hot pepper sauce, Worcestershire, and salt.
- Fold in whipped cream.
- Turn into an oiled springform pan and chill overnight or until set.
- Unmold and garnish with parsley sprigs.
- Serve with thin slices of ham rolled around blanched and chilled tender fresh asparagus spears.

Béchamel Sauce

2 cups milk
Sprig of fresh thyme
1 bay leaf
Sprig of parsley
5 peppercorns
Small wedge of onion
4 tbsp. unsalted butter
4 tbsp. flour
½ tsp. salt
Dash hot pepper sauce

- Put milk in saucepan and add all the ingredients through the onion. Scald and let sit for 30 minutes to infuse. Strain.
- Melt butter in a heavy saucepan.
- Stir in flour and cook, stirring, for 2-3 minutes, without browning.
- Whisk in infused milk and cook, stirring, until thickened.
- Season with salt and hot pepper sauce.
- Makes 2 cups.

Cinnamon Coffee

1 tsp. cinnamon
8 cups brewed coffee
1 cup sweetened whipped cream

- Stir cinnamon into hot coffee.
- Top with cream.
- Serves 8.

Heavy cream whips best at refrigerator temperature (38-40 degrees). For best results, use a chilled bowl and chilled mixer beaters. Most "ultrahomogenized" heavy creams will not whip into a fluffy mixture after they have been frozen.

For great-tasting coffee: always start with a clean pot. To extract the maximum flavor from the ground coffee without extracting the bitter oils, the water should be just under the boiling point, between 200 and 210 degrees. Aroma is an important part of the perfect cup of coffee. For the fullest and richest flavor, serve freshly brewed coffee as soon as possible after brewing. When making the first coffee in the morning, let the cold tap water run for a few seconds before drawing the coffee water. Fresh water makes fresher-tasting coffee.

Be a Guest at Your Own Party

Chicken Liver Pâté Spread

Marilyn's Holiday Pâté

Cheesy Tostada Appetizers
Easy Refried Beans
Marilyn's Salsa
and Guacamolé

Caponata Deluxe

Herbed Pita Triangles

Cocktail Pizzas
Easy Pizza Sauce

Baked Seafood Cakettes
with Zesty Tartar Sauce

Bleu Cheesecake

Vegetable Basket with
Three Dipping Sauces:
Chili Pepper Dipping Sauce
Watercress Dipping Sauce
Fresh Herb Dipping Sauce

Pecan Chicken Appetizers
with Chutney Mayonnaise

Piquant Pecans

Breaded Mushrooms
with Bavarian Tartar Sauce

Chilled Peppered
Tenderloin
with Green Peppercorn Sauce

Carmen's Canapé Bread

Shrimp Profiteroles

I'm writing this chapter to convince you that a successful cocktail party need not be so fancy and complicated that you cannot enjoy it along with your guests. Many people wouldn't think of giving any sort of cocktail party without hiring a caterer. I think you should be able to enjoy the planning of the party and the preparation of the food as well as the party itself. You don't have to buy out an entire watercress farm or make forty perfect tomato roses. Simply provide food that is fresh, tasty, and attractive. Then relax and enjoy it. Work at being a guest at your own party. If you designate someone else to help serve and clean up and you spend your energy on cooking, you'll find it can be a very creative and rewarding experience. To keep from becoming a hysterical host or hostess, make it a rule that if you're entertaining more than eight people, you should have help. It may just mean enlisting the services of a friend, or employing a neighborhood teen-ager looking to make a few dollars. Or, you may need to hire a professional from an agency that specializes in catering parties. This person will do all of the passing of food if you are having that type of cocktail party. He or she also replenishes the food on the table and, perhaps most importantly, keeps the kitchen clean and helps with the cleanup after the party is over. All of this allows you to relax during the entire party and enjoy socializing with your guests. That, after all, is why we have parties.

Cocktail parties of late rely less on mixed drinks and more on wine and champagne, or even wine punches. But, should you choose to have an open bar, you may also want to consider hiring a bartender. The party will run much more smoothly. Don't feel that you have to offer the ingredients for every drink in the "Bartender's Guide Book." Guests understand that they may choose from whatever selection you offer. Do remember to have some sort of non-alcoholic beverage for those who do not want wine or a mixed drink.

No matter what approach you choose for serving your party

food, you can make your party unique with the right sort of planning and by cooking all of the food ahead.

Whether you are giving an elegant and formal cocktail party with passers and bartenders and a beautifully garnished table, or whether you're simply putting out a rather hearty group of foods for a small group of good friends to graze their way through a relaxed evening, remember Marilyn's Rule No. 1: have fun! You're just hosting a party, not building the atom bomb, so relax!

Spicy Sweet-Potato Petite Pancakes

Piquant Beef Triangles

Asparagus in Phyllo with Dill-Cucumber Sauce

Pork and Pecan Stuffed Mushrooms

Savory Mushroom Tartlets with Sauce Béarnaise

Bleu Cheese-Walnut New Potatoes

Sun-Dried Tomato Spread on Zucchini Slices

Cheese-Filled Brussels Sprouts

Smoked Salmon Spread on Cucumbers

Chicken Liver Pâté Spread

I've done a lot of pâtés in the past, but this Chicken Liver Pâté is the one to which I always return. It can be made as long as three days ahead, covered, and chilled. The flavors simply improve. Set it out half an hour before the guests arrive so that it is spreadable.

1 stick + 2 tbsp. unsalted butter
¼ cup finely chopped yellow onion
1 lb. chicken livers, washed, dried, and trimmed
⅓ cup dry vermouth
½ tsp. salt, or to taste
1 tsp. Dijon mustard
¼ tsp. hot pepper sauce
2 tbsp. Cognac
Parsley or watercress, for garnish

- Melt the 2 tablespoons of butter in a non-aluminum skillet.
- Add the onion and sauté, stirring, for about 2 minutes.
- Add the livers and cook over medium heat, stirring, until all red is gone.
- Add vermouth, salt, mustard, and hot pepper sauce.
- Cover and simmer on low for 5 minutes.
- Remove cover and raise heat to medium. Cook until liquid is reduced by half.
- Cool.
- Place in a covered dish and chill for at least 2 hours.
- Soften the stick of butter. Cut into several pieces.
- Place the chilled liver mixture in the food processor.
- Add the butter and Cognac and process until smooth.
- Spoon into an attractive small crock or dish. Smooth the top.
- Cover loosely with plastic wrap and chill for several hours.
- Garnish with some sprigs of parsley or watercress to serve.
- Serve with thinly sliced party rye bread.
- Let soften at room temperature for about 30 minutes before serving so that it is a good spreading consistency.
- Makes about 2 cups.

Marilyn's Holiday Pâté

While searching through my twenty-year collection of recipe files with the purpose of choosing my favorite classic baked pâté, I kept returning to this tasty pork one with ham in the middle. I call it my "holiday pâté" because I have made it many times for my classes on holiday entertaining. I would like to point out, however, that it is tasty and appropriate any time of the year. It is even a good choice for hot-weather parties or picnics since it is served cold and can be made ahead in the evening when the kitchen is cool. The pork pâté is a traditional blend with an excellent seasoning. Though a bit time consuming, it never fails to be worth all of the effort when your guests taste it and discover that you have created it yourself. Try it with different mustards and chutneys. For the holiday party season, serve it with my Cranberry Chutney (see index).

   2½ lb. lean pork, cubed
   ½ lb. pork fat, rind removed and cubed
   ½ cup Madeira
   ½ cup heavy cream, well chilled
   2 large eggs
   ½ tsp. allspice
   1 tbsp. minced fresh gingerroot
   ½ tsp. freshly ground black pepper
   1½ tsp. salt, or to taste
   2 large cloves garlic, minced
   6 bay leaves
   ¾ lb. bacon
   ½ lb. lean smoked, cooked ham—¼ in. thick

- Put pork and pork fat in a large mixing bowl.
- Pour over the Madeira.
- Cover tightly and marinate at least 24 hours, or as long as 3 days in the refrigerator.
- In food processor with steel blade, purée the pork and salt pork, along with the Madeira, in small batches until very finely chopped.
- If the processor is a large one, return all of the pork and slowly pour in the cream with the processor running. Process until all cream is incorporated. (If processor is small, do this step in two parts.)

- Spoon the mixture into a large mixing bowl.
- Lightly beat the eggs and add.
- Stir in the allspice, gingerroot, pepper, salt, and garlic.
- Remove a spoonful and form into a patty. Fry in a small skillet, cool, and taste to check for correct seasonings. Add more salt or pepper, if needed.
- Mixture is enough to fill 2 small loaf pans (6" x 2½" x 2") or 1 pâté mold (approximately 12" x 4" x 3").
- Place 3 bay leaves an equal distance apart in bottom of the pans.
- Line each pan with the bacon, placing it crosswise and leaving ends to come up the sides of the pan.
- Spoon in enough pâté mixture to half-fill each pan.
- Cut the ham into julienne strips and place the ham, running lengthwise, on top of the pâté.
- Spoon remaining pâté mixture into each pan.
- Rap pans on counter top to pack mixture down firmly in pan.
- Bring bacon strips over top of mixture on each side and place 3 or 4 more strips lengthwise on top to cover.
- Cover and seal tightly with a triple layer of heavy-duty foil.
- Preheat oven to 325 degrees.
- Place the pâté pans in a shallow baking pan with enough hot water to come halfway up the sides of the pâté pan.
- Cook for 2 hours in the center of the oven.
- Remove.
- Remove foil and let cool for 30 minutes on a cooling rack.
- Replace foil and weight top with a foil-covered brick or something heavy enough to press down the pâté.
- Chill overnight.
- Remove from the pan.
- Cut into thin slices.
- Serve cold.
- Serves 24 as party food or first course.
- Serve with a good Dijon mustard, a mustard sauce, your favorite chutney, or Caponata Deluxe (see index).

Notes: "cornichons" are also a perfect complement to most pâtés of this type.

This pâté can be made 3 or 4 days before the party.

Cornichons are tart pickles made from tiny gherkin cucumbers. Other sour pickles may be substituted, but they are not likely to be as tasty as cornichons.

Cheesy Tostada Appetizers

Cheesy Tostadas are often my choice as the first course for a Mexican meal. Flanked by bowls of salsa and guacamolé to spoon on top, the tostadas are especially pretty and they can be completely assembled beforehand. When the flour tortilla (I prefer flour over corn for this particular recipe) is fried, it changes from a soft bread to a crisp one, somewhat resembling French pastry.

6 large flour tortillas
Vegetable oil, for frying
Easy Refried Beans (see below)
1 lb. natural Jack cheese, shredded
Marilyn's Salsa (see below)
Guacamolé (see below)

- Cut the tortillas into 6 wedges.
- Heat about 1 inch of the oil to 375 degrees in a heavy skillet.
- Fry the tortillas until crisp and golden brown.
- Drain well on soft white paper towels.
- Spread each "tostada chip" with a tablespoonful of the refried beans and place on baking sheets. Add a teaspoon of the shredded cheese on top of each chip.
- Set aside until ready to bake. (May be prepared up to this point as long as 1 hour ahead of serving time.)
- When ready to serve, bake in a preheated 425-degree oven for about 5 minutes or until heated through and cheese is melted.
- Serve hot with the salsa and guacamolé to spoon on top.
- Makes 36.

Easy Refried Beans

2 1-lb. cans pinto beans, drained (reserve liquid)
½ cup chopped yellow onion
3 tbsp. extravirgin olive oil
½ cup shredded Jack cheese
Pinch salt
½ tsp. hot pepper sauce
1 tsp. sugar

- Purée the beans in the food processor with about half of the liquid.
- In a medium-sized, heavy saucepan, sauté the onion in the oil until tender.
- Stir in the remaining ingredients and cook over low heat, stirring often, for 15 minutes.
- Makes about 4 cups.

Marilyn's Salsa

2 tbsp. extravirgin olive oil
1 cup chopped onion
2 cloves garlic, minced
4 large tomatoes, coarsely chopped
3-4 fresh jalapeño peppers, seeded and minced
3 mild green chiles (Anaheims), roasted, seeded, peeled, and chopped
3 tbsp. chopped fresh cilantro leaves
½ tsp. salt
1 tsp. sugar
2 tbsp. red wine vinegar

- Heat oil to medium in a heavy skillet and cook the onions and garlic for 2 minutes, just until the onions are translucent.
- Remove from heat and cool.
- Mix together all of the ingredients and chill for at least 4 hours before serving.
- Makes about 4 cups.

Notes: the salsa may be eaten immediately, but the flavors blend and mingle and create a much tastier salsa if the chilling time is allowed.

This amount of jalapeños makes a medium-hot salsa. If you want it to be very spicy, simply add more of the jalapeño peppers.

The jalapeño pepper is one of the spiciest of the hot chile peppers. The Serrano chile is also very piquant and may be used to add zip to the salsa. In my opinion the jalapeño is more flavorful. The seeds of all of the varieties of small, hot chile peppers are the hottest part and should be removed before the peppers are chopped. Take care when seeding these hot chile peppers. Avoid putting your hands in your eyes or mouth. People with very sensitive skin may want to use rubber gloves when seeding and chopping them. After handling, always wash your hands with plenty of soap and water.

Guacamolé

3 ripe medium avocados
⅓ cup finely chopped sweet salad onion
2 tbsp. fresh lime juice
Salt, to taste
¼-½ teaspoon hot pepper sauce
2 medium tomatoes, peeled and coarsely chopped
2 tbsp. chopped fresh cilantro

- Peel, seed, and mash avocados (reserve one of the avocado seeds).
- Stir in the remaining ingredients.
- Return the avocado seed to the mixture until ready to serve. Cover and chill.
- Makes about 2 cups.

Note: I prefer lime juice in this recipe, but when lemons are in season I substitute them.

Caponata Deluxe

Caponata Deluxe is based on a recipe I learned from a French chef in a course on "garde manger," the art of garnishing. I prefer this caponata over any I've made because it has a nice color and a lighter flavor than most. It can be made several days in advance—the flavor actually improves during this time. Consider using it as a cold relish with my Holiday Pâté.

2 1-lb. eggplants (fresh and tender)
1 large sweet red pepper
1 large sweet yellow pepper
1 large sweet green pepper
3 large ripe tomatoes
1 large Vidalia onion
4 large cloves garlic
½ cup golden raisins
¼ cup red wine vinegar
1 tbsp. sugar
½ cup (approximately) extravirgin olive oil
1 tbsp. chopped fresh basil
Salt, to taste

Roasting fresh peppers: wash and dry peppers. Preheat oven to 400 degrees. Place the peppers on the oven rack. Roast until peel is puffy and browned, turning to brown on all sides—10 to 15 minutes. Carefully remove and place in a plastic bag. Seal top of bag and let sit until peppers are cool enough to handle. Remove from bag. The peel is easily removed with your fingers. Take out stem and seeds. May be refrigerated or frozen until ready to use.

¼ tsp. cayenne pepper
1 bouquet garni composed of:
    3 sprigs fresh thyme
    3 sprigs parsley and a bay leaf
3 tbsp. capers

- Wash and trim the eggplants. Cut into small cubes without peeling.
- Core the peppers and cut into small strips.
- Peel and seed the tomatoes. Save the juice. Cut tomatoes into small strips.
- Coarsely chop the onion and mince the garlic.
- Place the raisins, vinegar, and sugar in a small non-aluminum saucepan and bring to boil. Let sit for 30 minutes to plump the raisins.
- Heat half of the oil in a large heavy skillet.
- Sauté the eggplant over medium-high heat, stirring often until translucent and tender. Remove to a paper-towel-lined dish.
- Add remaining oil to skillet and sauté the 3 peppers for 2-3 minutes, stirring.
- Add the onion and garlic. Cook 3-4 minutes longer, stirring.
- Stir in the tomatoes, basil and reserved juice.
- Return the drained eggplant.
- Season with the salt and pepper and add the bouquet garni.
- Cook over medium heat, uncovered, for 20 minutes, stirring occasionally.
- Discard the bouquet garni and add the capers and marinated raisin mixture.
- Let cool. Taste and correct the seasonings. Cover and chill.
- Serve cold.

Note: if fresh thyme sprigs are unavailable for the bouquet garni, substitute a teaspoon of dried thyme leaves.

Herbed Pita Triangles

These crunchy bread triangles are always nice to have on hand to serve as "munchies" with wine or cocktails.

> **6 6-7-in. pita breads**
> **1 stick (4 oz.) unsalted butter or margarine or ½ cup extravirgin olive oil**
> **½ tsp. dried dillweed**
> **½ tsp. dried oregano**
> **2 tbsp. chopped fresh parsley**
> **1 clove garlic, crushed**
> **Pinch salt**
> **Dash cayenne pepper**

- Wrap the pita in foil and heat for 2-3 minutes in a hot oven to make it easier to separate.
- Cut into fourths with a sharp knife.
- Separate each triangle into 2 pieces.
- Melt butter or slightly heat olive oil and add remaining ingredients. Let sit and "steep" for 30 minutes. (Reheat if butter hardens.)
- With a soft pastry brush, brush the butter or oil mixture onto the inside side of the triangles.
- Place on baking sheets and bake in a preheated 425-degree oven for a few minutes or until crisp and golden brown around the edges.
- Cool and store in a tightly sealed container.
- Makes 4 dozen.

Pita Triangles may be made 4-5 days ahead. They are excellent to have on hand for impromptu cocktail-hour goodies or just for snacks.

Cocktail Pizzas

Everyone loves pizza. It's a dish that can be very casual or very elegant. For casual pizza, use a large rectangular baking sheet and cut the pizza into squares. For the more elegant preparation, make the small rounds and top them with colorful and tasty tidbits. You can clean out your refrigerator for this recipe, using the last dabs of cheese that no one would eat, or forlorn anchovies or black olives. The caramelized onion and bacon recipe is always the No. 1 hit with my guests.

Easy Crust

1 envelope quick-rising yeast
1 cup warm water (105-115 degrees)
2 tsp. sugar
2½-2¾ cups bread flour
1 tsp. salt
1 tbsp. olive oil

- Stir together the yeast, water, and sugar until yeast is dissolved.
- Let sit for 5 minutes.
- Place 2½ cups of the flour and the salt in food processor with steel blade or in mixer with dough hook. Process just to blend.
- Add the yeast mixture. Mix well.
- Add enough extra flour, 1 tablespoon at a time, to make a soft dough.
- Mix in the oil.
- Knead for 1 minute in the processor or 5 minutes in the mixer, or until dough is smooth and elastic.
- Remove and place in a gallon-sized plastic bag. Press out the air and seal.
- Set in a warm place for 30 minutes.
- Punch down and place on a lightly floured board. Cover dough with plastic wrap and allow 15 minutes resting time.

A pizza should always be baked in the bottom one-third of the oven so that the crust is assured of being cooked through without burning the top. A dark pan will yield a browner, crisper crust.

For Pizza Squares

- Roll out dough and place in a generously oiled jelly-roll pan (15½" x 10½" x 1"). Press some of the dough halfway up the sides of the pan to make a rim.
- Spread with Easy Pizza Sauce (see below) and top with desired toppings.
- Bake in bottom one-third of a preheated 425-degree oven for 20-25 minutes, or until golden brown around the edges.
- Use a pizza cutter or sharp knife to cut into small squares.
- Serve warm.
- Makes about 4 dozen small pizza squares.

For Round Cocktail Pizzas

- After dough is rolled out to about ⅛" thickness, cut with a 2½"-3" biscuit cutter.
- Puncture each round a few times with a fork.
- Spread with some of the Easy Pizza Sauce, leaving a rim of dough around the edge.
- Top with desired topping.
- Place on a lightly greased baking sheet and bake in the bottom one-third of a preheated 425-degree oven for 6-8 minutes or until golden and crisp around the edges.
- Makes about 3 dozen.

Easy Pizza Sauce

1 28-oz. can Italian plum tomatoes
3 tbsp. tomato paste
1 tsp. salt, or to taste
1 tsp. sugar
2 tsp. dried oregano
1 tbsp. chopped fresh basil (or 1 tsp. dried)
2 tbsp. chopped fresh parsley
1 clove garlic, minced
¼-½ tsp. crushed red pepper flakes, to taste

- Drain the tomatoes.
- Place all ingredients in the food processor with steel blade. Process just to mix. Do not purée. There should be small pieces of tomato visible.
- Place in a covered container and chill until ready to use.
- Keeps a week to 10 days in the refrigerator. (Best if made the day before.)

Suggested Pizza Toppings

—Finely chopped Caponata olives with shredded mozzarella cheese and diced roasted red peppers.

—Oil-packed, marinated sun-dried tomatoes cut into small strips, small cubes of goat cheese, and chopped fresh basil.

—Caramelized Onion and Bacon: caramelize the onion by slicing a large yellow onion and sautéing it in 2 tablespoons olive oil with a sprinkling of light brown sugar and a pinch of thyme. Cook over low heat, stirring, until onion is very tender and golden brown. Finish with a small splash of red wine or balsamic vinegar and some salt and freshly ground pepper to taste. Cook bacon until very crisp and break into pieces. (This topping is best without pizza sauce. Simply brush the pizza crust with some good fruity olive oil.)

—Chopped boiled shrimp, chopped fresh cilantro, and mozzarella cheese.

—Sliced porcini or shiitake mushrooms, sautéed in a bit of olive oil with some minced garlic, topped with some provolone and freshly grated Parmesan cheese.

All pizza toppings should be previously cooked. In the case of vegetables, such as onions, peppers, or mushrooms, they are only lightly sautéed.

Baked Seafood Cakettes

These Seafood Cakettes are an economical and delicious way to introduce seafood into your party lineup. They can be assembled the night before or at least several hours before, chilled on a lightly greased baking sheet, and popped into a hot oven before the guests arrive. Make a lot—they always go quickly and, with the help of the food processor, they are easy to prepare.

> **2 tbsp. olive oil**
> **½ cup chopped onion**
> **2 cloves garlic, minced**
> **¾ lb. raw shrimp, peeled and deveined**
> **½ lb. raw scallops**
> **¼ cup mayonnaise**
> **1 egg, lightly beaten**
> **1 tbsp. fresh lime juice**
> **¼ tsp. hot pepper sauce**
> **½ tsp. salt, or to taste**
> **2 tbsp. chopped fresh cilantro**
> **2 cups fresh bread crumbs***

- Heat the oil in a skillet.
- Sauté the onion and garlic for 2-3 minutes. Remove and cool.
- Finely chop the shrimp and scallops in the food processor.
- Mix with the onion-garlic and add the mayonnaise, egg, lime juice, hot pepper sauce, salt, and cilantro.
- Stir in ½ cup of the bread crumbs.
- Form into small oval cakes.
- Roll in remaining crumbs to coat.
- Place on a well-greased baking sheet.
- Cover and chill until serving time.
- When ready to serve, place in a preheated 400-degree oven for 15 minutes or until golden brown.
- Serve warm with Zesty Tartar Sauce for dipping (see below).
- Makes about 24 small cakes.

*Use slightly stale white or whole-wheat bread. Break it into large pieces, including crusts, and place in food processor with steel blade. Process until fine crumbs are formed.

Zesty Tartar Sauce

1 cup mayonnaise
1 tbsp. fresh lime juice
1 tbsp. Dijon mustard
½ tsp. hot pepper sauce
2 tbsp. chopped cilantro
2 tbsp. chopped scallions
2 tbsp. capers

- Stir together the mayonnaise, lime juice, mustard, and pepper sauce until smooth.
- Fold in remaining ingredients.
- Cover and chill until ready to serve.
- Makes about 1¼ cups.

Bleu Cheesecake

I always tell my students that cooking is definitely a creative art. I have enjoyed knowing a lot of creative and talented people in many professions who share my love for cooking. A favorite example is John Chesteen. John is an extremely talented interior designer who practices what he preaches. He lives in a perfectly beautiful and interesting house and is a most charming host who enjoys cooking and entertaining. At the drop of a hat he will invite 20 or 30 people for dinner and do all of the shopping and cooking himself. He is very organized and insists that his entire house, including the kitchen, be in its usual perfect order when the guests arrive. This requirement causes John always to be on the lookout for dishes that can be done completely ahead.

One of his fabulous make-ahead dinner menus was featured in the "Great Cook" series in *Bon Appetit* magazine. When I asked John to give me one of his popular cocktail party recipes, it was no surprise to hear that this recipe also came from *Bon Appetit*. His friends, however, have come to think of this particular dish as John's own since he has made it so popular at his parties. John uses Roquefort cheese from France in this recipe. When I made it I used Gorgonzola and found the flavor to be quite scrumptious. Make this 2-3 days before the party. It's delicious served with slices of fresh pear and apple. Acidulate the fruit with lemon juice to prevent darkening.

2 tbsp. unsalted butter or margarine
½ cup fresh bread crumbs, toasted
4 tbsp. freshly grated imported Parmesan cheese
½ lb. good smoky bacon, diced
1 tbsp. olive oil
1 medium yellow onion, finely chopped
2 lb. cream cheese, softened
½ lb. good bleu cheese (Roquefort, Gorgonzola
    or your favorite domestic)
4 large eggs
½ cup heavy cream
½ tsp. salt, or to taste
¼ tsp. hot pepper sauce

- With the 2 tablespoons of butter or margarine. butter a 9- or 10-inch springform pan.
- Mix the bread crumbs and Parmesan and sprinkle over the butter to evenly coat.
- Chill until ready to fill.
- Cook the bacon over medium heat, stirring occasionally, until crisp. Drain on paper towels.
- Pour off all of the bacon fat.
- Add the olive oil to the skillet.
- Sauté the onion in the oil just until softened and translucent. Cool.
- In a food processor with steel blade, or with an electric mixer, beat the softened cream cheese with the bleu cheese until smooth.
- Add eggs, cream, salt, and hot pepper sauce. Beat until very smooth.
- Fold in the bacon and onion.
- Pour into prepared pan.
- Set into a shallow larger pan that has enough hot water added to come halfway up the sides of the cheesecake pan.
- Place in the middle of a preheated 325-degree oven.
- Bake for 1 hour and 30 minutes.
- Cool cheesecake in the hot water bath for 1 hour.
- Chill until ready to serve.
- Serves 24 people as cocktail food.
- Garnish with fresh fruit and sprigs of parsley or watercress.

Vegetable Basket
with Three Dipping Sauces

A vegetable basket, or crudités, has long been standard cocktail-party fare. Some may dispute that its popularity continues, but I still see my guests making a beeline for a beautiful arrangement of crunchy vegetables. Besides being healthy, the basket lends wonderful color to any party table. Part of the success depends on the dipping sauces and I include three of my favorites. A pretty vegetable arrangement can be fun to assemble, allowing you to use all of your artistic flair. Whether very simple and elegant or "baroque" and covering half of the cocktail table, the most important factor is to always have crisp, chilled vegetables. Remember, too, that all garnishes must be edible.

Use an interesting, attractive basket. I often use one with a handle to give some height to the party table. The vegetables may be prepped as long as 24 hours ahead of time. For the ones to be eaten raw: wash and dry well, cut or trim into desired shapes and sizes, and store in plastic bags that have a paper towel added to absorb excess moisture. Take care not to blanch the cooked vegetables longer than the times indicated. They should remain crisp. They, too, may be wrapped in soft white paper towels and stored in plastic bags in the refrigerator. Assemble the final basket as close to serving time as possible since freshness is such an important factor.

The finished "crudités basket" should look attractively arranged, but not too contrived or stiff. It is important to group each vegetable separately in the arrangement. Kale is an excellent choice for greens to use as a basket lining. Its ruffled edges look great and it stays crisp longer than most lettuces. Some of the new, colorful varieties are especially decorative. Any leafy fresh herb or edible flower may be used to garnish. The sauces may be placed in matching bowls or in hollowed-out red and green cabbages, squash, or large bell peppers.

Vegetables that are blanched and refreshed:
Asparagus—2 minutes
Broccoli, cut into 2-3-inch pieces—1-2 minutes
Cauliflower, cut into small florets—1-2 minutes
Green beans—3-4 minutes

Raw vegetables:
Turnips—cut into julienne strips
Red, green, and yellow peppers—cut into strips
Jicama—cut into julienne strips
Small whole mushrooms—stem and acidulate with lemon juice
Snow peas—remove strings
Radishes—cut large ones in half, soak in ice water
Fennel—cut into julienne strips
Carrots—cut into julienne strips
Zucchini—cut into julienne strips
Scallions—"feather" the crisp tops, soak in ice water
Cucumbers—slice or julienne

Chili Pepper Dipping Sauce

1 4-oz. can chopped mild green chiles, drained
1 large sweet red pepper or pimiento, roasted
   and chopped
1 tsp. Hungarian paprika
¼ tsp. cayenne pepper
1 tsp. mild chili powder
1 tbsp. fresh lemon juice
Salt, to taste
2 cups mayonnaise, homemade or a good
   commercial one
Chopped fresh cilantro

- Stir together all ingredients, except cilantro.
- Sprinkle cilantro on top.
- Chill for at least 1 hour before serving.
- Serve chilled.
- Makes about 2½ cups.

Hungarian paprika is the most flavorful paprika and comes in mild or sweet and hot varieties. The best ones are usually packed in large tins and tend to become stale before they are depleted. Place the freshly opened can in a small zip-top freezer bag and keep in the freezer to maintain freshness and flavor.

Watercress Dipping Sauce

2 large bunches watercress, stems removed and finely chopped
1 cup chopped parsley (flat-leaf variety if available)
4 scallions, trimmed and finely chopped
2 cups sour cream (regular or reduced fat)
1 cup mayonnaise
1 tbsp. fresh lemon juice
Dash hot pepper sauce and salt to taste

- Stir together until well blended.
- Chill until ready to serve.
- Best if chilled a couple of hours.
- Garnish with some extra chopped watercress or parsley.
- Makes about 3½ cups.

Fresh Herb Dipping Sauce

¼ cup chopped sweet salad onion
½ cup chopped fresh basil, dill, and marjoram
¼ cup chopped fresh parsley
1 tbsp. fresh lime juice
1½ cups mayonnaise
2 tbsp. Dijon mustard
1 tbsp. canned green peppercorns, drained
Salt, to taste

- Stir together and chill until serving time.
- Best if chilled at least 1 hour.
- Makes about 2 cups.

Pecan Chicken Appetizers

I promised my friend Bette Sherman that I would not do a cookbook without including her favorite: Pecan Chicken. And Bette, my friend who gets the award for being the most finicky eater I know, has always loved this recipe. (And I love her, in spite of the fact that she won't eat most of my food.) So, Bette, here's your favorite chicken recipe. I know you don't like the Chutney Mayonnaise, but I've included it for all of the other folks, who will probably appreciate it. By the way, you should try this same recipe on halved, boned chicken breasts that are pounded to an equal thickness. It makes a delicious main course for a luncheon or dinner party and is a dish that even Bette makes.

2 whole chicken breasts
2 eggs
2 tbsp. water
2 cups fresh bread crumbs
1 cup finely chopped pecans
½ cup flour seasoned with salt and cayenne pepper
Vegetable oil, for frying

- Wash the chicken in warm water and pat dry.
- Skin, bone, and cut, across the grain, into ½-inch strips.
- Whisk together the eggs and water.
- Mix together the bread crumbs and chopped pecans.
- Dredge the chicken in the seasoned flour to lightly coat.
- Dip the chicken pieces into the egg mixture and then coat them with the pecan-bread mixture.
- Place in a single layer on a tray. Cover with plastic wrap and chill for at least 30 minutes. (May be made as long as 12 hours ahead and chilled until ready to cook.)
- Heat 2-3 inches oil to 375 degrees in a heavy skillet.
- Fry the chicken pieces for 5-8 minutes, depending on their size, or until golden brown and cooked through.
- Keep hot at "warm" setting in oven until ready to serve.
- Best when not held longer than 1 hour before serving.
- Serve with Chutney Mayonnaise as a dipping sauce.
- Makes approximately 32.

When "breading" any foods, cover and chill for at least 30 minutes or as long as several hours before frying. It causes the breading to adhere more readily.

Chutney Mayonnaise

1 cup mayonnaise
2 tsp. Dijon mustard
½ tsp. hot pepper sauce
½ tsp. salt
1 tsp. lemon zest
1 tbsp. fresh lemon juice
¼ cup mango chutney

- Whisk together the mayonnaise, mustard, hot pepper sauce, and salt until smooth.
- Stir in the lemon zest, lemon juice, and chutney.
- Chill until ready to serve.
- Makes about 1½ cups.

Note: other fruit chutneys may be substituted for the mango chutney. Add according to taste.

Piquant Pecans

These flavorful pecans always go quickly when I set a dish before my guests. This recipe is mildly spicy. Add more cayenne pepper if you prefer them spicier.

¼ cup peanut oil
1 tbsp. mild chili powder
½ tsp. cumin
¼ tsp. cayenne pepper, or to taste
3 cups pecan halves
½ tsp. salt

- Combine oil and spices in a skillet.
- Heat over low heat until hot (approximately 350 degrees).
- Remove from heat.
- Add nuts and stir until coated.
- Line a baking sheet with 5 layers of soft white paper towel.
- Spread the nuts out on the towels.
- Bake in a 300-degree preheated oven for 10 minutes.

- Sprinkle with salt while hot.
- Let cool completely before serving.
- Store in tightly sealed jar.
- Makes 3 cups.

Note: walnuts or almonds may be substituted for the pecans. For almonds, extend cooking time to 15 minutes.

Breaded Mushrooms

These golden mushrooms can also be made a couple of hours ahead of serving time and successfully held in a keep-warm oven.

> **1 lb. medium-firm fresh mushrooms**
> **Flour**
> **3 large eggs**
> **¼ tsp. each, salt and white pepper**
> **Fine dry bread crumbs**
> **Vegetable oil, for frying**

- Clean mushrooms. Trim the stems.
- Dredge in flour, shaking off the excess.
- Lightly beat the eggs with the salt and pepper.
- Dip the mushrooms in the egg mixture, just to coat.
- Roll in bread crumbs.
- Place in a single layer on a tray.
- Cover with plastic wrap and chill for at least 30 minutes.
- Heat 3-4 inches of the oil in a heavy skillet or deep fryer to 375 degrees.
- Cook the mushrooms in the hot oil for about 3 minutes or until golden brown and crisp.
- Drain on paper towels.
- Place in a 150-degree oven to keep warm until ready to serve.
- Serve warm with Bavarian Tartar Sauce for dipping.
- Makes 18-20, according to size of mushrooms.

Note: following the same breading, chilling, and frying instructions, use thickly cut julienne strips of fresh eggplant, which are also delicious served with the Bavarian Tartar Sauce.

For dry bread crumbs, process some "day-old" or stale bread in the food processor until very fine crumbs are formed. Spread in a thin layer on a baking sheet. Toast in a 350-degree oven for a few minutes, turning and stirring often until evenly toasted. Cool and store in a freezer bag in the freezer for future use.

COOKING WITH MARILYN

Bavarian Tartar Sauce

Bavarian Tartar Sauce comes from a party dish I sampled while living in Germany. I liked it so much I went directly to the kitchen in my apartment after the party and worked to duplicate it. The yogurt gives it a very fresh and light flavor and allows it to be lower in calories than many such sauces. It is a versatile sauce and comes in most handy during hot weather. For example, try it spooned over whole, chilled hard-cooked eggs for a summer brunch.

> **1 cup mayonnaise**
> **½ cup finely chopped sweet salad onion**
> **2 tbsp. chopped sour pickles**
> **¼ cup chopped fresh parsley**
> **1 tbsp. chopped fresh dillweed (1 tsp. dried)**
> **2 hard-cooked eggs, finely chopped**
> **Salt, to taste**
> **Dash hot pepper sauce**
> **½ cup plain nonfat yogurt**

- Stir together the mayonnaise, onion, pickles, parsley, dill, and eggs.
- Season to taste with salt and add a small dash of the hot pepper sauce.
- Fold in the yogurt until mixture is smooth.
- Chill at least 2 hours before serving.
- Makes about 2 cups.

Chilled Peppered Tenderloin

Chilled Peppered Tenderloin with Green Peppercorn Sauce is another grazing favorite. Any leftovers are soon gobbled up the next day. The Angel Biscuits in the brunch chapter would be heavenly with the tenderloin, especially for a winter party. However, if you are short of time, the suggested French or party rye breads are just fine with this tasty meat dish. Be sure to slice the meat very thinly.

2 tbsp. canned green peppercorns, drained
2 large cloves garlic
1 tsp. coarse sea salt
2 tbsp. extravirgin olive oil
1 3-lb. beef tenderloin, well trimmed

- In a mortar and pestle, or in the food processor, make a paste from the peppercorns and garlic.
- Combine with the salt and oil and rub entire surface of the tenderloin with the mixture.
- Cover loosely with plastic wrap and set aside at room temperature for 1 hour.
- Or, make ahead, place in the refrigerator for several hours, and let sit at room temperature for at least 30 minutes before roasting.
- To roast: place on a rack in a shallow roasting pan.
- Place in the center of a preheated 425-degree oven for 25-35 minutes (25 minutes for rare and 35 for medium rare).
- Cool.
- Wrap in plastic wrap and chill for several hours.

To Serve

- Slice into thin slices and serve with Green Peppercorn Sauce and thinly sliced French bread or party rye bread.

Green Peppercorn Sauce

1 cup mayonnaise
2 tbsp. Dijon mustard
½ tsp. sugar
2 tbsp. drained green peppercorns
1 tbsp. minced scallions
1 cup sour cream (regular or reduced fat)

- Whisk together the mayonnaise and mustard.
- Fold in the sugar, peppercorns, scallions, and sour cream.
- Cover and chill for at least 1 hour before serving.
- Makes about 2 cups.

Carmen's Canapé Bread

Carmen Jones, well known across the country as an excellent cooking teacher, is a cheerful person with great innovative ideas. She made this Canapé Bread for a class at the Fourth Street Cooking School in Cincinnati. I've altered it a bit as I've enjoyed it through the years.

> 1½ cups sifted all-purpose flour
> 4 tsp. baking powder
> 1½ tsp. salt
> 1 tsp. freshly ground black pepper
> ½ cup yellow cornmeal
> ½ cup whole-wheat flour
> 3 tbsp. sugar
> 1 large egg
> 1½ cups milk
> ¾ cup vegetable oil
> 1 cup sliced pimiento-stuffed olives
> 1 cup chopped roasted and salted cashews

- Combine all dry ingredients in a large bowl.
- Mix together all liquid ingredients with olives and nuts.
- Pour together with dry ingredients and mix only until all flour disappears. Do not overbeat.
- Grease small or miniature loaf pans generously with butter or margarine.
- Pour batter into pans, filling about three-quarters full. Place in center of a preheated 375-degree oven and bake for 30-40 minutes or until cake tester plunged into center comes out clean.
- Remove from pans and let cool on a rack.
- Wrap in plastic wrap and store in refrigerator or freezer.
- Makes 5-6 small loaves, depending on pan size.

Note: this bread slices better when made 2-3 days before the party. It may be made a month ahead and frozen. (Wrap in freezer wrap if stored in freezer.) Thinly slice and spread with whipped butter and top with thinly sliced cheese like Swiss or sharp Cheddar. Or, spread with whipped cream cheese and top with thinly sliced ham or smoked turkey.

Shrimp Profiteroles

I used to make the puff pastry by hand for these Shrimp Prof-iteroles, and I could tell when the dough was done when my elbow could no longer move. The advent of the food processor has saved countless elbows. You can bake the unfilled puffs ahead of time for freezing. Thaw them and heat them for a few minutes in a hot oven to freshen and crisp before filling them.

Puffs

1 cup water
1 stick unsalted butter, cut into 8 pieces
½ tsp. salt
1 cup flour
4 large eggs

- In a medium saucepan, combine water, butter, and salt.
- Bring to a boil and add all of the flour at once. Cook over low heat, stirring vigorously with a wooden spoon, until mixture forms a ball of dough.
- Remove from heat.
- Let cool for 5 minutes.
- Place in food processor with steel blade and add the eggs.
- Process until mixture is very smooth and shiny.
- Using a rubber spatula, place the mixture in a large pastry bag that is fitted with a large plain tip (6-8 mm).
- Pipe small mounds of dough onto a lightly greased baking sheet.
- Place in top one-third of a preheated 400-degree oven and bake for 18-20 minutes or until puffed and golden brown.
- Turn off oven.
- Pull out baking sheet. Using a small knife, make a small slit in the side of each puff.
- Return to turned-off oven for 10-15 minutes.
- Let cool on a rack.
- Slice in half crosswise.

Cheese with a high butterfat content may be successfully stored in the freezer for several months. (Do not freeze low-fat cheeses such as cottage cheese.) Cream cheese may be stored in the freezer in its original foil package. The creamy texture is altered a bit, but it can still be used in most recipes with excellent results. It is best thawed overnight in the refrigerator, but for last minute needs may be thawed in the microwave oven. Be sure to remove the foil wrapping and cover with plastic wrap or waxed paper before placing in the microwave.

Filling

12 oz. cream cheese, softened (regular or light)
8 oz. boiled shrimp, peeled and deveined
1 tbsp. chopped fresh dill (or 1 tsp. dried)
1 tbsp. fresh lemon juice
¼ tsp. cayenne pepper
2 tbsp. chopped parsley

- In food processor with steel blade, process the cream cheese until light and fluffy.
- Add remaining ingredients and blend by turning on and off until mixture is well blended.
- Spoon into pastry bag fitted with same tip as for the pastry.
- Pipe a small amount onto the bottom half of each puff.
- Cover with top of puff.
- Makes about 4 dozen.

Spicy Sweet-Potato Petite Pancakes

These hot Spicy Sweet-Potato Pancakes come from my own recipe, inspired by my love for sweet potatoes as a child. Make them as spicy as you wish by adding more of those wonderful little jalapeño peppers.

1½ lb. fresh sweet potatoes, peeled
1 small yellow onion, minced
1 large jalapeño pepper, seeded and minced
⅔ cup flour
4 large eggs
½ tsp. salt
¼ tsp. cayenne pepper
Vegetable oil, for frying
Sour cream
Fresh cilantro sprigs, for garnish

- Shred the potatoes into fine shreds.
- Mix together with the onions and jalapeño.
- Beat together the flour and eggs. Season with salt and cayenne.
- Stir into the potato mixture.
- Heat about ½ inch of oil in a large heavy skillet.
- Drop the batter by small teaspoonfuls. Flatten with a metal spatula and cook 2-3 minutes on each side.
- Drain on paper-towel-lined baking sheet and place the baking sheet directly into a "keep-warm" oven until serving time.
- At serving time, top each with a dollop of sour cream and a cilantro leaf.
- Serve warm.
- Makes about 4 dozen.

Note: if these appetizer pancakes are made and kept warm as described above, they should not be held longer than 1 hour. They can be made several hours ahead and held, covered, in the refrigerator. They should be reheated on the baking sheet in a preheated 350-degree oven until hot and crisp around the edges.

Piquant Beef Triangles

My phyllo classes have always filled up quickly. Phyllo is a fun pastry that makes you look like an accomplished pastry chef without really being one. Like a lot of things, it can be made very easily if you follow the directions. It is time consuming to work with, but the effects are fantastic. These recipes can be made ahead and frozen, as long as they are well protected in proper freezer wrapping. Baking time always increases when the food starts out partially frozen or at refrigerator temperature.

If these spicy Beef Triangles are made ahead and frozen, they should thaw overnight in the refrigerator and sit for an hour or so at room temperature before being popped into the oven. Better piping hot rather than warm, they are ideal for passing at a cocktail party.

1 large onion, minced
3 tbsp. olive oil
2 cloves garlic, minced
1 lb. very lean ground beef (chuck or round)
¼ cup chopped pimiento-stuffed olives
½ tsp. crushed red pepper
⅓ cup white raisins
¼ cup tomato paste
Salt and freshly ground pepper, to taste
18 sheets phyllo dough
2 sticks unsalted butter, melted, or ⅔ cup olive oil

- Sauté the onions in the olive oil for about 5 minutes or until translucent.
- Add garlic and cook 2 minutes longer.
- Add beef and cook, stirring, until red is gone.
- Stir in remaining ingredients (except phyllo dough and butter) and cook, stirring, for 10 minutes.
- Set aside and let cool.
- Spread a sheet of phyllo dough on a large cutting board and brush lightly, using a soft-bristle pastry brush, with butter or oil.
- Top with a second sheet and brush in same manner.
- Finish with a third sheet for a triple thickness of pastry.
- Using a small sharp knife, cut the sheet of pastry into 4 equal lengthwise strips.
- Place a teaspoon of filling on the end of each strip and fold over the top corner to make a triangle shape.
- Continue to fold, as though folding a flag, until a small triangle of filled phyllo dough is formed.
- Place triangles on a parchment-paper-lined baking sheet.
- Cover well and chill until serving time.
- At serving time, place the baking sheet in the top one-third of a preheated 375-degree oven and bake for 12-15 minutes or until golden and crisp.
- Serve warm.
- Makes 24 appetizers.

Asparagus in Phyllo

The phyllo-wrapped fresh asparagus, obviously, would lose some quality if frozen ahead, but you can assemble the ingredients as many as 24 hours prior to a last-minute visit to the oven.

24 medium-sized fresh asparagus spears
4 sheets phyllo dough
1 stick unsalted butter, melted
1 recipe Dill-Cucumber Sauce

- Wash asparagus, break off tough ends, and peel with a vegetable peeler, starting about 2 inches below the tip.
- Blanch for 1 minute in a large skillet of rapidly boiling salted water. Refresh in ice water and pat dry on paper towels.
- Cut phyllo sheets into 6 rectangles. Brush each generously with melted butter.
- Place an asparagus spear in the center of each pastry rectangle.
- Fold ends over and roll sides to encase asparagus.
- Seal edge of pastry with butter and brush top of the final roll with butter.
- Place on parchment-paper-lined baking sheets.
- Cover and chill until ready to serve.
- At serving time, place in a preheated 375-degree oven for 6-8 minutes or until golden brown.
- Serve hot with Dill-Cucumber Sauce.
- Makes 24 appetizers.

Dill-Cucumber Sauce

1 cup "light" sour cream or plain yogurt
¼ cup mayonnaise
1 medium tomato, peeled, seeded, and chopped
½ cucumber, peeled, seeded, and chopped
1 tbsp. fresh chopped dill (or 1 teaspoon dried)
Pinch salt, or to taste
Generous dash hot pepper sauce

- Stir together all ingredients just to mix.
- Cover tightly and chill until ready to serve.
- Good made the day before the party.

Phyllo dough (sometimes spelled *filo*) is found in the freezer case at the grocery store. Keep it in its original wrapping until thawed. It may be thawed overnight in the refrigerator or in a couple of hours at room temperature. When it is opened, spread out the number of sheets needed for the recipe. Keep covered with a damp cloth. Take great care not to let it dry out. Fold up the unused dough, wrap in freezer paper, and refreeze for later use.

To peel and seed cucumbers: choose regular "American" cucumbers for sauces and cold soups where a true "cucumber flavor" is desired (as opposed to the European or seedless variety), and peel with a vegetable peeler. Cut in half lengthwise. Run a teaspoon down the center of each half to remove the seeds. Slice or chop as desired.

Pork and Pecan Stuffed Mushrooms

Stuffed hot mushrooms are a very hearty yet elegant dish. This is an especially good cold-weather party dish. They also make a wonderful starter course for a dinner party. I prefer buying a piece of pork loin and grinding it myself in the food processor.

> 24 medium mushrooms
> 3 tbsp. extravirgin olive oil
> 3 large shallots, minced
> ½ lb. ground lean pork
> ¼ cup good Cognac
> ¼ cup chopped parsley
> Dash freshly grated nutmeg
> 1 cup finely chopped toasted pecans
> 2 cups fresh bread crumbs
> Salt and freshly ground pepper, to taste

- Clean the mushrooms.
- Remove the stems and chop the stems finely; set aside.
- Heat the oil in a heavy skillet and sauté the shallots and chopped stems.
- Add the pork and cook, stirring for 5-6 minutes. Add the Cognac and cook over high heat to reduce to 1 tablespoon liquid.
- Stir in parsley, nutmeg, pecans, bread crumbs, and salt and pepper.
- Taste and correct seasonings.
- Spoon into washed and dried mushroom caps.
- Place in a buttered shallow baking dish, cover well with plastic wrap, and chill until ready to serve.
- At serving time, place in a preheated 375-degree oven, and bake for 20-25 minutes, or until hot through and lightly browned on top. (Mushrooms should be tender, but firm.)
- Serve warm.
- Makes 24 hors d'oeuvres.

Savory Mushroom Tartlets

I learned to make these tartlets while studying at the Cordon Bleu School in London. They are a very traditional "haute cuisine" type of appetizer. Your friends on a restricted cholesterol diet should be cautioned against too many of these succulent beauties, but they should certainly savor at least one.

I've included the tartlets to remind you what a treat it is to make tart shells. Such little tarts add a lot of class to a party tray. Forms are available at cooking stores, and even though they are time consuming, you can make them ahead and freeze them. I always tell my classes tart shells are a good rainy-day project.

The Béarnaise sauce in this recipe is made from scratch, but you can also make it in the food processor or blender. The Béarnaise can be made several hours ahead. The mushrooms, which may be sautéed earlier, should not be added to your delicate pastry until only one hour beforehand. Otherwise you will be serving soggy tarts.

Pastry

1½ cups unbleached flour
½ tsp. salt
1 egg yolk
1 stick chilled unsalted butter, cut into 8 pieces
5 tbsp. ice water

- In food processor with steel blade, place the flour, salt, egg yolk, and butter.
- Process until mixture resembles coarse meal.
- Add water and process until a ball of dough begins to form. (Do not overprocess.)
- Remove, pat into a disc, and wrap securely in plastic wrap.
- Chill for at least 2 hours.
- When ready to roll, let sit at room temperature until pliable enough to roll easily, but still cool.
- Roll out on a lightly floured board with a pastry rolling pin to ½-inch thickness.
- Place the rolling pin at the top of the rolled-out dough and roll the dough loosely up on the pin.
- Place the small tartlet molds in a group on a baking sheet and roll the dough over the top of them.
- Gently lift the dough so that it will fall into the molds. (Take care not to stretch the dough.)

"Blind baking" is prebaking a pastry shell without allowing it to puff up. This is accomplished by covering the raw pastry with parchment paper (or foil—parchment is better) and professional metal pie weights or dried beans or rice. After the initial baking process takes place, the paper and weights are removed. If a partially baked pastry is desired, return it to the oven for a minute or two. If the pastry is to be completely baked, it is then returned to the oven to finish baking. (If puffy pockets still occur in the pastry, gently and cautiously press them back down with a clean cloth or potholder.)

- When the dough is placed over the molds with enough dough to fit into each mold, roll over the top with the rolling pin.
- Remove the excess dough and gently press the dough into each mold.
- Cover each tart shell with a square of parchment paper and fill with some pie weights.
- Bake "blind" in a 425-degree oven for 8-10 minutes.
- Remove and take out parchment and pie weights.
- Return to oven for 2-3 minutes more to bake until golden and crisp.
- Remove and gently invert the molds onto a cooling rack to cool the pastry.
- Repeat to bake more tartlet shells.
- Makes about 24 tiny pastries.

Mushroom Filling

½ lb. mushrooms, thinly sliced
1 stick (4 oz.) unsalted butter
Salt and freshly ground pepper, to taste
2 tbsp. flour
3 tbsp. dry sherry

- In a heavy skillet, sauté the mushrooms in the butter. Season with salt and pepper.
- Add the flour and cook, stirring constantly, for 2-3 minutes without browning.
- Add the sherry and cook for 2 minutes longer.
- Remove from heat and put a small spoonful in each tart shell.
- Spoon over enough Béarnaise sauce just to cover and serve warm.

Note: if the Béarnaise is made ahead and has cooled, the finished tarts may be placed for a few minutes in a warm oven. Or, for a different look, but also an acceptable method, "glaze" the Béarnaise under a hot broiler just before serving.

Sauce Béarnaise

1 tbsp. chopped fresh tarragon (or 1 tsp. dried)
1 tbsp. chopped fresh parsley
2 shallots, finely chopped

3 tbsp. white wine vinegar
½ cup dry white wine
3 large egg yolks
1 tbsp. water
8 oz. (2 sticks) unsalted butter, cut into pieces
Salt, to taste
¼ tsp. hot pepper sauce

- Combine tarragon, parsley, shallots, vinegar, and wine in a non-reactive saucepan.
- Cook over high heat until reduced by half.
- Place mixture in double boiler with yolks and water.
- Whisk over hot, not boiling, water until light and fluffy.
- When mixture becomes very warm, start whisking in butter, a piece at a time, whisking briskly as sauce begins to thicken.
- Do not allow to become too hot or sauce will "break."
- Season to taste with salt and hot pepper sauce.
- Serve immediately.

Bleu Cheese-Walnut
New Potatoes

This little cocktail potato filled with bleu cheese and topped with a walnut half is an excellent and hearty treat. Potatoes are inexpensive, and new crop potatoes are always so wonderfully tasty, especially in early spring and early fall. You can make these hours ahead and cover them loosely with plastic wrap, but be sure not to serve them too cold.

18 small red new potatoes
4 oz. bleu cheese (Gorgonzola or Roquefort)

8 oz. cream cheese, softened
½ cup lightly toasted walnuts, chopped
2 tbsp. Cognac
18 walnut halves

- Scrub the potatoes.
- Boil them in well-salted water until just fork tender—15-20 minutes.
- Drain.
- Refresh with cold water and let cool and dry.
- Cut a thin slice from bottom of each potato so they sit up straight.
- With a melonballer, scoop out the top.
- Season inside potato shells with salt and pepper.
- Whip together the two cheeses in food processor or mixer until light and fluffy.
- Add chopped walnuts and Cognac.
- Spoon cheese mixture into a large pastry bag fitted with a large (7-8 mm) star tip.
- Pipe a small amount of the filling into each potato.
- Top each with a walnut half.
- Chill until ready to serve. Let return to room temperature to serve.
- Makes 18.

Note: to toast walnuts, spread walnut halves in a single layer on a baking sheet. Place in a 375-degree oven for 8-10 minutes. Let cool completely before using.

Sun-Dried Tomato Spread on Zucchini Slices

This trio of crunchy vegetables with toppings (this recipe and the next two) is nice set out or passed. A basic rule of arranging canapé trays is never to put more than three types of appetizers on a tray. They should be grouped together, and never in a random mix.

My friend Neal O'Donnell, whom you probably know as "Chef Cornelius," first did the Sun-Dried Tomato Spread on Zucchini Slices as a guest instructor at my cooking school. It is a colorful and very tasty spread that will keep a good ten days in the refrigerator. (Neal is not only a great cook, but his cheerful personality and natural teaching style always make him a favorite of my cooking students. He is also one of my very favorite friends from the culinary world.)

2 cloves garlic, minced
8 oz. cream cheese, softened
4 oz. fresh goat cheese
1 cup oil-packed sun-dried tomatoes, drained
1 tbsp. fresh basil (or 1 tsp. dried)
1 tbsp. capers, drained
¼ cup parsley leaves
Pinch cayenne pepper
4-5 small crisp zucchini, washed and chilled

- In food processor with steel blade, blend together the garlic, cheeses, tomatoes, basil, capers, parsley, and cayenne pepper until smooth.
- Trim the ends from the zucchini.
- Cut at a diagonal to form oval slices.
- Spread the cheese spread on the zucchini slices no sooner than an hour before serving.
- Cover and chill until ready to serve.
- Garnish with fresh basil or parsley leaves.

Sun-dried tomatoes can be purchased marinated in oil or in their original dried form. The most economical method is to buy them dried. (They are available in bulk in many gourmet specialty stores and in the produce departments of some grocery stores.) Place the dried tomatoes in a vegetable steamer and steam them until they are moist and plump (about 10-15 minutes, depending on how dry they are). Cool and place in a jar that has a tight-fitting lid. Add some dry black peppercorns and a mixture of dried herbs— thyme, oregano, marjoram, and basil. Pour over enough olive oil to completely cover the tomatoes. Seal tightly and store in the refrigerator. When the tomatoes are used up, the oil may be used for cooking or in salad dressings.

Cheese-Filled Brussels Sprouts

The lowly Brussels sprout is usually the stepchild of vegetables. Indeed, it seldom appears on the cocktail menu. My theory is that the reason it lacks respect is because it is usually overcooked, resulting in a mushy, strong-tasting food. It is, however, a most attractive vegetable and lends itself nicely to being filled. When cooked properly, you will find that its crisp texture, delicious nutty flavor, and beautiful green color may just be a surprise favorite at your next party. This herb-cheese filling is one of my favorites. I sometimes substitute Roquefort or Gorgonzola.

1½ lb. fresh Brussels sprouts
6 oz. herbed cream cheese
4 oz. cream cheese, softened
3 scallions, minced
1 tbsp. chopped parsley
Freshly ground pepper, to taste

- Wash and trim the Brussels sprouts.
- Bring a large pot of water to a boil.
- Add some salt and the Brussels sprouts. Cook for 8 minutes.
- Refresh in ice water and drain well.
- In food processor or mixer, cream together the cheese filling.
- Cut the bases of the sprouts completely flat and hollow out a deep well in the top with a small melonballer.
- Spoon the cheese mixture into a pastry bag fitted with a large plain tip and pipe the cheese filling into the hollowed tops.
- Cover lightly with plastic wrap and chill until serving time.
- Makes about 3 dozen.

This cheese filling is equally delicious piped onto artichoke bottoms. Canned ones are fine; rinse and dry them before adding the cheese filling. Another tasty appetizer can be created with fresh snow peas. Wash and dry the peas. String them on one side and, using a small piping tip, pipe a small strip of the cheese filling into the pea pod. Chill until ready to serve.

Smoked Salmon Spread
on Cucumbers

The following recipe offers a thrifty way to serve smoked salmon at a large party. The flavor of the salmon lends itself very nicely to the clean, crisp taste and texture of the cucumbers. It is a most elegant dish when made with the long, slender, "European"-type cucumbers. If they are not available, the normal garden-variety cucumber must be peeled, still yielding a tasty party food, though not as colorful.

> **12 oz. cream cheese, softened**
> **¼ cup cream**
> **8 oz. smoked salmon, cut into pieces**
> **2 tbsp. chopped scallions**
> **1 tbsp. chopped parsley**
> **1 tbsp. fresh lemon juice**
> **½ tsp. finely chopped lemon zest**
> **Generous dash hot pepper sauce**
> **2 European-style fresh crisp cucumbers**
> **Salmon caviar**

- In food processor with steel blade, blend together the cheese, cream, and salmon until smooth.
- Add the scallions, parsley, lemon juice and zest, and hot pepper sauce to taste.
- Spoon into a pastry bag fitted with a large star tip (7-8 mm).
- Wash and trim the cucumbers.
- Cut crosswise into ¼-inch slices.
- Pipe the cheese mixture onto the cucumbers and top each with a dollop of salmon caviar.
- Makes about 4 dozen.

If you want low-fat party food, substitute low-fat cream cheese for the regular cream cheese and whole milk for the cream in all of the above cheese spreads.

Salmon caviar is definitely the best garnish choice for this dish. The color as well as the salmon flavor best enhances the cheese filling. A very small amount on each cucumber will suffice.

The lemon "zest" is the yellow outer layer of the rind. Only the yellow part, with the flavorful citrus oils, should be used. Avoid the white part of the rind. The "zesting" may be done with a lemon zester (available in the gadget section of the kitchen department) or with a small grater. Always wash the lemon with warm water and dry before zesting.

Fun and Fancy Menus

"Yes, it does sound like a good recipe for my luncheon, but what do I serve with it?" How often I've heard that sort of question from students and radio listeners!

This chapter is filled with some of my longtime favorite, tried and true recipes. I have grouped them in menus comprised of the recipes I have served with good success and positive critiques from my family and friends.

Most of these menus are casual enough to be easily tried as something new and fun for the family to enjoy. They also come in handy for less formal occasions and gatherings because they are certainly fancy enough to set before your favorite guests. I bet you don't know anyone who wouldn't appreciate a delicious home-cooked lunch or supper.

You will find some light and healthy foods in the following pages as well as some more indulgent dishes—from soup to dessert—that are perfect to make when you know there will be hungry guests to assist in consuming them at one sitting.

My main intention in sharing these menus is for you to savor the experience of both cooking and eating, as well as sharing them further in your circle of family and friends. Most are not difficult, making the enjoyment even greater for those of you who are the designated cooks.

Whether you choose to follow my menu suggestions and cook an entire meal or pick and choose from some of the recipes that happen to strike your fancy, I do hope you will have fun.

MENU 1

Guacamolé Soup

Amanda's Chicken Taco Salad

Orange Flan

Sangria Blanc

Returning the avocado pit to a puréed avocado mixture prevents darkening. Cover the mixture well with plastic wrap so that it is as air-tight as possible.

Peeling an avocado: cut the unpeeled avocado in half by running a small sharp knife lengthwise around the avocado, cutting all the way through to the pit. Twist each half in opposite directions to separate. Remove the pit from its half. Slide a large oval-shaped serving spoon between the peel and avocado pulp. Rotate to remove the half of avocado in one piece. It may now be served intact to be filled as a salad or placed flat side down on a cutting board to be sliced or cubed.

Guacamolé Soup

This first menu, with its definite Southwestern influence, is especially good for warm-weather months. Because I enjoy cooking this type of food almost as much as I enjoy eating it, my friends have often requested all of the dishes in this menu for lunch when invited to my house. I couldn't count the times I have served this Guacamolé Soup. It's great for lunch on a hot summer day. I've changed it a bit over the years, but I think I am offering you the best version yet.

> **3 medium ripe avocados***
> **¼ tsp. salt**
> **¼ tsp. hot pepper sauce**
> **1 tbsp. fresh lime juice**
> **2 cups chilled chicken stock**
> **2 cups sour cream****
> **2 tbsp. chopped salad onion**
> **2 medium ripe tomatoes, peeled, seeded, and chopped**
> **2 tbsp. chopped cilantro**
> **1 very thinly sliced lime**
> **Cilantro leaves**

- Peel the avocados. Cut into slices. (Save the pits to return to finished soup.)
- In food processor or blender, purée the avocado with the salt, hot pepper sauce, and lime juice.
- Blend in the chicken stock.
- Add the sour cream and process just long enough to blend well.
- Pour into a bowl.
- Fold in the onion, tomatoes, and chopped cilantro. Add the avocado pits.
- Cover and chill for at least 2 hours.
- Taste and correct seasonings.
- Serve ice cold. Top each bowl with a very thin slice of lime with a cilantro leaf in the center.
- Serves 6-8 as a first course.

*The Haas variety avocado is best for this recipe. The avocados should be very ripe and soft, but without dark or mushy spots.

**The light or reduced-fat sour cream will do just fine for this recipe. Plain yogurt may also be substituted.

Amanda's Chicken Taco Salad

My first restaurant consulting job was for my dear friend Mary Sue Morris. I developed this chicken taco salad recipe for her restaurant and it is still one of my favorite main-dish salads. You'll want to use this approach for poaching the chicken in other chicken salad recipes, too. It's easy, low fat, and most flavorful.

> **6 corn tortillas**
> **Vegetable oil, for frying**
> **3 whole chicken breasts, skinned and boned**
> **1 recipe Poaching Stock (see below)**
> **1 small head iceberg lettuce, coarsely shredded**
> **3 large tomatoes, diced**
> **¾ lb. Jack cheese, shredded**
> **1 recipe Picante Dressing (see below)**
> **Small tomato wedges**
> **Fresh cilantro sprigs**

- In a large heavy skillet, fry the tortillas until very crisp in about two inches of oil that is heated to 375 degrees.
- Drain thoroughly on paper towels.
- Place on a paper-towel-lined baking sheet and put in a 125-degree oven to keep warm until you are ready to assemble the salad.
- Place the boned chicken breasts between two sheets of plastic wrap.
- Pound with a veal pounder, or some heavy flat object, until they are the same thickness throughout.
- Place in the Poaching Stock.
- Cover with a sheet of parchment paper, carefully pressing the paper in around the edges to hold in the steam.
- Poach for 8-10 minutes or until just opaque and done through.
- Remove from liquid.

- Cool and cut, across the grain, into ½-inch strips.
- Place a tortilla on a luncheon-sized plate. Sprinkle with a layer of shredded lettuce.
- Top with a layer of diced tomatoes.
- Cover with a layer of shredded cheese.
- Arrange chicken strips on top of the cheese.
- Spoon over enough Picante Dressing to cover.
- Garnish with tomato wedges and cilantro or parsley sprigs.
- Serve immediately.
- Serves 6 as a main course.

Poaching Stock

2 cups dry white wine
1 medium onion, coarsely chopped
1 tsp. dry black peppercorns
1 clove garlic, crushed
1 bouquet garni composed of:
3 sprigs fresh thyme
3 sprigs parsley and a large bay leaf
1 tsp. salt
Generous dash hot pepper sauce sauce
1 cup water

- Bring all ingredients to a boil and boil for 5 minutes before adding the chicken.

Picante Dressing

1 cup mayonnaise (regular or reduced fat)
½ cup sour cream (regular or reduced fat)
1½ cups Picante Sauce
1 tbsp. fresh lime juice

- Stir together. Cover and chill for at least 2 hours to blend flavors.
- Makes 3 cups.

Picante Sauce

1 large yellow onion, finely chopped
2 large cloves garlic, minced
2 tbsp. extravirgin olive oil
4 fresh jalapeño peppers, seeded and minced
3 mild green chiles, roasted and chopped
3 large tomatoes, peeled and finely chopped
½ tsp. cumin
3 tbsp. chopped fresh cilantro leaves
1 tsp. salt, or to taste
1 tsp. sugar
2 tbsp. red wine vinegar

- Sauté onions and garlic in the oil for 2-3 minutes, stirring (just until onions are translucent).
- Remove from heat and cool.
- Stir together all of the ingredients.
- Cover and chill for at least 2 hours.
- Taste and correct seasonings.

Sangria Blanc

Sangria is the traditional Spanish wine punch. This one is made with white rather than red wine and is a refreshing complement to the food in this menu. Make your sangria base in the morning or even the evening before so the flavors will become more pronounced. Sangria Blanc is a perfect hot-weather drink and it can be very elegant if served poured over cracked ice in large-stemmed wineglasses.

2 tbsp. sugar
2 cups water
2 cups freshly squeezed orange juice
2 cups dry white wine
Orange and lemon slices
Mint leaves (optional)

- Dissolve the sugar in the water.
- Stir together with the orange juice and wine.
- Chill until ready to serve.
- Serve on the rocks garnished with the fruit slices and mint leaves.
- Serves 6-8.

Orange Flan

The menu concludes with the flan, a velvety egg custard that the Spanish love very much. With a caramelized sugar topping, flan is a kissing cousin of crème caramel, and is the perfect finale for a spicy menu. The Grand Marnier and grated orange zest add just the right touch of elegance.

> ¾ cup sugar
> 6 whole eggs
> 2 egg yolks
> ⅔ cup sugar
> 2 tbsp. orange zest
> ½ tsp. lemon zest
> 2 tbsp. Grand Marnier
> 2 cups light cream

- In a heavy skillet (preferably an iron skillet) melt the ¾ cup of sugar over moderate heat. Shake the skillet as the sugar melts to allow it to caramelize evenly.
- When dark-golden syrup forms, remove from heat and quickly pour into a 9-inch, metal, layer-cake pan (not necessary to grease the pan).
- Very carefully tilt the pan to coat the bottom evenly. (Sugar melts at a very high temperature, so mixture will be very hot.)
- Set aside.
- Whisk together the whole eggs, egg yolks, ⅔ cup sugar, orange and lemon zest, and Grand Marnier until well blended.
- Whisk in the cream. (Do not overbeat.)
- Pour into the caramel-lined pan.
- Place in a large shallow baking pan that has enough hot water to come halfway up the sides of the flan pan.
- Bake in the center of a preheated 350-degree oven for 30-35 minutes, or until puffed and set.
- Remove from heat and carefully take the pan from the water bath.
- Cool on a rack for 15 minutes.
- Place in refrigerator and chill until completely cold . . . for several hours. (Best made the day before.)
- Run a small, flexible, metal spatula around the edge of the pan.
- Invert onto a rimmed serving plate. (Plate must be deep enough to hold the caramel sauce.) Cut into wedges and serve.
- Serves 6-8.

Fresh Tomato Bisque

The fresh tomato soup is best in the summer when you can find vine-ripened tomatoes and fresh herbs. But it's not bad in winter made with canned plum tomatoes. The seasoned whipped cream topping is truly a "fun and fancy" touch.

8 large ripe tomatoes
3 tbsp. unsalted butter or extravirgin olive oil
2 medium yellow onions, chopped
3 ribs celery, chopped
2 cloves garlic, minced
2 tbsp. flour
5 cups chicken stock
1 tbsp. chopped fresh basil (or 1 tsp. dried)
1 tsp. chopped fresh marjoram (or ⅓ tsp. dried)
¼ cup chopped fresh parsley
1 bay leaf
¼ tsp. hot pepper sauce
Salt, to taste
1 cup whipping cream, chilled
Salt and cayenne pepper
Extra chopped parsley for garnish

- Peel and seed the tomatoes, reserving the juice.
- Place tomatoes and juice in food processor or blender and finely chop. (Do not purée until smooth. There should be small pieces of tomato in the finished soup.)
- Melt butter in a heavy, non-aluminum pot.
- Sauté the onions and celery, stirring, for 5 minutes over medium heat.
- Add the garlic and cook 2 minutes more.
- Stir in the flour and cook, stirring constantly, for 2 minutes.
- Add the tomatoes and their juice.
- Whisk in the stock and add the basil, marjoram, parsley, and bay leaf.
- Season with hot pepper sauce and salt.
- Bring to a boil. Partially cover and simmer for 20 minutes.
- Remove the bay leaf.

MENU 2

Fresh Tomato Bisque

**Salad Niçoise
with Fresh Tuna Filet**

**Dainty Whole-Wheat
Dinner Rolls**

**Cream Puffs
Extraordinaire**

- Taste and correct seasonings.
- Whip the cold cream until stiff. Season to taste with a bit of salt and cayenne.
- Serve the soup hot topped with a dollop of the cream and a sprinkling of fresh parsley.
- Serves 6-8.

Note: for a very light soup, the cream may be omitted and only chopped parsley used as a garnish.

Salad Niçoise
with Fresh Tuna Filet

The main-dish salad has often been featured in my fish and seafood classes. When I first started making Salad Niçoise, I used canned tuna. Now with the greater availability of fresh fish, this dish takes on an entirely new look and taste. It's a perfect entrée for the most exquisite of luncheons or a light summer supper.

2 lb. fresh tuna filets
Mayonnaise
Salt and freshly ground pepper
2 lb. small red new potatoes, scrubbed
2 cups chicken stock
1 cup white wine
1 lb. small fresh whole green beans, trimmed
2 cups cherry tomatoes, washed and halved
5 hard-cooked eggs, peeled and cut into wedges
¼ cup chopped parsley
½ cup Niçoise olives (or Kalamata olives)
1 large head leaf lettuce, washed and crisped
1 medium red Spanish onion, thinly sliced
Small parsley sprigs

The basic rule for cooking fish filets, whether on the grill, in the broiler, or in the oven: figure 10 minutes cooking time for each 1-inch thickness. Always cook about two-thirds of the total cooking time on the first side before turning. Turn only once! As soon as the fish flakes easily with a fork, it is done. Do not overcook!

Dressing

¾ cup extravirgin olive oil
¼ cup red wine vinegar
1 tbsp. good Dijon mustard
1 large clove garlic, finely minced
Pinch sugar
Salt and freshly ground pepper
1 tbsp. each chopped fresh dill and parsley

- Spread both sides of the tuna filets with a light coating of mayonnaise.
- Season with salt and freshly ground pepper.
- Grill on an outdoor grill or broil in a preheated broiler until just done through.
- Set aside to cool (or do ahead, wrap, and chill).
- Trim a slice of peel from each end of the potatoes and slice them into ¼-inch slices. Steam in a vegetable steamer for 8 minutes, or until just tender, but not falling apart.
- Stir together the chicken stock and wine.
- Remove the hot potatoes from the steamer to the stock mixture.
- Let marinate for 20-30 minutes.
- Steam the green beans for 7 minutes. Refresh in cold water.
- Pat dry.
- Whisk together the dressing ingredients.
- Cut the fish into large pieces and drizzle with a bit of the dressing.
- Toss the green beans with just enough dressing to coat.
- Toss tomatoes with dressing to coat.
- Drain the potatoes thoroughly and toss with enough of the dressing to coat.
- Sprinkle the egg wedges with the chopped parsley.

To Assemble the Salad

- In a large shallow bowl (or individual salad bowls or plates), place the crisp lettuce leaves.
- Top with the potatoes.
- Arrange the green beans on the potatoes.
- Top with onion slices and cherry tomato halves, reserving a few for garnishing the top of the finished salad.
- Place the fish in the center.
- Arrange the parsley-coated egg wedges and olives around the fish.
- Drizzle over any remaining dressing. Garnish with the reserved onion slices, tomato halves, and some parsley sprigs.
- Serve immediately.
- Serves 6 as a main dish.

Dainty Whole-Wheat Dinner Rolls

1 pkg. quick-rising dry yeast
1 tbsp. sugar
¼ cup warm water (105-110 degrees)
2-2½ cups unbleached flour
¾ cup whole-wheat flour
1 tsp. salt
2 tbsp. melted butter or margarine
¾ cup water

Topping

4 tbsp. melted butter or margarine
1 tsp. mixed dried herbs (thyme, oregano, and dill)
1 clove garlic, crushed
Coarse sea salt

Quick-rising yeast will save about half the time required when using regular yeast. In my experience the final results for most breads are the same as with regular yeast, making it a great convenience and time-saver.

- Dissolve yeast and sugar in the warm water. Let stand for 5 minutes.
- Stir together 2 cups of the unbleached flour, the whole-wheat flour, and the salt.
- Stir in the yeast mixture and melted butter. Add the ¾ cup of water and mix well.
- Add enough remaining flour so that the dough is not sticky.
- Knead until smooth and elastic.
- Place in a gallon-sized plastic bag. Press out air and seal.
- Put the bag in a warm place and let rise until doubled—about 30 minutes.
- Punch down and turn out onto a lightly floured board.
- Roll into a long roll that is about 2 inches in diameter.
- Cut the roll in half and then into fourths.
- Cut each fourth into 6 equal pieces. Roll each piece into a round ball.
- Butter two 9-inch round baking pans.
- Place rolls in each pan.
- Cover with lightly oiled plastic wrap and place in a warm place until rolls are doubled—about 30 minutes.
- Mix together the butter and herbs in a small saucepan. Add the crushed garlic clove and heat until the butter is melted and begins to bubble. Remove from heat and let steep for 30 minutes.
- Remove and discard garlic.
- After rolls have risen, lightly brush on the butter mixture with a soft-bristle pastry brush.
- Sprinkle with a bit of the coarse salt.
- Place in the center of a preheated 375-degree oven for 12-15 minutes or until rolls are golden.
- Serve hot or at room temperature.
- Makes 2 dozen small dinner rolls.

If kneading by hand, knead for 10 minutes. In mixer with dough hook, knead for 5 minutes. This entire recipe may also be made using the steel blade in the food processor. The kneading time in the food processor is only 1 minute.

Always note the date on the yeast package. Using the yeast close to or after the expiration date is likely to result in a bread that does not rise properly.

An accurate temperature of the first liquid in which the yeast is dissolved is crucial for good results in bread baking. If the liquid is too cool, the rising times will extend beyond what the recipe recommends, making the total preparation time difficult to calculate. If the liquid is too hot, the yeast will lose some or all of its ability to grow and raise the dough, resulting in a flat, unpalatable baked product.

A good source for soft, natural-bristle pastry brushes is your local hardware store. Buy natural-bristle paintbrushes in all sizes. To care for them, clean in warm sudsy water and dry well before storing. Do not put into the dishwasher.

Cream Puffs Extraordinaire

My Cream Puffs Extraordinaire are a Marilyn variation of an old favorite, using a lightly sweetened pâte au choux pastry with a traditional crème Chantilly or whipped cream filling. You can either prepare one large puff for each serving or several tiny ones, giving your guests the feeling that one more little one won't be horridly indulgent. The puffs themselves are just the basic, classic recipe. It's the apricots flavored with the liqueur and the grated orange rind that make this cream filling so special. The chocolate adds a heavenly touch; in fact, I think the combination of chocolate, apricots, and oranges has no equal in the world of sweetdom.

Pâte au Choux (Pastry)

1 cup water
1 stick unsalted butter or margarine,
 cut into 8 pieces
1 tbsp. sugar
¼ tsp. salt
1 cup unbleached flour
4 large eggs

- Mix the water, butter, sugar, and salt together in a small heavy saucepan.
- Bring to a rolling boil. (Butter should be completely melted.)
- Add the flour all at once, stirring vigorously with a wooden spoon until the mixture leaves the sides of the pan and forms a smooth ball.
- Remove from heat and let cool for about 2 minutes.
- Place in food processor with steel blade.
- Add the eggs and process until mixture is smooth and shiny. (Mixture will be very sticky.)
- Spoon into a large pastry bag that is fitted with a large (7-8 mm) plain metal pastry tip.
- Pipe mounds of dough about 1 inch in diameter onto a lightly greased baking sheet.
- Place in the upper one-third of a preheated 425-degree oven for 20-25 minutes, or until puffed and golden brown.
- Turn off oven.

- Remove baking sheet and make a slit with a small paring knife in the side of each puff.
- Return to turned-off oven for about 10 minutes.
- Cut each puff in half.
- Remove any moist dough from centers.

The Creamy Apricot Filling

½ cup Grand Marnier
6 oz. glazed apricots*, finely chopped
2 cups whipping cream, chilled
¼ cup confectioners' sugar
Zest of 1 large orange

- Pour the liqueur over the chopped apricots and let marinate at room temperature for at least 1 hour.
- Drain and reserve liqueur.
- Whip the cream in a chilled bowl with chilled beaters until very stiff. Gradually add the sugar after the cream starts to stiffen.
- Add 1 tablespoon of the reserved liqueur. When stiff, fold in the apricots and orange zest.
- Spoon into a large pastry bag that is fitted with a large (7-8 mm) star pastry tip.
- Pipe a large pouf of cream filling onto base of a puff and gently replace the top of the puff. (The filling will be visible in the middle.)
- Drizzle with the chocolate topping and chill until ready to serve.
- Can be prepared 3-4 hours before serving.
- Makes about 2 dozen small puffs.

*Glazed apricots, sometimes called "Australian apricots," are available in fine candy stores or gourmet shops. Be sure to specify the glazed, and not just dried, apricots. They add a more elegant touch.

Chocolate Topping

6 oz. good semisweet chocolate

- Melt the chocolate in a double boiler over hot, not boiling, water.
- Stir occasionally. The melted chocolate should be very creamy and very shiny.
- Drizzle over the puffs while chocolate is still warm.
- Chill to set.

MENU 3

**Vegetarian Black
Bean Soup**

**Stuffed Flank Steak
with Soy-Ginger Sauce**

Herbed Tomatoes

Foolproof French Bread

Chocolate Mousse Torte

Vegetarian Black Bean Soup

Black bean soup traditionally has meat in it and can be very rich and heavy. My own version uses only water and dry red wine. Consequently, it's very light. And it makes a lot of soup, which will keep for a good week in the refrigerator. Or you can store it 6-8 weeks in the freezer without actually altering the flavor.

> **2 cups dried black turtle beans**
> **Warm water to cover**
> **2 large yellow onions, chopped**
> **4 large cloves garlic, minced**
> **3 ribs celery, chopped**
> **3 medium carrots, chopped**
> **⅓ cup extravirgin olive oil**
> **9 cups water**
> **1 cup dry red wine**
> **2 bay leaves**
> **2 sprigs thyme**
> **2 sprigs parsley**
> **2 tsp. salt, or to taste**
> **¼ tsp. hot pepper sauce, or to taste**
> **Sour cream**
> **1 small red Spanish onion, chopped**
>   **(or other sweet salad onion)**
> **Chopped parsley or cilantro**

- Wash beans well and place in a large pot. Pour over enough warm water to cover and soak overnight.
- Drain.
- In a heavy soup pot, sweat the vegetables in the olive oil, covered, for 10 minutes.
- Pour over the 9 cups of water.
- Add the beans.
- Add wine.
- Tie together the bay leaves, thyme sprigs, and parsley sprigs with some kitchen twine to make a bouquet garni. Add to pot along with salt and hot pepper sauce.
- Bring to boil and cook over low heat, covered, for about 4 hours, or until beans are very tender.

- If mixture becomes too thick, add some more water.
- Taste and correct seasonings. Remove bouquet garni.
- Top with a dollop of sour cream, some chopped sweet salad onion, and a sprinkling of chopped parsley or cilantro.
- Serves 8-10.

Stuffed Flank Steak

The stuffed flank steak happens to be my husband's favorite. Flank steak is a less tender cut of meat but a good choice for beefsteak because of its low fat content. It normally requires several hours of marinating in a marinade that tenderizes as well as flavors. Putting a pocket in it or fileting it and rolling it will result in a thinner piece of meat and thus eliminate the need for marinating. You can prepare it through the searing stage then let it cool, chill it, and pop it in a hot oven the next day. The cooking time will be doubled when it is chilled.

1½ to 2 lb. flank steak
1 lb. fresh spinach leaves
3 tbsp. extravirgin olive oil
1 large clove garlic, minced
Salt and freshly ground pepper
3 medium carrots
3 scallions

- With a sharp boning knife, remove all visible fat from the steak.
- Place steak on a cutting board with the grain running vertically.
- Carefully cut, with the grain, just halfway through the thickness, the full length of the steak.
- Slowly cut, holding the knife flat against the steak, through the center of each side to "butterfly" the steak.
- Lay back the two sides. (You now have a piece of meat which is approximately half of the original thickness and twice as wide.)
- Cover and refrigerate until ready to stuff.
- Remove coarse stems from the spinach. Wash and dry.
- Heat 1 tablespoon of the olive oil in a skillet.

- Sauté the spinach, stirring, for 2 minutes. Add the garlic and sauté a minute more. Season to taste with salt and pepper.
- Remove from skillet and cool. Squeeze out excess liquid. Place down center of the steak (in the center, with the grain of the meat—where the first cut was made).
- Peel and cut the carrots into thin julienne strips.
- Chop the scallions.
- Sauté the carrots in 1 tablespoon of the oil, stirring for 3 minutes or until "crisp-tender."
- Add the scallions and cook a minute longer, stirring. Remove from heat. Season lightly and arrange in an even fashion in the center of the spinach.
- Carefully roll the meat, ending with a roll that is 3 to 3½ inches in diameter.
- Tie in 4 or 5 places with kitchen twine.
- Heat the remaining 1 tablespoon of oil in a large heavy skillet.
- Sear all sides of the rolled meat until it is well browned.
- Place on a rack in a shallow pan in a preheated 425-degree oven for 10 minutes (for medium rare . . . if you desire a well-done steak, leave it in the oven 5 minutes longer).
- Place on a cutting board. Remove the string.
- Cut with a very sharp carving knife into 1-inch rounds.

Soy-Ginger Sauce

½ cup thin Chinese soy sauce
1 tbsp. water
1 tbsp. toasted sesame oil
1 tsp. finely minced gingerroot
¼ tsp. finely minced fresh garlic
Few drops hot pepper sauce
¼ cup dry sherry

- Mix together.
- Heat just until hot.
- Do not boil.
- Serve hot or cold.
- Makes about ⅔ cup.

Chinese soy sauce is usually the best choice for marinades and sauces. It is available in different strengths, from thick to thin. The thin ones are best to use as "all-purpose" soy sauces. The Chinese soy sauce is more flavorful and less salty than many other soy sauces, though the saltiness and flavor can vary depending on the brand. The best-quality soy sauces are usually found at specialty Asian food shops.

To Serve

- Spoon a small amount of the Soy-Ginger Sauce onto the dinner plate. Place the steak slice flat on the plate in the sauce. May be served hot or chilled.
- If served cold, cool the cooked meat to room temperature, wrap well in plastic wrap, and chill for several hours. Slice just before serving.
- Serves 4-6.

Herbed Tomatoes

There is hardly a better way to eat very good, ripe tomatoes than this recipe for herbed tomatoes. The tomatoes can be prepared ahead of time, covered and chilled, ready to broil just before serving time.

8 medium tomatoes, ripe but firm
Salt and freshly ground black pepper, to taste
1 stick unsalted butter or unsalted margarine
2 large cloves garlic, minced
1 tsp. chopped fresh thyme leaves (or ½ tsp. dried)
1 tsp. chopped fresh marjoram (or ½ tsp. dried)
1 tbsp. chopped fresh basil (or 1 tsp. dried)
4½ cups fresh bread crumbs

- Pierce the tomatoes with a cooking fork and place for 30 seconds in a pot of boiling water.
- Plunge into cold water.
- Core and peel.
- Cut the tops off so that they are flat.
- Cut a small slice from the bottom so that they sit flat.
- Season tops with salt and pepper to taste.
- Melt the butter, add the garlic, and let sit to steep for ½ hour.
- Stir in the herbs and bread crumbs and mix well.
- Spread butter mixture on top of tomatoes.
- Just before serving time, broil under a preheated broiler until golden and just hot through.
- Serve immediately.
- Serves 8.

Delicious with all steaks and chops.

All fresh herbs should be submerged briefly in lukewarm water to remove any dirt and grit. Dry with absorbent paper or cloth towels. Wrap in absorbent white paper towels and seal in a plastic bag. Store in the crisper drawer of the refrigerator. The herbs should stay fresh and ready to use for at least a week.

Foolproof French Bread

6 cups bread flour
1 tbsp. salt
2 pkg. quick-rising dry yeast
2 cups warm water (105-115 degrees)
1 egg
1 tbsp. water

- In food processor or heavy-duty mixer fitted with dough hook, mix together flour, salt, and yeast. Process to blend.
- Add the water and mix into a soft but firm dough.
- To knead, process for 1 minute in the food processor, or 5 minutes in the electric mixer. Dough should be smooth and elastic.
- Place in a gallon sized zip-top plastic bag. Place in a warm spot (80-90 degrees) to rise.
- Let rise for 1 hour.
- Punch down.
- Place on a lightly floured board and divide into 2 equal parts.
- Roll out each into a rectangle approximately 15 x 5 inches.
- Roll up in a tight roll to make a long *baguette* approximately 15 inches long.
- Pinch ends and seam firmly to seal well.
- Place, seam side down, in a lightly oiled double French-bread pan.
- Repeat with second loaf.
- Loosely cover with oiled plastic wrap, sealing sides.
- Let rise in a warm place until doubled—about 30 minutes.
- Slash with a very sharp knife to make three or four 2-3-inch diagonal slashes.
- Beat together the eggs and water and brush the "egg wash" lightly on the bread using a soft pastry brush.
- Place in the center of a preheated 425-degree oven.

- Place a shallow pan of boiling water on the rack just beneath the bread.
- Bake for about 40 minutes or until golden and crisp.
- Remove bread loaves from pan as soon as it comes from the oven.
- Cool on a cooling rack.
- Makes 2 loaves.

Notes: for an extracrisp crust, turn the oven off and let it cool down for 10-15 minutes. Lay the loaves directly on the oven shelves in the turned-off oven for a few minutes.

This recipe requires a large food processor. If you have a small one, divide the ingredients in half and make one loaf at a time.

Bread flours vary. If the dough is too stiff, add a bit more water, a little at a time until the dough is the proper consistency.

Chocolate Mousse Torte

I couldn't have done this book without including the Chocolate Mousse Torte. It's been a favorite of my cooking students over the years. After tasting it at a dinner party in California, I copied down the recipe on an old checkbook cover and have been making it ever since. It's a must if you're entertaining anyone who loves chocolate.

8 oz. semisweet chocolate
8 oz. (2 sticks) unsalted butter
1¼ cups sugar
6 large eggs
1 tsp. pure vanilla extract
1 cup heavy cream, chilled
2 tbsp. confectioners' sugar

- Melt chocolate in a double boiler with hot, not boiling, water in bottom of boiler.
- Cut butter into 1-tablespoon-size pieces. Add to chocolate and whisk until melted.
- Whisk in sugar and stir until mixture is smooth . . . about 10 minutes.
- Beat eggs until foamy and stir into the chocolate mixture along with vanilla.
- Butter a 9-inch round cake pan, line bottom with parchment paper, and generously butter the paper.
- Pour in chocolate mixture and place the cake pan in a shallow baking pan filled with enough hot water to come halfway up the sides of the cake pan.
- Place in the middle of a preheated 350-degree oven for about 1¼ hours—or until the torte is puffed and set.
- Remove from oven and cool in pan on a rack until lukewarm. Invert onto a serving plate. Remove paper.
- Chill until serving time.

To Serve

- Whip the chilled heavy cream with the 2 tablespoons confectioners' sugar until very stiff.
- Cut the torte into 8 or 10 wedges.
- Garnish each slice with a spoonful of whipped cream.
- Or, if you wish, spoon the cream into a pastry bag fitted with a large (7-8 mm) star tip. Pipe a rosette onto the base of each wedge of torte.
- Chocolate curls or candied violets may be placed on the cream rosettes to make an elegant dessert for a special occasion.

To make a perfectly formed rosette of stiffly whipped cream, spoon the cream into a pastry bag fitted with a large (7-8 mm) star tip. Visualize a clock face, hold the pastry bag at 10 till 12, and, in an easy motion squeezing only from the top and slowly moving the bag clockwise, make a complete circle and stop at 10 after 12.

Melon with Prosciutto

I want to remind you that cantaloupe or honeydew and prosciutto is a wonderful starter for almost any luncheon or dinner. I like to add extra zing by putting freshly ground black pepper on the prosciutto and garnishing it with a lime slice.

1 large chilled cantaloupe or honeydew melon
12 very thin slices prosciutto*
Freshly ground black pepper
6 wedges fresh limes

- Cut the melon in half.
- Remove seeds and pee!.
- Cut each half into 6 slices.
- Place 2 slices of melon on individual plates.
- Place a slice of prosciutto over each melon slice.
- Sprinkle the ham with freshly ground pepper.
- Garnish with a lime wedge. Serve chilled.
- Serves 6.

*Prosciutto is dry-cured Italian ham. Other "dry-cured" hams, such as Westphalian ham, may be substituted. For best flavor, it is important to have the ham very thinly sliced.

Cheese-Filled Homemade Manicotti
with Fresh Tomato Sauce

As it happens, manicotti is not a traditional Italian dish. It is, however, a popular main dish at my house. The filling can easily be made the day before, as can the sauce and the manicotti. The manicotti is best if assembled on the same day it is to be served. And of course, imported Parmesan always tastes better. Remember this wonderful tomato sauce for plain spaghetti or other pastas.

MENU 4

Melon with Prosciutto

Cheese-Filled Homemade Manicotti
with Fresh Tomato Sauce

Fresh Artichoke Salad

Lemon-Lime Tart

The Manicotti

2 cups water
4 large eggs
½ tsp. salt
2 cups unbleached flour
2 tbsp. olive oil

- Place all ingredients in food processor or blender. Blend for 1 minute or until smooth.
- Cover and chill for at least 2 hours.
- The batter should be the consistency of heavy cream. If it is too thick, add a bit more water; if too thin, whisk in a bit more flour. (Take care that the flour is completely incorporated.)
- Lightly grease a 7-8-inch crepe pan (or small nonstick skillet).
- Heat the pan until very hot, but not smoking.
- Lift pan from heat and over to the bowl of batter.
- Use a small ladle or large spoon which holds enough batter to just coat the bottom of the pan. Ladle the batter into the center of the pan.
- Rotate wrist to tilt pan to allow batter to completely coat the bottom of the pan.
- Pour off any excess batter.
- Return to heat and cook for a few seconds over medium-high heat until batter is set and the mixture is dry on top.
- Turn and cook for about 15 seconds on the second side.
- Invert pan to remove onto a holding plate.
- Repeat the procedure until all batter is used up.
- Keep covered with a dishcloth or foil to prevent drying.

You can make all types of crepes several weeks in advance and put them in the freezer in a carefully sealed heavy-duty foil package (no more than 12 in a stack). When you're ready, take them from the freezer and let them thaw at room temperature for a few hours. Then place the whole package into a 350-degree oven for 10 minutes, just until they can come apart. It's not necessary to put waxed paper between the crepes as some cookbooks instruct.

The Cheese Filling

16 oz. low-fat ricotta (or cottage cheese, well drained)
8 oz. "light" cream cheese
4 oz. freshly grated Parmesan cheese
3 large eggs
½ tsp. salt, or to taste
½ tsp. freshly ground black pepper
¼ cup chopped parsley
2 tbsp. chopped fresh dill (or 2 tsp. dried)
1 tbsp. chopped scallions

- In food processor fitted with steel blade, add ricotta and cream cheese.
- Blend until smooth and add the Parmesan.
- Blend.
- Add the eggs and process until light and fluffy.
- Add seasonings and blend.
- Remove from processor, cover, and chill until ready to use.

Fresh Tomato Sauce

6 large ripe tomatoes
2 tbsp. extravirgin olive oil
1 large yellow onion, chopped
2 large cloves garlic, minced
1 rib celery, chopped
2 tbsp. tomato paste
1 tsp. salt
1 tsp. sugar
Freshly ground pepper
1 tbsp. chopped fresh basil (or 1 tsp. dried)
1 bouquet garni composed of:
   2 sprigs fresh thyme
   2 sprigs parsley and 2 bay leaves
1 tsp. dried oregano leaves
½ cup chicken stock
¼ cup dry white wine

When counting calories or reducing fat in your diet, use a good nonstick skillet or spray a regular skillet with a nonstick spray. It allows you to sauté with far less fat.

- Peel and seed the tomatoes. Reserve tomato juice to add to the sauce.
- Heat the oil in a heavy skillet.
- Sauté the onion just until translucent.
- Stir in the garlic and celery. Cook, stirring, for 2-3 minutes.
- Stir in the tomatoes, tomato paste, salt, sugar, pepper, basil, bouquet garni, oregano, chicken stock, and wine. Add the reserved tomato juice.
- Cook, stirring occasionally, uncovered and over medium heat for 20 minutes.
- Taste and correct seasonings.
- Remove bouquet garni.
- Cool, cover, and chill if not used right away.

When good-quality fresh tomatoes are not available, substitute a 28-ounce can of Italian plum tomatoes. Purée the entire contents, including juice, in food processor or blender.

To Assemble

- Place an unfilled manicotti flat on a plate.
- Spoon a heaping tablespoonful of the cheese filling onto the inside (the second side that was cooked). Distribute evenly and roll up.
- Place, seam side down, in a lightly greased shallow baking dish. (May be assembled several hours before cooking and serving. Cover well and chill if made ahead.)
- When ready to bake, spoon over the tomato sauce. Sprinkle with the extra Parmesan. Place in the center of a preheated 350-degree oven.
- Bake until sauce is bubbly and manicotti is hot through . . . 30-40 minutes, depending on temperature of the manicotti when placed in the oven.
- Makes approximately 20 filled manicotti.

Note: this Fresh Tomato Sauce is an excellent pasta sauce for spaghetti or any of your favorite pastas. For a completely vegetarian sauce, the chicken stock may be omitted and V-8 or tomato juice substituted.

Fresh Artichoke Salad

On one of her trips from California, Sharon Shipley brought me some baby artichokes along with assorted other produce. In fact, she arrived with a suitcase crammed with fresh foods. I called up a group of my friends who are good eaters for an impromptu dinner. Sharon and I composed this delightful artichoke salad for that party. You could substitute Kalamata or Greek olives for the Niçoise, but don't use those bland canned black olives or you won't get the good, full-bodied flavor.

> **6 fresh large artichokes, or 12-15 baby artichokes**
> **1 lemon, halved**
> **1 sweet red or yellow pepper**
> **4 scallions**
> **½ cup whole Niçoise olives**
> **¼ cup chopped parsley, preferably flat-leaf variety**
> **½ cup extravirgin olive oil**
> **3 tbsp. balsamic vinegar**
> **Salt, to taste**
> **¼ tsp. freshly ground black pepper**
> **Crisp lettuce leaves**
> **Parsley sprigs, for garnish**

To Prepare Artichokes

- With a sharp knife, slice each artichoke stem even with the bottom of the artichoke.
- Rub with a lemon half to prevent darkening.
- Squeeze the lemon halves into a bowl of cold water.
- As the artichoke hearts are cut, place in the lemon water until ready to cook.
- Break away all of the leaves.
- Cut in half, exposing the prickly "choke."
- Place, cut side down, on a cutting board and slice away the pointed top just above the purple portion.
- With a small sharp knife, remove the choke and the coarse purple leaves just above the choke.
- Trim the ragged edges where the leaves were removed.

- For large artichokes, cut each half of the trimmed "heart" in half or (for very large ones) into thirds.
- Return to the lemon water until ready to cook.
- For baby artichokes, simply halve the small "hearts."

To Cook Artichokes

- Bring 3-4 cups of water to a boil in a non-aluminum pot.
- Salt lightly.
- Add the artichoke hearts and simmer until the meaty base is just fork tender—20-25 minutes, depending on the size.
- Drain and cool.
- Wash, core, and cut the pepper into small julienne strips.
- Wash, trim, and thinly slice the scallions into tiny "rounds."
- Add to the drained artichoke hearts, along with the olives and chopped parsley.
- Add oil, vinegar, and seasonings. Let marinate for 30 minutes at room temperature.
- Taste and correct seasonings.
- Cover and chill until ready to serve.
- Spoon on a crisp lettuce leaf. Top with a couple of parsley sprigs.

Lemon-Lime Tart

Lemon-Lime Tart is my own version of a recipe created in France. I was privileged to take several classes in Lyons restaurants and found shopping, cooking, and eating there one of my most fun culinary experiences. Quite simple to make, this tart actually tastes better when done the day before. I like to serve it very well chilled and topped with lightly sweetened whipped cream and a thin slice of lime or lemon. My friend Amy Hoffman had long maintained that she would never learn to do pastry, but she gave in just so she could make this tart. Amy, this one's for you.

The Pastry

1½ cups unbleached flour
1 tbsp. sugar
½ tsp. salt
1 large egg yolk
1 stick very cold unsalted butter,
    cut into 8 pieces
3-5 tbsp. ice water*

- Place the flour, sugar, salt, egg yolk, and butter in the bowl of the food processor with the cutting blade in place (or put it in a mixing bowl).

- If the food processor is used, simply process for a few seconds, turning on and off until the butter is cut in tiny pieces and the mixture resembles "coarse meal."

- When making "by hand," use two table knives with serrated edges. Cut rapidly in an *X* motion, continuing to push the mixture to the center of the bowl. (This ensures that all of the butter is cut in as quickly as possible.) If the butter starts to soften, set the bowl in the freezer for a few minutes.

- To add the ice water: for the food processor, pour in with the machine running and let process just until a dough forms. Do not overprocess. Remove and press into a disc. Wrap in plastic wrap and chill for at least 2 hours.

- For the "by hand" method: make a well in the center of the dry mixture and add the water gradually, gathering up the dry mixture until a rough dough is formed. Gather together and place on a lightly floured board. Knead with the heel of the hand by sliding forward until the mixture is smooth. Gather into a ball. Press into a disc. Wrap and chill.

*The amount of water in pastry will vary according to the flour. Flours with higher protein content will absorb more water.

When kneading pastry that should be flaky, it is important not to melt the tiny butter flakes. Use the fingertips and the heel of your hand instead of your palm. The higher temperature in the palms will soften the butter.

To Roll

- Let the cold pastry sit at room temperature for a few minutes, until pliable enough to roll—but still cool.
- Using a pastry rolling pin, roll from the center out, taking care not to overmanipulate or stretch the pastry.
- Roll to a large circle ⅛ inch thick.
- Place rolling pin at top of circle and roll toward you to roll up the pastry on the pin.
- Working quickly, place an 11-inch removable-bottom tart pan directly under the rolling pin and release the pastry from the pin over the top of the pan.
- Gently lift the edges and allow the pastry to fall into the pan. (Try not to stretch the pastry while placing it into the pan. This will cause shrinkage when it is placed into the hot oven.)
- Loosely drape the excess pastry over the sides of the pan.
- Roll the rolling pin over the top of the pan, cutting away the excess pastry.* Press the sides of the pastry so that they adhere to the pan.

*This method of rolling off the excess works only with a removable-bottom metal tart pan because of the sharp edges. If a glass or ceramic pan is used, cut away the excess with kitchen shears.

To Bake Blind

- Place a sheet of parchment paper or foil on top of the unbaked pastry.
- Form to fit the inside of the tart pan.
- Fill with dry beans (or metal pie weights*).
- Place in the bottom one-third of a preheated 425-degree oven and bake for 10 minutes.
- Remove the paper and weights and return to oven for 1 minute— or just until the pastry looks dry and "sealed."
- Let cool.
- Fill with the filling.

*Metal pie weights are available in kitchen specialty stores or housewares departments in department stores.

Lemon-Lime Filling

2 large lemons
2 large limes
1 stick unsalted butter, softened
1 cup sugar
4 large eggs
3 tbsp. heavy cream
Sweetened stiffly beaten cream
Thin slices of lemon or lime

- Remove the zest from the 2 lemons and 2 limes.
- Juice the 2 lemons and 2 limes. In an electric mixer, beat together the butter, sugar, and eggs until very light and fluffy.
- Mix in the cream, zest, and juices.
- Pour into the prebaked and cooled pastry shell.
- Place in the bottom one-third of a preheated 350-degree oven for 30-35 minutes or until puffed and golden brown.
- Cool and chill.
- Cut into 8-10 slices.
- Garnish each slice with a puff or rosette of whipped cream, topped with a twisted slice of lemon or lime.
- Serves 8-10.

Light and Lovely

After spending December attending my traditional holiday classes, many of my cooking students would be waiting at the door in January for my annual offering of "Light and Lovely" classes. That is the origin of this chapter title. Whatever the title, it is not much fun to think of calorie counting as a permanent regimen, but many of us find it an occasional necessary evil. I seek to add a positive touch to the dreaded reducing diet with some truly tasty morsels for you. The challenge, as I see it, in this diet dilemma is to devise menus to lessen one's daily caloric intake without total culinary deprivation.

There are many fancy health spas around the world that have gotten much attention in the press by serving foods that are so attractive and tasty that their caloric content becomes secondary. I have tried to convey some of this. I have chosen favorite foods from my recipe files and I have also polled various dinner and house guests and students for their opinions. And though my intention was to pick light and healthy selections appropriate to this section, I hope you will look upon them as toothsome treats and not just low-calorie foods.

I think that we all know that the real answer to this diet business is to try to maintain a life-style of eating in a healthy manner every day rather than to dread the beginning of next Monday's diet. It is with that lofty goal in mind that I offer the three following menus.

MENU 1

Zippy Gazpacho

Grilled Lime Chicken

Grilled Herbed Vegetable Kabobs

Instant "Chocolate Mousse"

Zippy Gazpacho

When I told my friend Susan Wooley that I had a new recipe for gazpacho, she said she didn't want to hear it. "I always expect too much from gazpacho; it never follows through," she said. I know what she means. Most gazpachos have too little zip and too much indigestion. After many years of this problem, I've managed to come up with a nearly perfect recipe. In my opinion, the secrets are removing the seeds from the tomatoes and cucumbers, omitting the green peppers and substituting the sweeter and lower-in-acid ripe red pepper, having enough liquid, and adding some zip with jalapeño peppers. This gazpacho recipe with only one tablespoon of olive oil is also in keeping with our "light" theme.

> 6 large, very ripe tomatoes, peeled, seeded*, and finely chopped
> 2 large cucumbers, peeled, seeded, and finely chopped
> 1 large Vidalia onion (or other sweet salad onion), finely chopped
> 1-3 jalapeño peppers, cored and finely chopped
> 1 large red bell pepper, cored and finely chopped
> 2 12-oz. cans Spicy V-8 Juice
> 1 tbsp. red wine vinegar
> 1 tbsp. extravirgin olive oil
> 1 tsp. salt, or to taste
> 3 tbsp. chopped fresh cilantro
> Light sour cream (optional)

- Stir together all of the finely chopped vegetables.
- Add the juice and season with the vinegar, oil, salt, and cilantro.
- Cover and chill for at least 2 hours.
- Taste and correct the seasonings.
- If desired, serve topped with a dollop of light sour cream garnished with some more chopped cilantro.
- Makes 8-10 generous servings.
- Will keep, well covered, in the refrigerator for a week.

*Seed the tomatoes over a sieve and reserve the juice to add to the soup when the V-8 Juice is added.

Notes: the food processor may be successfully used to chop all of these vegetables. It is best, however, to chop each separately and stir together to finish the soup.

The number of jalapeño peppers used in this soup determines how much "zip" it has. Start with at least 1 medium to large pepper and add more according to your taste. Allowing the mixture to sit and chill for 2 hours will bring out more of the spicy note.

Grilled Lime Chicken

A lot of my recipes evoke memories of the occasions when they were cooked. I've prepared this chicken for a number of people in both small and large groups. The one I remember best was the Cincinnati Symphony fund-raiser that we did with our friends Kitty and Peter Strauss. It was a large and lively group, but we had the chicken marinated and ready to grill, so we enjoyed the party, too. It is a people-pleasing dish, easy on the hostess and light enough for serving on a hot day.

> **4 whole chicken breasts, halved, skinned, and boned**
> **¼ cup fresh lime juice**
> **1 tbsp. lime zest**
> **2 tbsp. finely chopped gingerroot**
> **2 tbsp. chopped fresh cilantro**
> **1 tbsp. honey (or artificial sweetener)**
> **1 tbsp. extravirgin olive oil (or vegetable oil)**
> **Dash cayenne pepper**
> **Dash salt**
> **Slices of fresh lime and sprigs of cilantro**

- Flatten chicken breasts between two sheets of plastic wrap.
- Stir together the lime juice, lime zest, gingerroot, chopped cilantro, honey, oil, pepper, and salt. Pour into a gallon-sized heavy plastic bag with a zip top.
- Add chicken to the marinade, seal the bag, and place in the refrigerator for at least 2 hours.
- Grill on a hot grill, or broil under a preheated broiler, for 5-6 minutes on the first side and 3-4 minutes on the second side. Allow more time if the chicken breasts are very large. They must be done through—but should not be dry.
- Serve hot or at room temperature.
- Garnish with the lime slices and sprigs of cilantro.
- Serves 8.

Fresh gingerroot is available at specialty produce markets as well as in the produce section of many grocery stores. It is often referred to as a "hand" of ginger since the shape of a section of it resembles a palm with fingers. It should be firm and very crisp and the outside peeling should be smooth and blemish-free. To maintain the freshness, store uncovered in the crisper drawer of the refrigerator. To use, cut off the amount needed and peel with a small paring knife. It can then be grated with a ginger grater, finely chopped with a knife, or finely minced in the food processor.

Grilled Herbed Vegetable Kabobs

"Ratatouille on a stick," as one of my students calls the grilled vegetables on a skewer, is an easy and delicious way to serve summer vegetables. The oil drips off of the vegetables as they cook on the grill. This causes this dish to be as low in calories as it is tasty.

> **1 small eggplant, washed and trimmed**
> **2 tsp. salt**
> **2 small yellow summer squash, washed and trimmed**
> **2 small zucchini, washed and trimmed**
> **1 medium Vidalia or other sweet salad onion, peeled**
> **1 sweet red pepper, cored**
> **1 green pepper, cored**
> **3 tbsp. extravirgin olive oil**
> **¼ cup coarsely chopped fresh basil leaves**
> **1 clove garlic, minced**
> **Freshly ground black pepper**
> **Pinch salt**
> **Bamboo skewers**

- Cut the eggplant into 1-inch cubes. Sprinkle eggplant with the 2 teaspoons salt and place in colander in the sink to drain. Allow to sit for 30 minutes. Rinse and pat dry.
- Cut the squashes into ½-inch rounds.
- Cut the onion into fourths and separate into single layers.
- Cut the peppers into 1-inch squares.
- Mix together the oil, basil, garlic, salt, and pepper.
- In a large shallow bowl, lightly toss the oil mixture with the vegetables, coating each vegetable well.
- Cover and let marinate, at room temperature, for at least 1 hour.
- Soak the bamboo skewers in cold water for 1 hour.
- Thread the vegetables onto the skewers.
- Grill on a hot grill, turning often, for 12-15 minutes or just until the vegetables are lightly browned and cooked through. (The squashes should be "crisp-tender.")
- Serves 8.

Note: it is important to use a small tender eggplant. The salting process causes the eggplant to give off excess liquid and absorb less oil.

Instant "Chocolate Mousse"

Even when people are dieting they need a little treat. This chocolate mousse may not be quite as good as a typical French dessert, but it's certainly far lower in calories. And it's quick to fix. Make it right before you sit down to eat and it's ready to serve when you are ready for dessert. Put it in tall-stemmed wineglasses and add a lovely mint leaf or a candied violet for the perfect light touch.

> **2 envelopes unflavored gelatin**
> **1¼ cups skimmed milk**
> **6-oz. pkg. semisweet chocolate chips**
> **½ cup boiling coffee**
> **⅔ cup sugar***
> **1 tsp. vanilla extract**
> **1 heaping cup ice cubes**
> **Grated semisweet chocolate, for garnish**

- In food processor with steel blade or in blender, add the gelatin and ¼ cup of the milk. Let sit a bit to soften and process to mix.
- Add the chocolate bits.
- With machine running, pour in the very hot coffee. Process until a smooth mixture is formed, stopping to scrape the sides of the container.
- Add sugar, vanilla, and remaining milk. Process to mix.
- With machine running, add the ice cubes, one at a time, and process until all ice is mixed in.
- Immediately pour into a serving dish, or individual dishes. Garnish with grated chocolate.
- The mousse will be ready to eat after 30 minutes in the refrigerator.

*For an even lower caloric content, substitute an equivalent amount of Nutra Sweet or other artificial sweetener.

MENU 2

Carrot-Walnut Soup

**Baked Fresh
Salmon Steaks**

Sautéed Dilled Cucumbers

**Green Beans with Roasted
Red Pepper Sauce**

**Strawberries
with Black Pepper
and Balsamic Vinegar**

Make chicken stock the day before it is needed. Refrigerate overnight. The fat will rise to the top and coagulate, making it very easy to remove. Homemade stocks are best when dieting, because the salt content can be controlled. Never add salt until the stock is finished.

Carrot-Walnut Soup

A light broth-based soup is a good starter when one is cutting back—it is filling and satisfying. Carrot-Walnut Soup has been in my repertoire for many years. This is also a very attractive soup, especially when served in clear glass bowls.

¼ cup finely chopped onion
1 clove garlic, minced
1 tbsp. unsalted butter or extravirgin olive oil
1 cup thinly sliced carrots
3 tbsp. chopped parsley
6 cups de-fatted chicken stock
½ cup raw long-grain white rice
Dash hot pepper sauce
¼ cup chopped walnuts
Extra chopped parsley

- Sauté onion and garlic in the butter, stirring constantly for 2 minutes.
- Add carrots, parsley, and stock and bring to a rolling boil.
- Stir in the rice and hot pepper sauce.
- Cook, partially covered, for 20 minutes or until rice is just tender.
- Just before serving, add walnuts and extra parsley as garnish.
- Serves 6-8.

Baked Fresh Salmon Steaks

You won't even need to tell people that the salmon is low calorie; it's so elegant it stands on its own. You can use this recipe with any kind of meaty fish, such as red snapper, halibut, or swordfish. The cucumbers, which are sautéed in a minimun amount of fat, serve as a tasty garnish.

1 tsp. sweet Hungarian paprika
Dash cayenne pepper
¼ cup fresh lemon juice
1 tsp. finely chopped lemon zest
1 clove garlic, finely minced
2 tbsp. chopped parsley
6 fresh salmon steaks, 1 inch thick

- Mix together all of the seasoning ingredients and rub on both sides of the salmon steaks.
- Place in a shallow dish and cover. Let sit at room temperature for at least ½ hour or in the refrigerator for at least 2 hours.
- Place on a rack in a shallow baking pan and bake in a preheated 375-degree oven for 10 minutes.
- Garnish with more chopped parsley and some parsley sprigs. Serve hot.
- Serves 6.

Sautéed Dilled Cucumbers

If you've never tried cooked cucumbers, you're in for a pleasant surprise. They are wonderful with any baked, grilled, or broiled fish.

> **3 medium cucumbers, peeled, seeded,**
> **   and cut into ½-in. slices**
> **6 scallions, thinly sliced**
> **1 tbsp. butter, margarine, or olive oil**
> **Freshly ground black pepper**
> **Dash salt**
> **2 tbsp. chopped fresh dill (or 2 tsp. dried)**

- In a nonstick skillet, sauté the cucumbers and scallions in the hot butter or oil, stirring constantly, for about 3 minutes.
- Add the seasonings and cook a minute longer. Taste and correct seasonings. Serve hot.
- The cucumbers should be cooked, but still crisp. They may be piled on top of the cooked salmon or served as a side dish.

Green Beans with Roasted
Red Pepper Sauce

Here is a pretty, different preparation of one of our most popular green vegetables, low in calories and fat and high in flavor.

Fresh green beans remain greener when cooked uncovered. If steaming, lift the lid of the steamer for a minute or two about halfway through the cooking time. This rule also applies to other green vegetables, such as broccoli, Brussels sprouts, etc.

For best flavor, color, and texture, start all fresh green vegetables in boiling, never cold, water. Root vegetables like potatoes may start cooking in cold water with good results. One basic rule of cooking that is often taught is: all vegetables that grow above the ground start in boiling water and all vegetables that grow below the ground start in cold water. It is a good rule to follow.

Balsamic vinegar is a dark, aged Italian vinegar that is good to have around when dieting. Its rich, full flavor adds great taste to salads without the addition of very much, if any, oil.

1½ lb. fresh whole green beans,
   washed and trimmed
1 large red bell pepper
2 tsp. extravirgin olive oil
2 tbsp. minced onion
1 small clove garlic, minced
¼ cup minced celery
Pinch salt
Dash hot pepper sauce
Fresh basil leaves, cut into strips, for garnish
   (or fresh parsley leaves)

- Cook the beans in just enough boiling, lightly salted water to cover, for 7-8 minutes. Drain and keep warm.
- Roast the pepper (see Guacamolé recipe), peel, and purée.
- In a small heavy pan, heat the oil, add the onion, garlic, and celery. Cover and sweat the vegetables for 3 minutes or until the celery is tender.
- Stir in the puréed pepper, salt, and hot pepper sauce. Cook for 1-2 minutes over medium heat, stirring. Taste and correct seasonings. Toss the beans in the pepper mixture and garnish with fresh basil or parsley.
- Serves 6-8.

Strawberries with Black Pepper and Balsamic Vinegar

The sweetness of the strawberries is enhanced by the spiciness of the pepper and the gentle acidity of this elegant, aged vinegar.

1 qt. fresh whole strawberries
Freshly ground black pepper
Balsamic vinegar

- Wash strawberries quickly in water or white wine. Let drain.
- Remove strawberry hulls.
- Place in a large serving bowl or individual dessert dishes.
- At serving time, lightly sprinkle with the pepper and vinegar.
- Serve immediately.
- Serves 6.

Skinny Remoulade Sauce
with Fresh Artichokes

6 whole fresh artichokes
1 large lemon
Salt

- Wash the artichokes in cool water.
- With a sharp knife, cut off each stem even with the base of the artichoke.
- With kitchen shears, trim the thorns off of leaf tips.
- Rub all cut surfaces with half of the lemon.
- Squeeze the remaining lemon into a large non-aluminum pot of water. Bring water to a rolling boil. Salt lightly.
- Add the artichokes and cover with a soft dish towel or a triple layer of strong white paper towels.
- Boil for 30-45 minutes, depending on the size of the artichokes, or until a leaf pulls out easily and the artichoke bottom is just fork tender.
- Remove artichokes and invert to drain well.
- Cool and chill until ready to serve.
- To serve: twist out each middle section, exposing the purple leaves and the "choke" underneath. Pull out the purple leaves.
- With a grapefruit spoon, remove the choke. Gently pull back the side leaves, making a "bowl" in the center of the artichoke. Spoon some Remoulade into the center of each artichoke. Garnish with a couple of fresh parsley leaves. Serve immediately.
- Serves 6 as a first course.

Disposable paper towels can be a handy cooking aid. Just be sure to choose a brand that does not fall apart when wet. When the towel comes in contact with food, it is also best to use plain white ones.

MENU 3

Skinny Remoulade Sauce
with Fresh Artichokes

Chicken Supreme
Poached in Fresh
Tomato Sauce

New Potatoes
in White Wine

Fresh Pineapple
with Kirsch

Skinny Remoulade Sauce

1 cup light or fat-free mayonnaise
½ cup plain fat-free yogurt
1 tsp. Dijon mustard
1 tbsp. fresh lemon juice
1 tsp. lemon zest
1 tbsp. drained capers
1 tbsp. chopped fresh tarragon (or 1 tsp. dried)
1 tbsp. chopped parsley
1 tbsp. chopped cornichon
Dash hot pepper sauce

- Lightly whisk together the mayonnaise and yogurt until smooth.
- Stir in the remaining ingredients.
- Cover and chill until ready to serve.
- Will keep in the refrigerator for a week.

Chicken Supreme
Poached in Fresh Tomato Sauce

3 whole chicken breasts, split, skinned, and boned

- Place the boned chicken breast halves between two sheets of plastic wrap and pound with a veal pounder to a consistent thickness.
- Make the Fresh Tomato Sauce according to the following recipe. (Sauce may be made the day before and chilled.)
- Heat the sauce in a large skillet that has a lid.
- Place the chicken breasts in the heated sauce. Spoon over enough sauce to cover each chicken breast.
- Place a sheet of parchment paper over the chicken, pushing down on the sides.
- Cover the pan and cook for 15 minutes over medium heat.
- Serve hot or cold garnished with some fresh herbs.

Fresh Tomato Sauce

**2 lb. very ripe tomatoes, peeled and seeded
    (reserve juice)
1 cup finely chopped yellow onion
2 cloves garlic, minced
½ cup finely chopped celery
1 tbsp. extravirgin olive oil
1 tbsp. tomato paste
1 tsp. sugar (or artificial sweetener)
Salt (or salt substitute), to taste
Freshly ground pepper, to taste
2 tbsp. each chopped fresh basil and oregano
    (or 2 tsp. dried)
¼ cup chopped parsley
1 tsp. chopped fresh thyme
    (or ⅓ tsp. dried thyme leaves)
1 cup de-fatted chicken stock
Splash dry white wine**

- Coarsely chop the tomatoes.
- In a skillet covered with a tightly fitting lid, sweat the onion, garlic, and celery in the oil for 5 minutes.
- Stir in the chopped tomatoes with their reserved juice. Cook, uncovered, over high heat for 3-4 minutes, stirring.
- Add remaining ingredients. Bring to boil. Cover, reduce heat, and cook for 10 minutes. Uncover, cook 10 minutes longer.
- Taste and correct seasonings.
- Makes about 2 cups.

New Potatoes in White Wine

Don't overlook the potato. Additions, as you know, are what make the potato high in calories. Not only are potatoes composed of good and filling carbohydrates, but they have lots of vitamins and minerals as well.

2 lb. small red new potatoes, well scrubbed
1 tbsp. butter
⅔ cup dry white wine
Salt, to taste
Freshly ground black pepper
3 tbsp. chopped fresh parsley
2 tbsp. chopped fresh dill

- Cut away a small strip of peel around the center of each potato with a vegetable peeler.
- Place in a saucepan and cover with lightly salted cold water.
- Bring to boil and cook until fork tender—about 20 minutes (depending on size of the potatoes).
- Drain in a colander.
- Melt the butter in a skillet.
- Add the drained potatoes and roll around to coat well.
- Add the wine, raise heat, and cook until wine is reduced to 1 tablespoonful.
- Sprinkle with salt, pepper, and the parsley and dill.
- Stir gently to coat the potatoes.
- Serve hot.
- Serves 6-8.

Cooking new potatoes that have a strip of peeling removed in a well-seasoned, de-fatted chicken stock infuses the potatoes with enough flavor to omit the addition of butter or margarine. If the stock has been salted, no additional salt should be necessary.

For a fancy new-potato dish, cut the potatoes in the shape of mushrooms. Using a small sharp paring knife, make a horizontal cut a little above center around the raw potato, cutting about halfway into the potato. Trim off the bottom by cutting in a downward motion, paring away the potato, and forming the shape of a mushroom stem. Cut a slice from the bottom of the stem to make it flat. Leave the peeling on the "mushroom cap."

Fresh Pineapple with Kirsch

One of my favorite desserts is fresh strawberries and wedges of pineapple with a little bit of kirsch, a very aromatic and flavorful liqueur made from cherries. Let this mixture sit in the refrigerator for several hours to blend the flavors. Garnish with some fresh mint.

> **1 fresh ripe pineapple**
> **Kirsch**
> **Fresh mint leaves**

- Peel the pineapple and cut into bite-sized wedges.
- Sprinkle with kirsch.
- Cover and chill for at least 1 hour.
- Serve in individual dessert bowls or wineglasses, topped with some fresh mint leaves.
- Serves 6-8.

Southern Comfort Suppers

A food trend that has managed to snare a fair amount of attention from the food press is "comfort food." Not long ago, I sat through a seminar at a food conference where the topic was current food trends. When the speaker referred to "comfort food" and gave some examples of such foods as meatloaf with mashed potatoes and cream gravy, I couldn't keep myself from leaning over to the person next to me and whispering, "Hey, he's just talking about supper!" Seriously, what all of this seems to mean is that we have seen a renewed interest in what I call "real" food. There is a special emphasis on fresh ingredients; baking real breads, muffins, etc., from scratch; and serving all sorts of food with a straightforward and honest approach. This is, you must admit, a far cry from the craze not so long ago that featured artistic food composed of tiny portions of exotic ingredients displayed on an oversized plate and often leaving the diner to wonder whether to dine or write a critique. I don't want to appear too cynical about some of the artistic creations of some of our talented chefs—both here and abroad. There's no doubt the innovative chefs of those movements made rich contributions to our culinary heritage. My point is that I cannot help but experience a warm feeling when I know that some of those big-name chefs are now endorsing the brand of cooking I know so well from my own heritage. This is "real" food to me. I think you, too, will admit that when you are tired and hungry after a long, hard day, you don't yearn for a plate of cold marinated raw fish and some "al dente" baby vegetables on the supper table to comfort you.

There is also a certain comfort in the psyche that goes along with rolling up the old sleeves and cooking up a tasty repast for the people you love. It is a special, nurturing act that makes for a warm atmosphere and some happy folks. That is why the activity in so many Southern homes has always centered around the good-smelling kitchen.

My intention in this chapter is to recreate some of those great flavors and to allow you to fill your kitchen with aromas that will delight the folks you enjoy feeding. The recipes I offer you are, for the most part, my own updated versions of old favorites. I have attempted to keep the simplicity and to capture some of those "honest" favors while offering foods that have been adapted to our current healthier, lighter eating patterns. I propose that you will find that you too can have fun "rolling up your sleeves" and cooking up some of these dishes, and you can even do it without having to spend the whole day in the kitchen.

MENU 1

Hearty Cabbage Soup

Oven-Barbecued
Chicken Breasts

French-Fried
Sweet Potatoes

Succotash Salad

Spicy Corn-Bread Muffins

Golden Peach Strudel

Hearty Cabbage Soup

Cooked cabbage has gained a bad reputation with many folks. I think that's because Southern cooks have always cooked it to death. Overcooking turns this sweet-flavored, crunchy vegetable into unattractive mush that has an unpleasant aroma. Please note that the coarsely shredded cabbage in this soup is added only in the last 10 minutes of cooking time. The cabbage shreds should be tender but still slightly crisp. It's a wonderful soup for a cool evening. It's also chock full of ingredients that are very good for you.

6 tbsp. unsalted butter
1 cup chopped yellow onion
4 cloves garlic, minced
4 oz. smoked country ham, cut into small cubes
6 cups unsalted chicken stock
3 medium carrots, peeled and coarsely shredded
3 large red potatoes, peeled and cut into small cubes
1 bay leaf
½ tsp. thyme leaves
1 medium head green cabbage, trimmed,
    quartered, and coarsely shredded
Dash cayenne pepper, or to taste
1 cup light cream
½ cup chopped parsley

- Melt butter in a large heavy pot.
- Add onion and sauté for 5 minutes, stirring.
- Stir in the garlic and ham. Cook 2-3 minutes more, stirring.
- Add the stock, carrots, potatoes, bay leaf, and thyme.
- Bring to boil, partially cover, lower heat, and simmer for 20 minutes.
- Stir in the cabbage and cook uncovered for about 10 minutes longer, or just until the cabbage is crisp-tender.
- Stir in the pepper, cream, and parsley.
- Reheat, but do not boil.
- Taste and correct seasonings.
- Makes 8-10 generous servings.

Oven-Barbecued Chicken Breasts

Of course it wouldn't be a complete Southern chapter without some sort of barbecue recipe. Southern cooks all have their own ideas about what constitutes the ultimate barbecue sauce. It is not my intention to enter myself into the "best" or "most authentic" barbecue sauce contest. I decided to include this recipe because it is so handy to make on days when you don't want to go outside to the barbecue grill. This chicken is tangy and juicy and can be done easily and quickly in the oven. Of course, you can feel free to try it on the grill, too.

> **4 whole chicken breasts, cut in half**
> **Barbecue Sauce (see below)**

- Wash the chicken in lukewarm water. Pat dry with paper towels.
- Place in a shallow baking dish, skin side up.
- Brush generously with the sauce.
- Turn, and brush with more sauce to coat well.
- Place in a preheated 400-degree oven.
- Bake for 20 minutes.
- Using tongs, turn and brush the skin side with more sauce. Bake 15 minutes longer or until chicken is done through. (Large chicken breasts may require 20-25 minutes on the second side.)
- Heat any remaining sauce and serve on the side.
- Serves 8.

Barbecue Sauce

1 stick (4 oz.) butter
1 cup finely chopped yellow onion
3 cloves garlic, minced
¼ cup honey
1 cup catsup
2 tbsp. Worcestershire sauce
1 tbsp. Dijon mustard
2 tsp. hot pepper sauce
¼ cup fresh lemon juice
½ tsp. salt, or to taste

- Melt the butter in a small heavy saucepan. Add the onion and garlic to the hot butter. Simmer for 5 minutes. (Do not allow the butter to brown.) Remove from the heat and allow to cool.
- Whisk together all of the ingredients until thoroughly mixed.
- Cook over low heat for 10 minutes, stirring.
- Cool, cover, and chill until ready to use.

Note: this chicken is also good served cold. It's great picnic fare.

French-Fried Sweet Potatoes

I was served a lot of sweet potatoes while growing up in Mississippi. The bright-colored, creamy tubers were baked (with lots of butter added), mashed, shredded, formed into patties, or put into pies. I never had them French fried until recently. I have enjoyed eating them in several good "American-style" restaurants and have had fun trying them in my own kitchen. Sweet potatoes never become as crisp as white potatoes, even with the soaking in ice water. The positive side of this is that you can make them an hour before dinner and keep them warm without changing the texture very much.

> **3 large sweet potatoes**
> **1 qt. peanut or vegetable oil**
> **Coarse sea salt**
> **Freshly ground black pepper**

- Wash potatoes thoroughly.
- Dry and trim off any blemishes.
- Cut into large julienne strips, leaving on the peel. Soak in ice water for 30 minutes.
- Pat dry with paper towels.
- Heat the oil in an electric fryer or in a heavy deep pan, to 375 degrees.
- Add the potatoes, a few at a time.

- Fry for 6-8 minutes, or until golden brown and tender. Drain on plenty of soft white paper towels.
- Line a baking sheet with paper towels and spread the potatoes on it.
- Place in a 200-degree warm oven to hold until serving time (no longer than 1 hour).
- Sprinkle with coarse sea salt and freshly ground pepper before serving.
- Serves 8.

Succotash Salad

The mixture of fresh-cut corn kernels and tender little lima beans has long enjoyed this interesting American Indian name. I've always been taken with this vegetable mixture, which is traditionally served as a hot dish. I also like it lightly chilled and dressed with a tangy dressing. It's a great picnic salad or a good side salad for all sorts of grilled meats and poultry.

6 medium ears tender white corn,
**   trimmed and washed**
2 cups shelled fresh baby lima beans
**   (or 1 10-oz. pkg. frozen)**
1 or 2 large jalapeño peppers,
**   seeded and minced**
¼ cup chopped cilantro or parsley
1 tsp. salt, or to taste
½ cup extravirgin olive oil
3 tbsp. fresh lime or lemon juice
4 ripe tomatoes
Bibb or leaf lettuce leaves, washed,
**   dried, and chilled**
Cilantro or parsley sprigs, for garnish

- Bring a large pot of water to boil.
- Add a pinch of sugar and the corn.
- Boil, uncovered, for 7-8 minutes. Do not overcook.
- Drain and refresh in ice water.
- Cut the kernels from the cob.
- Cook the lima beans in a small amount of lightly salted water until just tender.
- Drain and refresh in ice water.
- Toss together the corn, lima beans, jalapeño, and cilantro.
- Whisk together the salt, oil, and lime juice. Stir into the vegetable mixture. Let marinate for at least 30 minutes at room temperature.
- Cut the tomatoes into small wedges. Lightly season with some salt and pepper.
- Spoon some of the corn-bean mixture onto some crisp lettuce leaves.
- Surround with tomato wedges.
- Garnish with cilantro or parsley sprigs.
- Serves 8.

Note: the corn and lima beans can be successfully cooked in a microwave oven for this recipe. Follow instructions for times depending on the wattage of the oven.

Spicy Corn-Bread Muffins

In my opinion, one cannot even think about writing about Southern food, or "comfort" food, without at least one recipe for corn bread. Hot bread is an essential component in any acceptable Southern meal. (Angel Biscuits would also be appropriate for either of these meals; see index.) Anyway, I chose this particular corn bread because it is a necessary ingredient for the pork chops later in this chapter. It is also very tasty. If you don't want the spicy note, just omit the jalapeño pepper. The secret ingredient is a good-quality cornmeal: the coarse-grind meals will yield crunchier corn bread. Always serve corn bread piping hot!

1 stick (4 oz.) unsalted butter
½ cup finely chopped onion
1 large jalapeño pepper, seeded and minced
2 large eggs
1½ cups buttermilk or sour cream
2 cups self-rising yellow cornmeal
1 tbsp. sugar
¾ tsp. baking soda
1 tsp. paprika

- Melt the butter in a small, heavy saucepan.
- Take out 2 tablespoons of the melted butter and brush into a 12-cup muffin pan.
- Add the onion and pepper to the remaining butter. Heat to bubbling. (Do not allow to brown.) Turn off the heat and allow the mixture to sit for 15 minutes.
- Lightly beat the eggs.
- Stir the eggs and buttermilk into the cooled butter mixture.
- Stir together all of the dry ingredients.
- Pour the liquid ingredients into the dry ingredients. Fold together with a rubber spatula just until no dry ingredients are visible.
- Place the buttered muffin pan in a preheated 450-degree oven for 2-3 minutes, or just long enough to heat.
- Spoon the muffin batter into the hot muffin pan, filling each cup almost to the top.
- Place in the center of the 450-degree oven.
- Bake for 20-25 minutes, or until muffins are puffed and golden brown.
- Run a small flexible metal spatula around each muffin to loosen.
- Gently invert onto a rack.
- Serve hot.
- Makes 1 dozen large muffins.

Note: if regular, rather than self-rising, cornmeal is used, add 1 tablespoon baking powder and 1 teaspoon salt.

Golden Peach Strudel

The juicy, aromatic peach plays an important role in summer-time Southern desserts. As a matter of fact, the following recipe can be enjoyed year 'round when good-quality frozen peaches are available. This, of course, is not an authentic and traditional Southern recipe. I like to think of it as "the best of all worlds." While living in Germany, I became very fond of good strudel and thought it would be a good idea to combine it with the flavor I remember from the peach pies of my childhood. The peach schnapps is a new addition. When I first tasted this liqueur, a few years ago, I thought right away that it would be an interesting addition for this dish to enhance the peach flavor. This recipe is not nearly as labor intensive or time consuming as the old-fashioned pie. Frozen phyllo (or filo) pastry allows it to be quickly assembled. It can be made ahead, placed on a baking sheet, and refrigerated until time to bake. Serve it warm with freshly whipped cream or vanilla ice cream. (I have one friend who loves it with chocolate ice cream!)

> **2 lb. fresh, ripe peaches**
> **2 tbsp. fresh lemon juice**
> **1 tsp. finely chopped lemon zest**
> **2 tbsp. peach schnapps**
> **1 cup sugar**
> **Pinch allspice**
> **1 tbsp. cornstarch**
> **10 frozen phyllo pastry sheets**
> **2 sticks unsalted butter, melted**
> **Fine dry plain bread crumbs**
> **1 cup heavy cream, chilled**
> **1 tbsp. confectioners' sugar**
> **1 tbsp. peach schnapps**
> **Fresh mint leaves (optional)**

- Peel and thinly slice the peaches.
- Stir together the lemon juice, zest, and schnapps.
- Add the peaches and lightly toss to coat each slice.
- Stir together the sugar, allspice, and cornstarch. Toss with peaches.
- Let sit at room temperature for at least 30 minutes, or until the sugar dissolves.

- Using a soft, natural-bristle pastry brush, brush a sheet of phyllo with a light coating of the melted butter.
- Lightly sprinkle with bread crumbs.
- Repeat until 5 sheets of pastry are stacked to form 1 sheet.
- Lay out the layered pastry sheet lengthwise.
- Mound half of the peach mixture in the center of the pastry leaving a 5-inch border on the ends and a 2-inch border on each side.
- Fold the sides over the filling.
- Fold up the far end and roll toward you, forming a round roll with the filling enclosed.
- Seal the ends by brushing generously with butter.
- With a small sharp knife, cut 2-inch-long slits across the top.
- Repeat with remaining phyllo and filling.
- Place strudels on a parchment-lined baking sheet.
- Bake in the center of a preheated 350-degree oven for 30 minutes, or until golden brown.
- Let sit for 10 minutes before cutting into slices.
- Whip the chilled heavy cream until slightly thickened.
- Gradually add the sugar and remaining peach schnapps.
- Top each warm slice of strudel with the whipped cream.
- Garnish with a mint leaf, if desired.
- Each strudel makes 5-6 servings.

Variation: Apple Strudel—substitute tart cooking apples for the peaches. Peel, core, and thinly slice the apples; toss them with the lemon juice and zest. Instead of the peach schnapps, add an orange liqueur like Cointreau or Triple Sec to both the filling and the whipped cream. Toss ½ cup coarsely chopped pecans or walnuts into the filling just before assembling the strudel.

When buttering the phyllo pastry leaves, use a soft, natural-bristle pastry brush. Since they dry out so quickly, it is best to brush the edges first. Then, working quickly, butter the center. Use just enough unsalted butter to moisten the pastry. Too much butter will cause it to become soggy and difficult to handle.

MENU 2

Rutabaga Soup

Pork Chops with Zesty Corn-Bread Stuffing

Southern Summer Squash

Spinach-Orange Salad with Celery-Seed Dressing

Toasted Pecan Soufflé with Bourbon Custard Sauce

Rutabaga Soup

I know a lot of people who have a die-hard prejudice against any member of the turnip family. Before you turn the page and write off this recipe, give it a second consideration. The combination of apples, ginger, and cream with the rutabaga contributes such great flavor that it won't even be necessary to mention the soup's main ingredient, the lowly rutabaga—at least, not until your dinner guests have eaten it.

6 tbsp. unsalted butter
2 medium rutabagas, peeled and diced
2 Yellow Delicious apples, peeled and diced
1 cup chopped yellow onion
1 tsp. grated fresh gingerroot (or ¼ tsp. dry)
1 tsp. dark brown sugar
1 tsp. salt, or to taste
¼ tsp. hot pepper sauce
6 cups chicken stock
1 cup cream (heavy or light)
Chopped parsley, for garnish

- In a large, heavy pot, melt the butter over low heat. Stir in the rutabagas, apples, and onion.
- Cover and sweat the vegetables in the butter for 15 minutes.
- Add the ginger, sugar, salt, and hot pepper sauce.
- Stir in the stock; bring to a boil. Partially cover and reduce to simmer.
- Cook for 30 minutes.
- Purée in the blender.
- Return to a cleaned pot.
- Add cream. Reheat, but do not boil.
- Taste and correct seasonings.
- Serve hot with fresh parsley sprinkled on top.
- Serves 8-10.

Pork Chops
with Zesty Corn-Bread Stuffing

Pork has long been the favored meat on the Southern dinner table. And, although no one could argue with its unmatched flavor, many methods of preparation were too fat laden for our updated approach to eating. Pork has changed in recent years and the fat content has been reduced. By selecting lean center-cut pork chops (which have very little marbling of fat in the lean section), cutting away most of the outside rim of fat, and browning them in vegetable oil, you can keep the flavor and reduce the fat. Both the lemon and wine give this dish a light and elegant flavor addition. This is a super company dish because the entire preparation can be done hours ahead.

8 center-cut pork chops, cut 2-3 in. thick
Salt and freshly ground pepper
½ recipe Spicy Corn-Bread Muffin batter
   (see above)
6 tbsp. unsalted butter or margarine
1 cup chopped scallions
2 cloves garlic, minced
½ cup chopped celery
1 tsp. finely chopped lemon zest
1 tbsp. fresh lemon juice
½ cup chopped parsley
¼ tsp. cayenne pepper
Salt, to taste
1 large egg, lightly beaten
1 cup chicken stock
¼ cup vegetable oil
¾ cup dry white wine
8 thin lemon slices, cut on one side to the center
   and twisted
8 parsley sprigs

As soon as scallions are unpacked from the grocery bag, trim off the root ends, cut off the tough and stringy green tops (leave the tender portion of the green tops), and plunge into a basin of cool water. Let soak for a bit and then rinse to be sure to remove all grit. Pat dry with soft white paper towels and wrap in more towels to store. Place in a plastic bag and store in the crisper drawer of the refrigerator. You will have fresh and crisp green onions ready to chop for several days.

- Cut away most of the rim of fat on the outside of the chops. With a sharp knife, cut a pocket in the side of the pork chops. (Or ask your butcher to do this for you.)
- Season inside of pocket with salt and freshly ground pepper.
- Bake the corn-bread batter in a well-greased 8-inch square pan in a 425-degree oven for 25-30 minutes, or until golden and crisp around the edges. Let cool and cut into small cubes. Place in a mixing bowl.
- Heat the butter in a heavy skillet.
- Sauté the scallions, garlic, and celery, stirring, for 5 minutes over medium heat.
- Remove from heat, cool, and add to corn bread.
- Stir in the lemon zest and juice, parsley, pepper, salt to taste, and the egg.
- Add enough chicken stock, a tablespoon at a time, to moisten well. (Reserve remaining stock.)
- Stuff the pork chops.
- Fasten edges together with wooden toothpicks.
- Heat the oil in a large, heavy skillet. Brown the pork chops to a deep golden brown on each side.
- Place pork chops in a shallow baking dish.
- Pour off excess oil from skillet.
- Over high heat, reheat the skillet and add the wine and then the remaining chicken stock. Reduce by one-third.
- Pour reduction over the chops.
- Cover the dish with a double layer of heavy-duty foil and bake in the center of a preheated 350-degree oven for about 40 minutes (or until an instant thermometer reads 155-160 degrees when plunged into the center of a chop).
- Serves 8.
- Garnish each chop with a thin lemon slice and a parsley sprig.

Note: for a "Southern-style" stuffed turkey, try this corn-bread stuffing. Double the recipe to have enough stuffing for a 10-12-pound turkey.

Southern Summer Squash

I still think of these little golden cylindrical squashes as "summer" squash, because that was the only time they were available. And summer was really the only time they were eaten, because, with their high water content, they do not retain their texture and flavor after being frozen or canned. Nowadays they are usually called "yellow" squash and can be purchased in the fresh produce department year 'round (though I still like them best in summer when locally grown). I created this recipe from flavors that I remember. The leftovers make a delicious warmed-over lunch.

> ¼ lb. bacon, cut into small pieces
> 2 tbsp. olive or vegetable oil
> 1 large onion, thinly sliced
> 2 lb. small yellow summer squash, washed,
>   trimmed, and thinly sliced
> 3 medium tomatoes, peeled, seeded,
>   and coarsely chopped
> Salt and freshly ground black pepper, to taste
> 1 tbsp. chopped fresh basil leaves (or 1 tsp. dried)
> 1 cup shredded mild Cheddar cheese

- In a heavy skillet, cook the bacon pieces over medium heat, stirring, until crisp. Remove with a slotted spoon.
- Pour off all of the bacon fat. Add oil to the skillet and heat.
- Sauté the onion in the oil until translucent.
- Add the squash and cook, stirring often, for about 10 minutes, or until crisp tender.
- Stir in the tomatoes, salt and pepper, and basil.
- Cook 5 minutes more.
- Sprinkle the cheese evenly over the top of the vegetables.
- Cover the skillet for 2-3 minutes, or until the cheese melts.
- Serve immediately.
- Serves 8.

Spinach-Orange Salad
with Celery-Seed Dressing

If you have done much eating in the Southern part of our country, or read many Southern-style cookbooks, you know of the outrageous Southern sweet tooth. Your palate may find this dressing a bit on the sweet side and you may want to add only half as much honey for dressing this spinach salad. If, however, you need a dressing for an all-fruit salad, try it first as is. Either way, I think that you will find the rather unlikely combination of flavors in this recipe to be quite scrumptious.

1 lb. fresh spinach, washed, dried, stemmed, and chilled
Celery-Seed Dressing (see below)
2 large navel oranges, peeled* and thinly sliced
½ cup lightly toasted sliced natural almonds or lightly toasted pine nuts**

- Just before serving, toss the spinach with just enough dressing to coat.
- Garnish with orange slices and sprinkle with the nuts.
- Makes 8 small side salads or 4 large salads.

*Peel the oranges with a sharp, flexible-bladed knife. Cut through both peel and pith to reveal the orange pulp.

**Toast sliced almonds or pine nuts in a shallow baking pan in a preheated 350-degree oven for 6-8 minutes or until just lightly golden. Cool completely.

Celery-Seed Dressing

½ cup peanut oil
1 tsp. salt, or to taste
¼ cup cider vinegar
¼ cup honey
1 tsp. celery seed

- Combine all ingredients in the blender or food processor and blend until smooth. Makes 1 cup.

Toasted Pecan Soufflé
with Bourbon Custard Sauce

A surefire way to dazzle your guests is to whip out a soufflé to conclude a meal. They'll think you are a culinary magician, full of intrigue and drama. Actually, none of the above need be true. There is no mystique to a successful soufflé. As I've told my classes over and over, cooking is chemistry, and as with many things in life you must first master the basic rules. Once you do, you'll find that the soufflé works every single time. Read this recipe carefully, even though it seems a bit long. It'll be worth it, I guarantee. Bourbon is one of my favorite flavors. Splurge a bit and use a good one. Like wine, there is a big difference in the flavor with a higher-quality bourbon. The alcohol will cook off but the flavor remains: rich, mellow, and prominent. The Bourbon Custard Sauce is delicious. There's something special about the combination of bourbon and vanilla. You'll find it marvelous as well spooned over a plain cake such as pound cake.

The Soufflé

2 tbsp. bourbon whiskey
1-in. piece vanilla bean
¼ cup flour
1 cup milk
½ cup + 2 tbsp. sugar
5 large eggs, separated
3 tbsp. softened butter
¾ cup toasted, finely chopped pecans
2 large egg whites
Softened butter, for greasing dish
Sugar, for sugaring dish

- Pour the bourbon into a small saucepan.
- Slit the piece of vanilla bean down the center. Place in the bourbon.
- Heat the bourbon just until bubbles form around the edge. Turn off the heat and let sit for at least 30 minutes.
- Place the flour in a heavy, non-aluminum, medium saucepan.

- Gradually add the cold milk, whisking to make a smooth mixture.
- Whisk in the ½ cup sugar.
- Cook the mixture, whisking constantly, over medium heat until mixture comes to a boil and thickens. (Will be very thick.)
- Remove from heat and cool slightly.
- Beat in the egg yolks, one at a time, beating vigorously after each addition.
- Strain the bourbon and whisk in along with the butter.
- Add the pecans.
- If the soufflé is being made ahead of time (before dinner), stop at this point and cover the mixture with a round of buttered waxed paper. Place paper, buttered side down, directly on the mixture. May sit at room temperature for 1-2 hours. If longer time is needed, cover so that it will be airtight and refrigerate. The 7 egg whites should be room temperature before beating. Take care that the bowl for the egg whites is free of any grease, room temperature, and dry.
- When you are ready to assemble the soufflé, beat the 7 egg whites until bubbly. Gradually add the remaining 2 tbsp. sugar and beat until very stiff, but still very shiny. (Egg whites must not be dry.)
- With a spoon, stir in one-quarter of the whites into the base mixture. Mix well.
- Gently fold in remaining whites.
- Prepare a 2-quart soufflé dish that has been generously buttered with the softened butter and sprinkled with granulated sugar. (Tap against the side of the sink to remove excess sugar.)
- Prepare a collar for the soufflé dish by cutting a piece of parchment paper (or foil) that is long enough to wrap around the dish with 4 to 5 inches' overlap. Butter one side and place this side toward the center of the dish. Fasten the end with a metal paper clip and tie around the circumference of the dish with a piece of kitchen twine. When the collar is in place, carefully spoon in the soufflé mixture.
- Place in a preheated 400-degree oven so that the top of the soufflé dish is in the center of the oven.
- Close door and reduce heat to 375 degrees.
- Cook for 40-45 minutes, or until soufflé has risen to the top of the collar and is golden brown on the top.

- Do not open the oven door until the last 10 minutes of cooking time . . . or the soufflé may fall.
- When soufflé is done, carefully remove from the oven.
- Remove paper clip and snip string.
- Gently remove the collar and take soufflé dish immediately to the table.
- Serve hot with Bourbon Custard Sauce spooned over each serving.
- Serves 8.

Bourbon Custard Sauce

3 large egg yolks
⅓ cup sugar
Pinch salt
1 cup heavy cream
½ tsp. vanilla extract
3 tbsp. bourbon whiskey

- In electric mixer, beat egg yolks with the sugar and salt until very thick and lemon colored.
- Scald the cream in a heavy non-aluminum saucepan.
- Gradually beat cream into the egg mixture.
- Return to the pan and cook, stirring constantly, until mixture is just thick enough to coat a wooden spoon. Do not allow to boil.
- Whisk in the vanilla and bourbon.
- Strain.
- May be served warm or chilled.
- Makes about 1½ cups.

Dinner in a Dish

**Chicken Salad Deluxe
with Fresh Asparagus**

Seashell Salmon Salad

Creamy Lemon Dressing

Summertime Pasta Skillet

**Spaghetti with Fresh
Tuna-Caper Sauce**

Spanish Chicken

Creole Stuffed Eggplant

Zesty Red Beans and Rice

I knew from the start that I wanted to include a chapter on food that was easy to prepare and that featured all the ingredients in one dish/one pan/one pot. The only question I had was what to call this section. *Dinner in a Dish* won, as you can see, but the food is actually just as appropriate for lunch or for a late-night supper or for a picnic and you may use any vessel that serves the purpose. It's a delightful way to entertain informally, or simply to get dinner together, whether made ahead or cooked all at the last minute.

I want to dispel the myth that all one-dish meals have to be casseroles that taste like wallpaper paste and don't look very appetizing either. The following dishes can make an attractive appearance on your table while offering something for your taste buds as well. I've included some dishes to be served hot, some cold, and some at room temperature. Most of these dishes can be used year 'round, whether you're dining on the patio, heading for a weekend on the boat, or need a cozy dinner for a frosty day. Any of these recipes would fit all of the above situations and should do so with a minimum of fuss and preparation.

Chicken Salad Deluxe
with Fresh Asparagus

My file of chicken-salad recipes is a hefty one. Chicken salads were habitual visitors at my always popular Main Dish Salad classes, appearing in many guises and garbed in many dressings. My students may have tired of hearing me sing the praises of the boneless chicken breast, but I can't help it. It makes life easier. A boneless chicken breast lets you control the cooking time so that you need not have overcooked, threadlike chicken, which can only result in a soggy and unappetizing chicken salad.

The Chicken Salad Deluxe with Fresh Asparagus is not only very tasty but is also attractive. It's perfect for an elegant dinner party for a large group as well as for your family dinner. You'll notice I have included my recipe for "Cheaty Chicken Stock" here. My husband, a scholar, assures me there is no such word. Of course, I agree, and I hasten to point out that its nonexistence relieves me of the responsibility for spelling it correctly. My classes have always accepted the word, the spelling, and the technique, and I'll wager you will too, especially after you have found how flavorful and time saving it is on busy days.

For a sweeter onion, soak the sliced onion in ice water for 30 minutes before assembling a salad. Pat dry with paper towels before adding to the salad.

1½ cups chicken stock
½ cup dry white wine
2 large cloves garlic, peeled and crushed
8 boneless chicken breast halves, skinned, well trimmed, and pounded flat
1 lb. fresh asparagus
1 cup mayonnaise
1 tbsp. fresh lemon juice
¼ cup chopped parsley
1 tsp. chopped fresh thyme leaves (or ⅓ tsp. dried)
1 tbsp. chopped fresh basil leaves (or 1 tsp. dried)
½ tsp. salt, or to taste
¼ tsp. cayenne pepper
1 medium sweet red pepper, cored and washed
1 sweet salad onion, thinly sliced
½ cup sliced black olives
Leaf lettuce leaves, washed, dried and crisped
Parsley sprigs or basil leaves, for garnish
8-10 cherry tomatoes, halved, for garnish

- In a large, nonreactive skillet which has a lid, heat the stock and wine with the garlic cloves to boiling.
- Add the chicken breasts and cover with parchment paper or waxed paper, pressing down around the sides of the skillet.
- Cover with the pan lid.
- Turn to simmer and cook for 8-10 minutes, depending on the size of the chicken breasts. They should be just done, or springy to the touch. Do not overcook.
- Remove chicken to a side dish. Cover to prevent drying and set aside to cool.
- Reduce the stock mixture over high heat by one-half. Strain and reserve.
- Wash the asparagus. Break off the tough ends.
- Blanch in a large skillet about half-filled with lightly salted, boiling water covered with a triple layer of soft white paper towels.
- Cook, without a lid, for 3-4 minutes, or until crisp-tender.
- Immediately refresh in very cold water and drain. Pat dry with paper towels.
- Cut, on the diagonal, into 2-inch pieces.
- Make the dressing by whisking together the mayonnaise, 2 tablespoons of the reduced poaching liquid, lemon juice, parsley, thyme, basil, salt, and pepper.
- Cover and chill until ready to assemble the salad.

To Assemble the Salad

- Cut the chicken, across the grain, into approximately ¾-inch strips.
- Cut the red pepper into 4 or 5 strips and cut each strip, crosswise, into small julienne strips.
- Combine chicken, pepper strips, sliced onion, and olives with three-quarters of the dressing.
- Toss lightly. Line a large platter with the lettuce leaves.
- Mound the chicken mixture in the center of the platter.
- Lightly toss the asparagus with the remaining dressing. Arrange around the chicken.

When selecting fresh asparagus, look for spears that are at least ½ inch thick at the base. The "fatter" asparagus spears are more tender and tasty. The very slim ones are likely to be stringy and not as succulent. Also look for firm, smooth asparagus with tips that are very tightly closed.

- Garnish with parsley or basil leaves and cherry tomato halves.
- Cover and chill until serving time.
- Serves 8 as a main course.

Notes: when a recipe calls for *sweet salad onion*, my preference is the "Vidalia" from Georgia. It, however, has a short season in the early summer. When it is not available, use the salad onion that is in season, such as: "Walla-Wallas" from Washington, "Texas Sweets," or the Maui onion from Hawaii. The red Spanish onion is also good, though not as mild as some of the other onions, which are best when eaten raw.

My preference for black olives in this salad would be a very flavorful variety such as the Kalamata (sometimes spelled Calamata) or one of the other large, round, and very flavorful black Greek olives. (All of the above are usually best when purchased in bulk from a specialty food store.) However, if you are reducing the salt in your diet, you may prefer to use ordinary canned and pitted black olives.

In hot weather, or to save time, make what I call "Cheaty Chicken Stock." Just combine a good-quality reconstituted stock base or some canned chicken broth with the following and cook, uncovered, for 20 minutes. Strain and it is ready to use. For a more concentrated flavor, reduce strained stock by one-third. The end result is a time-saving stock of good quality. This cheaty recipe comes in handy for many occasions.

Cheaty Chicken Stock

Add to 8 cups of chicken broth:
1 bouquet garni composed of:
    3 sprigs fresh thyme (or 1 tsp. dried thyme leaves)
    3 sprigs fresh parsley and a bay leaf
1 large onion, coarsely chopped
2 medium carrots, coarsely chopped
2 ribs celery, with leaves, coarsely chopped
1 tsp. black whole peppercorns
½ cup dry white wine

Seashell Salmon Salad

The Seashell Salmon Salad is very pretty, and it is an economical way to serve something special for a large group. I like to use salmon in this dish when it is in season, but this salad is also very good with any firm fish such as swordfish or fresh tuna. You can multiply this recipe two or more times if you're having a crowd. It's perfect for an informal buffet.

1½ lb. fresh salmon steaks, cut 1 in. thick
½ cup mayonnaise
1 tsp. finely chopped lemon zest
Salt and freshly ground pepper, to taste
1 lb. small pasta shells
2 tbsp. extravirgin olive oil
2 medium cucumbers, peeled, seeded,
    and thinly sliced
½ cup thinly sliced scallions
3 tbsp. chopped fresh dill (or 1 tbsp. dried)
3 tbsp. chopped parsley
Hot pepper sauce, to taste
1 recipe Creamy Lemon Dressing
Crisp lettuce leaves
Dill and/or parsley sprigs
Lemon slices

- Generously spread both sides of the salmon with the mayonnaise, which has been combined with the lemon zest.
- Add salt and pepper, to taste.
- On a hot grill, or in a preheated broiler, grill the salmon for 6 minutes on the first side. Turn once and grill for 4 minutes on the second side (for 1-inch steaks—adjust accordingly for thicker or thinner cuts but do not overcook).
- Cool.
- Remove skin and bones. Flake flesh into large flakes.
- Chill, well covered, until ready to assemble the salad.
- Cook the pasta in a large pot of lightly salted water until done, but still firm.
- Drain.

- Toss, while still hot, with the 2 tablespoons of olive oil.
- Place the sliced cucumbers in ice water for 30 minutes.
- Drain well and pat dry.

To Assemble the Salad

- Gently toss together the salmon, pasta, cucumbers, scallions, chopped dill, parsley, and hot pepper sauce with the dressing. Season to taste with salt, if desired, and pepper. Line a platter or large shallow bowl with lettuce leaves. Mound the salad in the center.
- Garnish with parsley and/or dill sprigs and lemon slices. Serve chilled or at room temperature.
- Serves 8 as a main course.

Creamy Lemon Dressing

1 cup mayonnaise
½ cup all-natural sour cream (regular or reduced fat)
1 tsp. finely chopped lemon zest
¼ tsp. hot pepper sauce
1 tbsp. fresh lemon juice
3 tbsp. drained capers

- Gently whisk together all of the ingredients until smooth.
- Cover and chill until ready to use.
- Makes about 1½ cups.

Note: for a lower caloric content, substitute a low-fat mayonnaise and a plain nonfat yogurt in this dressing recipe.

Summertime Pasta Skillet

Summertime Pasta Skillet has existed in my home cooking repertoire for years without a name. It's best with prosciutto or Westphalian ham (a dry cured ham from Germany), but you can also make it with any kind of leftover ham or turkey. The flavor is not only especially interesting with smoked turkey, but it makes the dish lighter as well.

3 tbsp. extravirgin olive oil
½ cup finely chopped scallions
1 large clove garlic, minced
1 lb. small zucchini, washed and cut
   into a fine julienne
1 lb. fresh tomatoes, peeled, seeded, and coarsely
   chopped
1 tsp. chopped fresh oregano
1 tbsp. chopped fresh dill
3 tbsp. chopped flat-leaf Italian parsley
1 lb. fresh homemade pasta (spaghetti,
   fettucini, or linguine)
6 oz. prosciutto, cut into small strips
Salt, to taste
¼ tsp. hot red pepper flakes, or to taste
½ cup freshly grated imported Parmesan cheese

- In a large skillet, heat the oil. Sauté the scallions for 2 minutes.
- Add the garlic and zucchini and sauté, stirring, for 2 minutes more. Add the tomatoes and herbs.
- Cook for 10 minutes, stirring occasionally.
- Meanwhile, cook the fresh pasta in a large pot of lightly salted boiling water for just 1 minute, or until tender, but still firm.
- Drain thoroughly.
- Add the prosciutto to the skillet.
- Season with salt and pepper to taste.
- Toss the drained pasta into the skillet.
- Top with the Parmesan cheese.
- Serve immediately.
- Serves 6-8 as a main dish.

   Notes: smoked turkey or cooked smoked ham may be substituted for the prosciutto.
   Dry, "factory" pasta may be used. Cook it according to directions on the package, making sure that it is done through but still firm.

Dried herbs have a shelf life of about 1 year. When they lose their pungent aroma they should no longer be used, since their seasoning power is diminished. If stored for a very long time they either lose their flavor completely or take on unpleasant "off" flavors.

In order to release the maximum flavor from dried herbs, rub them between your thumb and forefinger as they are being added to the other ingredients.

Spaghetti with Fresh Tuna-Caper Sauce

I have lots and lots of spaghetti dishes, but this one, with fresh tuna-caper sauce, has stood the test of time. It's appropriate for the pasta course of a traditional Italian meal, but I think it's most useful as a one-dish meal, and it makes a great supper. It's a fine way to make one pound of fresh tuna filet go a long way. If fresh tuna is not available, a good grade of canned tuna (use two 7-ounce cans) can be used.

1 cup dry white wine
¼ cup water
1 tsp. dried black peppercorns
1 bay leaf
1 small yellow onion, cut into fourths
Pinch salt and dash hot pepper sauce
1 lb. fresh tuna filets, 1 in. thick
3 tbsp. extravirgin olive oil
1 large yellow onion, chopped
2 cloves garlic, minced
1 carrot, peeled and minced
1 rib celery, chopped
½ cup dry red wine
1 28-oz. can Italian plum tomatoes, well drained
    and coarsely chopped
¼ cup drained capers
½ tsp. dried oregano leaves
2 tbsp. chopped fresh basil (or 2 tsp. dried)
¼ cup chopped parsley
Salt and freshly ground pepper, to taste
1 lb. dry spaghetti
Whole Kalamata olives
Chopped parsley, for garnish

- In a large, nonreactive skillet, bring to boil the wine and water with the peppercorns, bay leaf, onion, salt, and hot pepper sauce.
- Add the tuna, in a single layer, and cover with parchment paper.
- Cover the skillet and poach for 10 minutes.
- Remove tuna from poaching liquid, let cool, and break into large flakes.
- Heat the oil in a large skillet and sauté the onion, garlic, carrot, and celery for about 10 minutes, stirring.
- Add the wine and tomatoes and cook for 5 minutes, uncovered.
- Stir in the capers, oregano, basil, and parsley.
- Toss in the tuna.
- Season with freshly ground pepper and salt, to taste.
- Cook for just a few minutes to heat the fish and blend the flavors.
- Cook the spaghetti in a large pot of lightly salted boiling water until done through but still firm.
- Drain thoroughly.
- In a large heated bowl, toss together the tuna sauce with the spaghetti.
- Serve immediately garnished with the olives and chopped parsley.
- Serve with crusty Italian or French bread.
- Serves 6 as a main course.

Spanish Chicken

This whole chapter could have been subtitled *A Chicken in Every Pot*, I realized as I pored over my one-dish meal recipes. I have tried to choose something you may not have in your repertoire. Again, my paean to the versatile boneless chicken breast: it has no cholesterol, very few calories, no fat when trimmed, and it cooks up quickly when time is critical. Spanish Chicken looks absolutely beautiful with the asparagus, olive, and almond garnishes. It's wonderful made ahead and reheated in the microwave. If anything, the flavors improve when it sits around for a while. Add a salad and some crusty French bread and you have dinner. I have inserted another chicken-stock recipe—this time a "noncheaty" one. It's good to have several recipes for chicken stock because it forms the basis for so many dishes. If you bone your own chicken breast—and remember the sooner the chicken is used after being boned, the more juicy and succulent it is—make some quick chicken stock with the bones. I enhance mine with chicken stock base. I prefer the paste-type base from the refrigerator section over the dry kind, which I find too salty. If you can't find the paste type, throw in a can of concentrated chicken broth.

> **4 whole chicken breasts, skinned and boned**
>   **(bones reserved)**
> **1 cup flour**
> **1 tsp. salt**
> **½ tsp. cayenne pepper**
> **½ cup extravirgin olive oil**
> **1 large yellow onion, thinly sliced**
> **3 cloves garlic, minced**
> **1 28-oz. can plum tomatoes, drained**
>   **and coarsely chopped**
> **2 cups long-grain raw rice**
> **Large pinch saffron threads**
> **4 cups chicken stock**
> **1 bay leaf**
> **Generous dash hot pepper sauce**
> **1 lb. fresh asparagus**
> **½ cup chopped parsley**
> **2 tbsp. drained capers**
> **½ cup toasted sliced natural almonds**
> **12 large pimiento-stuffed olives, sliced**

- Make Easy Chicken Stock according to following recipe.
- Pound boned chicken breasts between two sheets of plastic wrap with a veal pounder until they are an even thickness. Cutting across the grain, cut into 1-inch strips. Make seasoned flour by combining the flour with the salt and cayenne. Dredge the chicken pieces in the seasoned flour. Shake off the excess, leaving just enough flour to lightly coat.
- Heat 6 tablespoons of the olive oil in a large heavy skillet that has a well-fitting lid.
- Sauté the chicken, in small batches, for 4-6 minutes, or until golden brown. Remove to a side dish. Add remaining oil to skillet and heat until hot.

- Sauté the onion until translucent, stirring constantly.
- Add the garlic and sauté for 2 minutes.
- Add tomatoes and rice. Stir to coat rice well.
- Add the saffron to the warm stock and let sit for a few minutes.
- Strain to remove the saffron threads.
- Stir in the stock, bay leaf, and hot pepper sauce.
- Bring to a boil, stirring once or twice only.
- Cover, turn to simmer, and cook for 25 minutes.
- Wash the asparagus and break off the tough ends. Blanch in just enough boiling water to cover until crisp-tender. Cut on the diagonal into 2-inch pieces.
- After the tomato mixture has cooked for 25 minutes, all of the liquid should be absorbed. Toss in the chicken and let sit over the low heat for 2-3 more minutes to allow the chicken to heat through.
- Spoon the mixture into a serving dish or onto a platter.
- Garnish with the chopped parsley, cooked asparagus pieces, capers, almonds, and sliced olives. Serve immediately.
- Serves 8 as a main course.

Easy Chicken Stock

Bones and chicken trimmings from the boned chicken breasts (not the skin)
8 cups water
2 ribs celery, with leaves, coarsely chopped
2 carrots, coarsely chopped
2 medium yellow onions, coarsely chopped
3 sprigs parsley
2 sprigs fresh thyme
1 bay leaf
1 tsp. whole dried black peppercorns
1 tbsp. good chicken stock base
½ cup dry white wine

- Combine all ingredients in a large pot.
- Cook, uncovered, for 30 minutes over medium-high heat.
- Strain through a fine sieve.

Note: for a more concentrated stock, reduce by half after straining.

Creole Stuffed Eggplant

My New Orleans recipes keep popping up, and one of my favorites is the Creole Stuffed Eggplant. It's very pretty stuffed back in the shell, but if you're in a hurry you could discard the shell after scooping out the eggplant and put the ingredients in a buttered 1½-quart casserole. Add some extra herbs or even grated cheese on top, and it is truly a dinner in a dish.

> 2 small eggplants (approximately 1 lb. each)
> 6 tbsp. extravirgin olive oil
> 1 large yellow onion, chopped
> 3 cloves garlic, minced
> 1 large green pepper, cored and cut into small strips
> 3 large tomatoes, peeled, seeded, and cut
>   into small strips
> ¼ cup chopped parsley
> ¼ tsp. hot pepper sauce
> 1 tsp. salt
> 1 tsp. chopped fresh thyme leaves (or ½ tsp. dried)
> 1 large egg, lightly beaten
> 1 cup cubed cooked ham
> 6 oz. boiled medium shrimp
> ¾ cup coarse fresh bread crumbs
> 3 tbsp. melted butter
> ¼ cup freshly grated Parmesan cheese

- Wash the eggplants and cut in half lengthwise. Score the cut sides with a sharp knife, cutting about ⅛ inch into the eggplant surface.
- Pour 2 tablespoons of the olive oil into a baking pan, spreading evenly on the bottom of the pan.
- Place the eggplants, cut side down, on the pans.
- Place in a preheated 375-degree oven for 30-40 minutes, or until fork tender.
- Remove and let cool.
- Spoon the pulp from the eggplant halves, taking care to leave the shells intact.
- Coarsely chop the pulp.
- Heat remaining oil in a large skillet.

- Sauté the onions, stirring, for 5 minutes.
- Add the garlic and green pepper; sauté 3 minutes longer.
- Add the tomatoes; cook, stirring, for 2 minutes.
- Remove from heat and stir in the chopped eggplant, parsley, hot pepper sauce, salt, thyme, and egg. Mix well.
- Add the ham and shrimp.
- Mix together the bread crumbs, butter, and Parmesan.
- Spoon the eggplant mixture into the reserved eggplant shells.
- Top with the bread-crumb mixture.
- Place in a lightly greased large baking dish.
- Bake in a preheated 375-degrees oven for 20 minutes or until golden brown on top. Serve hot.
- Serves 6-8 as a main course.

Note: serve with crusty French bread.

Zesty Red Beans and Rice

Finally, my Zesty Red Beans and Rice. In New Orleans, Red Beans and Rice is served every Monday, first because it's laundry day with no time to cook, and second because there is usually a hambone left over from one of the weekend's meals. Legend has it that Creoles, true to their thrifty French ancestors, never threw anything away in the kitchen. There are probably as many recipes for this dish as there are Creole cooks, but this is my favorite because of its seasonings. On cold days, and even on not-so-cold ones, it's very hard to beat this "down-home" dish for real "comfort food."

If you can't soak dried beans overnight, use the quick method: wash and rinse them, put them in a saucepan, and cover them with water. Bring to a boil, cover the pot, turn off the heat, and let sit for one hour. They are now ready to be cooked to the desired tenderness. (It may be necessary to add extra water during the cooking time.)

To make **Homemade Pepper Sauce**: take a handful of very spicy, small chile peppers, such as Serrano peppers, and wash them. Pour a bottle of vinegar into a non-aluminum saucepan and heat to boiling. Push the peppers into the empty vinegar bottle. Using a funnel, pour the very hot vinegar over the peppers. Seal and let marinate at room temperature for at least 10 days. Use the vinegar as the "sauce"—not the peppers themselves. New hot vinegar may be added as many as 3 times to the same peppers to make new Pepper Sauce. Also delicious on boiled fresh greens, like collards or kale.

2 lb. dry red beans
3 qt. water
1 lb. leftover cooked, smoked ham with bone,
    or 1 lb. dry cured "country ham"
4 large cloves garlic, minced
2 cups coarsely chopped onion
2 large bay leaves
1 tsp. hot pepper sauce
1 tsp. sugar
Salt, to taste (none needed if country ham is used)
2 cups raw long-grain rice, cooked
Chopped red Spanish or other sweet onion
Homemade Pepper Sauce (see at left)
    or commercial hot pepper sauce

- Rinse the beans well. Drain. Put in a large pot, add the water, and soak overnight. Remove the bone from the ham and cut up the ham. Add the bone to the beans and bring to boil. Simmer for an hour, partially covered. Add the cut-up ham, garlic, onions, bay leaves, hot pepper sauce, and sugar. Cook, covered, for about 2 hours more, or until very tender. (Add more water, if necessary.)
- Remove bay leaves.
- Remove about 2 cups of the beans. Purée in food processor and return to the pot.
- Simmer the mixture for 5 minutes, just to reheat.
- Taste and correct seasonings.
- Serve hot over the rice.
- Garnish with a spoonful of the chopped onion and pass the Homemade Pepper Sauce or hot pepper sauce bottle.
- Serves 8-10 as a main course.
- Serve with crusty French bread or corn bread.

One-Fork Buffets

There are many occasions when we want to feed people more than cocktail munchies, but, for various reasons, we do not want to set a formal table. This chapter is directed toward those times. Maybe you are entertaining 40 people and setting enough places at a table or tables is simply not possible. Even if you are only feeding a small group, there are times when it is appropriate and more convenient to sit around and simply eat with the plate on a lap tray. This is definitely not the time to serve dishes that require a lot of cutting. Wielding a knife while balancing a plate can take all of the fun out of eating even the most delectable dishes. But please don't think that the meals have to be planned around pots of finely chopped and stewed mystery meat. This is the time to plan dishes that, when set out on a dining table or kitchen counter, will compose an attractive buffet. You want to plan the sort of meal where the guests can comfortably help themselves on one plate, pick up one fork and a napkin, and be all ready to sit down and enjoy eating. I often use boneless chicken breasts cut into pieces for these buffet suppers. It is a safe choice because almost everyone likes chicken and boneless chicken breasts can be used in a virtually endless variety of tasty dishes. This chapter features some of my favorite chicken recipes. There are also some fun "finger food" appetizers and easy-to-serve-and-eat desserts.

When I arrived in Cincinnati from New Orleans in the late 1960s, few people in the area were interested in Creole cooking, or knew what it was for that matter. Since I learned my first cooking skills while living in Mississippi and Louisiana, much of my cooking was inspired by this colorful and tasty cuisine. Today, Louisiana cuisine has gained great popularity all over the country. I am still cooking my old favorites and my guests keep enjoying them. Some dishes, like the Shrimp Remoulade, are standard, classic recipes that I brought with me from New Orleans and have never changed. Many of the dishes, which I still enjoy time and again bringing out for a dinner party, have changed a bit over the years and have become my own recipes. They, too, are very much inspired by the authentic flavors of the wonderful and colorful cuisines of Louisiana.

MENU 1

Shrimp Remoulade

Ham and Chicken Jambalaya

Tossed Salad Greens
with Fabulous
Salad Dressing

Foolproof French Bread
(see index)

Praline Cheesecake Squares

Shrimp Remoulade

This is what I think of as "real" remoulade. That doesn't actually mean that the creamy French one is in any way not authentic. I simply find that it tends not to excite the taste buds like this colorful, piquant sauce does. In the last century, when the French actually inhabited the "French Quarter" in New Orleans, this dish was made only by professional chefs and required proper technique to create a successful smooth and emulsified sauce. With the invention of the electric blender, it became a snap for the home cook to make. I make mine now in the food processor. Remoulade also tastes great on cold poultry, cold sliced pork roast, and, of course, other chilled seafood like crabmeat. Mix it half and half with some mayonnaise to create a tasty dressing for all types of vegetable salads. The real secret of success in this recipe is to cook the shrimp in a flavorful "broth" seasoned with the "Shrimp Boil" that follows the recipe. Do not be shy when adding the salt. A good Creole chef always strives to have the salt level in the shrimp pot the same as sea water. It is also important not to overcook the shrimp so they are tender and succulent.

> 1½ lb. boiled, peeled, and deveined shrimp
> 1 small head iceberg lettuce, shredded
> ½ cup coarsely chopped scallions
> ¼ cup canned tomato sauce
> 1 tbsp. paprika
> 4 tbsp. Creole mustard*
> 1 large clove garlic, peeled
> 1 tsp. salt
> ½ cup tarragon wine vinegar
> ½ cup coarsely chopped celery
> ½ tsp. cayenne pepper**
> 1 cup vegetable oil
> Sprigs of parsley or tarragon

- Place the shrimp on a bed of the shredded lettuce, either on individual serving plates or on a large platter.
- Blend all of the remaining ingredients, except the oil and parsley or tarragon, together in a blender or food processor until smooth.
- With the motor running, pour in the oil in a slow stream, until all oil is incorporated and sauce is smooth.

- Pour enough sauce over the shrimp to lightly coat each shrimp.
- Garnish with parsley or fresh tarragon sprigs.
- Serves 6 as an appetizer.

*Creole mustard is "whole grain" horseradish mustard.

**For a less spicy sauce, you may want to cut the amount of cayenne pepper in half.

Shrimp can be purchased fresh or frozen. It tastes best when cooked in the shell. For the most flavorful boiled shrimp, season a large pot of water with the following homemade "Shrimp Boil." It is best to prepare the shrimp boil and let it boil for at least 20 minutes before adding the shrimp. Do not overcook the shrimp. As soon as it becomes opaque and pink, it is done. Drain immediately. Cool, peel, and devein. Chill until ready to assemble the dish.

Shrimp Boil: for each quart of water add the following: 2 tbsp. salt, ½ lemon, 12 whole allspice, 2 sprigs thyme, 1 bay leaf, 1 tsp. crushed hot red pepper, 1 tsp. celery seed, ½ tsp. mustard seeds, and ½ tsp. whole black peppercorns. This same recipe may be used for cooking fresh live crabs. Cool whole crabs for 20-25 minutes after the mixture has boiled for 20 minutes.

Ham and Chicken Jambalaya

The Creoles were the offspring of the French and Spanish settlers who settled in the Gulf states, mostly in and around New Orleans. They brought the distinctive flavors of each culture to their kitchens and produced dishes that have no equals in the culinary world. Jambalaya is the epitome of the intermarrying of French and Spanish cuisines. The word means a combination of one or more kinds of meat or seafood. This recipe calls for a flavorful cured country ham. The bouquet garni is essential for the true "Creole" flavor. However, if fresh thyme sprigs are not available, dried thyme leaves may be substituted.

When adding a bouquet garni to a thick and chunky mixture such as jambalaya, tie the little bundle of herbs with a long string. Tie the end of the string to the pot handle before covering the pot. This eliminates the need to search for it later and it is easily removed.

Rice should always rest for at least 15 minutes after cooking so that each grain is separate and fluffy.

1½ lb. boneless chicken breasts
Salt and freshly ground black pepper
3 tbsp. olive oil
1 large yellow onion, sliced
1½ tbsp. flour
½ lb. cured country-style ham
3 large cloves garlic, minced
3 cups peeled, seeded, and chopped tomatoes*
½ cup tomato juice
½ cup dry white wine
1 cup chicken stock
1 large red bell pepper, chopped
1 large green pepper, chopped
3 ribs celery, chopped
1 bouquet garni composed of:
    2 sprigs fresh thyme
    2 sprigs parsley and a large bay leaf
Pinch sugar
½ tsp. hot pepper sauce
Salt, to taste
1½ cups raw long-grain rice

- Cut the chicken breasts across the grain into 1-inch strips. Season lightly with salt and pepper.
- Heat the oil in a large heavy pot.
- Sauté the chicken, one layer at a time, for 3-4 minutes or until lightly browned.
- Remove to a side dish and reserve.
- Sauté the sliced onion in the remaining oil until just tender. Stir in the flour. Cook for 2 minutes, stirring constantly.
- Cut the ham into small pieces and add along with the garlic.
- Cook 2 minutes more, stirring.
- Stir in the tomatoes and tomato juice, wine, chicken stock, red and green pepper, and celery.
- Add the bouquet garni, sugar, hot pepper sauce, and salt.
- Stir in the rice, making sure that all of the rice grains are pressed into the liquid.
- Bring to a boil, cover, and reduce to a simmer. Simmer for 25 minutes.
- Stir in the chicken and cook 10 minutes longer.

- Remove from heat and let rest for 15 minutes.
- Serve hot.
- Serves 8.

*When fresh tomatoes are not available, use 3 cups of drained and coarsely chopped canned Italian plum tomatoes.

Tossed Salad Greens
with Fabulous Salad Dressing

I don't even remember when I first ate this dressing. It was a favorite when I lived in New Orleans. Easily made in the blender or food processor, it is a great dressing for very flavorful greens like watercress, Belgian or curly endive, spinach, romaine, or arugula. Use sparingly, making sure there is just enough dressing to very lightly coat each leaf. It is the most flavorful with imported Pecorino Romano cheese and a very good grade of cold-pressed, extravirgin olive oil. Fresh lemon juice is a must. This dressing keeps for two to three weeks in a tightly covered container in the refrigerator.

¼ lb. Romano cheese
1 cup extravirgin olive oil
Juice of 1 large lemon
2 large cloves garlic, peeled

- Cut cheese into small pieces.
- Place all ingredients in the blender or food processor and blend until smooth.
- Toss with 3 different varieties of chilled, crisp lettuce leaves. Use just enough dressing to lightly coat the greens.
- Serve immediately after tossing.
- Makes 1½ cups of dressing.

Praline Cheesecake Squares

This praline dessert is a traditional American cheesecake with a wonderful New Orleans twist. Pralines are a very popular pecan and caramelized brown sugar candy. This is also a perfect casual dessert because it can be cut into easy-to-serve and easy-to-eat bars. Best made the day before, it's wonderfully reminiscent of those yummy, if a bit sinful, New Orleans pralines. (Southerners say "praw-leens." Yankees say "pray-leens.")

Crust

1 cup flour
¼ cup dark brown sugar
1 cup chopped pecans
1 stick unsalted butter, melted

- Mix together in food processor.
- Press into bottom of 13" x 9" baking dish.
- Bake for 15 minutes in a 350-degree oven.
- Cool.

Filling

16 oz. cream cheese
1 cup sugar
1 tsp. vanilla
3 eggs

- In food processor, beat cream cheese, sugar, and vanilla until smooth.
- Add eggs and process until mixture is smooth and fluffy.
- Pour over crust.
- Bake in the center of a 350-degree oven for about 20 minutes or until set and puffed.
- Remove and spread with Topping.

Topping

2 cups sour cream
6 tbsp. sugar
1 tsp. vanilla
Pecan halves

- Stir together (except pecans) gently with a fork to mix.
- Spread on baked filling and return to oven.
- Bake 5 minutes more. Remove and cool on a rack.
- Chill.
- Cut into squares. Place a pecan half in the center of each square.
- Keep chilled until ready to serve.

Endive Appetizers

A few years ago when we were on sabbatical in Berlin, we resided in a charming little apartment near the Botanical Gardens. Unfortunately, for a cook like me, "little" was the perfect adjective to describe the kitchen. My dear husband was in Berlin to do research and write a book. But I, for the first time in many a year, had the luxurious role of "doing as I pleased." That meant that I had all the time I wanted to shop in the fabulous international gourmet shops and charming local markets that Berlin has to offer, plus the time to cook to my heart's content. You guessed it, I made the most of that small kitchen. I managed to squeeze far more people into that tiny little apartment for parties than any European would dream of inviting. And I managed to serve up much more interesting fare than dip and chips.

One of my standbys for fresh and attractive cocktail munchies was this cheese-filled endive. Belgian endive is so plentiful and inexpensive in Europe. (In fact, in the past few years it has gotten much easier to find and less expensive in this country.) And, of course, the French "chèvre" or goat cheese was plentiful and wonderful. With my trusty pastry bag and a couple of large star tips, I turned out an amazing number of these and other varieties of filled vegetables. That's when this appetizer gained so much popularity on my table and I still often serve it when I need an attractive, easy-to-eat first course or party food.

Try the filling as a piped-in stuffing for cherry tomatoes, hollowed-out cucumber, or zucchini rounds. As a bit of a footnote, I would add that the pastry bag is the secret weapon here. It takes only a small amount of skill and practiced technique to create really attractive and impressive appetizers, desserts, etc., with the greatest of ease. I don't recommend trying to run a kitchen without at least one large (15-16") nylon pastry bag.

2 large heads Belgian endive

- Wash the endive.
- Separate into individual leaves, roll in paper towels, and place in a plastic bag in crisper drawer of the refrigerator. Chill for at least 1 hour.

MENU 2

Endive Appetizers

**Chicken Florentine
with Lemon-Tarragon
Wine Sauce**

**Tomato-Stuffed Avocado
with Fresh Tomato French
Dressing**

**Pepper and Herb
Flat Bread**

The Ultimate Brownie

Filling

1 large red bell pepper, roasted
2 tbsp. chopped scallions
1 tbsp. chopped fresh dill (or 1 tsp. dried)
1 tbsp. chopped fresh parsley
1 tsp. fresh lemon juice
4 oz. fresh goat cheese
4 oz. cream cheese
Pinch cayenne pepper
Dill or parsley sprigs

- Peel, seed, and finely chop the red pepper.
- Cream together in the food processor, or in electric mixer, the herbs, pepper, lemon juice, and cheeses. Stir in the pepper.
- Taste and correct the seasonings.
- Spoon the cheese filling into a large pastry bag that is fitted with a large (7-8 mm) star tip.
- Pipe the mixture into the chilled endive leaves.
- Garnish with small sprigs of dill or parsley.
- Cover and chill until ready to serve.
- May be made as long as 2 hours before serving.
- Serves 8.

Chicken Florentine
with Lemon-Tarragon Wine Sauce

One of my very most interesting and fun cooking experiences, and, I might add, one that lasted for several years, was teaching at Hurrah. Hurrah was one of Cincinnati's first "real" kitchen shops. It was an intriguing shop with a charming owner—Jane Miller—and a full line of just about every kitchen gadget, pot and pan, etc., any cook could ever want to own. When Jane started the shop, she told me that she was planning a cooking school and invited me to teach there. And that was the beginning of a lot of fun times and many, many cooking classes. The shop is long gone, but I am still very much in contact with many people I got to know as students there, not to mention Jane and several members of her former staff. This chicken recipe reminds me of Hurrah because I originally developed it for a class there. The recipe has changed a bit over the years, but like Jane and crew, it has only gotten better.

4 whole chicken breasts, split and boned
Freshly ground pepper and salt
2 eggs
2 tbsp. water
Flour
2 cups fine fresh bread crumbs*
5 tbsp. unsalted butter
5 tbsp. vegetable oil
¾ cup dry white wine
Juice of 1 large lemon (approximately 2 tbsp.)
2 tbsp. chopped fresh tarragon (or 2 tsp. dried)
1 lb. fresh mushrooms, cleaned, stemmed, and sliced
2 large shallots, finely chopped
2 lb. fresh spinach, washed and stemmed
Chopped parsley

- Trim the boned chicken breasts.
- Place between two sheets of plastic wrap and pound with a veal pounder to a consistent thickness.
- Cut chicken, across the grain, into 1-inch pieces.
- Season with salt and pepper.
- Lightly beat eggs with water.
- Dredge the chicken in the flour, quickly dip into egg mixture, and coat with the bread crumbs. Cover and chill for at least 1 hour.
- Melt 2 tablespoons of the butter in a large heavy skillet. Add 2 tablespoons of the oil and heat until very hot. Sauté the chicken, a few pieces at a time, until golden brown and cooked through— about 5 minutes.
- Place on a serving platter and keep warm in a warm oven.
- Pour any excess fat from skillet.
- Over high heat, reheat the skillet and add the wine. Deglaze the pan with a wooden spoon or spatula.
- Reduce wine by one-half and stir in the lemon juice and tarragon.
- Season to taste with salt and pepper. Set aside to reheat later or keep warm.

COOKING WITH MARILYN

- Heat 2 tablespoons each of the remaining butter and oil in a second skillet. Over high heat, quickly sauté the mushrooms—for 3-4 minutes, stirring. Arrange on top of the chicken.
- Heat the remaining butter and oil in the skillet.
- Sauté the shallots, stirring, for 1-2 minutes.
- Add the washed spinach leaves, with the water clinging to the leaves, and sauté, stirring, for 2-3 minutes or just until wilted.
- Season to taste with salt and pepper.
- Ladle the warm sauce over the mushrooms and chicken.
- Surround the mushrooms and chicken with a ring of the sautéed spinach.
- Sprinkle mushrooms with chopped parsley.
- Serve immediately.
- Serves 8.

*Use "day-old" bread to make bread crumbs. I don't toast them for this recipe, but they should be dry.

Tomato-Stuffed Avocado
with Fresh Tomato French Dressing

A good choice for such a buffet, these filled avocado halves look beautiful when arranged on an attractive platter. They are easy to eat and go nicely with many main dishes. In fact, they can become a main luncheon dish with the addition of some cooked cold seafood such as shrimp or scallops.

> 1 cup Fresh Tomato Sauce (see index)
> 8 medium ripe tomatoes
> Parsley or thyme sprigs
> 3 tbsp. white wine vinegar
> ⅔ cup avocado oil (or olive oil)
> 1 tbsp. chopped parsley
> 1 tsp. chopped fresh thyme leaves (or ⅓ tsp. dried)
> 1 tbsp. chopped fresh chives
> 4 large ripe avocados
> Juice of 1 lemon

- Make the tomato sauce according to the recipe.
- Place tomato-sauce pan in ice water and stir sauce until cool. Measure 1 cup. (Reserve and chill or freeze remainder for later use.)
- Peel the 8 tomatoes by piercing them with a fork and plunging into boiling water, then in ice water.
- Cut in half crosswise and remove seeds and pulp.
- Cut into julienne strips and chill until ready to serve.
- Combine the 1 cup of tomato sauce with the remaining dressing ingredients to make the dressing.
- Taste dressing and correct seasonings.
- Toss the tomato slices with just enough of the dressing to coat.
- Cover and chill.
- At serving time, cut the avocados in half horizontally.
- Using a large spoon, carefully remove the avocado from the skin.
- Remove seed.
- Acidulate the avocados with a light coating of lemon juice to prevent darkening.
- Spoon the tomatoes into the cavity of the avocado.
- Drizzle some of the extra dressing over the top.
- Garnish with fresh thyme or parsley sprigs.
- Serves 8.

Pepper and Herb Flat Bread

Flat Bread is so much fun to make. Since it is merely a ball of dough that is flattened, it requires only a simple baking sheet and no special bread pan. Add the convient factors of quick-rising yeast and the food processor and it is fast and easy, too. I always recommend it for beginning bread bakers. It is Mediterranean in origin, but I think this recipe has wandered a bit from its ethnic roots. It is definitely tasty! I know, because I have never had much left after a dinner party or cooking class.

2½ cups unbleached flour
1 pkg. quick-rising dry yeast
1 tsp. salt
2 tsp. sugar
3 tbsp. extravirgin olive oil
1 large clove garlic, minced
1 cup warm water (105-115 degrees)
½ tsp. dried thyme leaves
½ tsp. dried oregano leaves
½ tsp. dried basil leaves
2 tsp. freshly ground coarse black pepper

- In food processor with steel blade (or in mixer with dough hook), stir together 2 cups of the flour with the yeast, salt, and sugar.
- Heat 1 tablespoon of the oil and "sweat" the garlic in covered pan over low heat. Do not brown. Cool.
- Add the water, garlic, and 1 tablespoon oil to flour mixture.
- Mix well.
- Add herbs and pepper and enough of the remaining flour to make a stiff dough.
- Knead until dough is smooth and elastic (about 1 minute in food processor or 6 minutes in mixer).
- Place dough in a gallon-sized plastic bag. Press out air and seal at top.
- Place in a warm place and let rise for 30 minutes, or until doubled.
- Punch down dough and shape into a ball.
- Place on a greased baking sheet and flatten to a 9- to 10-inch-diameter disc.
- Prick with a fork and brush with remaining tablespoon of olive oil.
- Cover with plastic wrap and let rise for 15-20 minutes in a warm place.
- Place in the center of a preheated 375-degree oven and bake for about 30 minutes or until golden brown.
- Cool on a rack.
- Cut into small wedges or thick slices and serve warm or at room temperature.
- Makes 1 loaf.

The Ultimate Brownie

    I knew that I could not put a bunch of my favorite recipes in a book without including a brownie recipe. The question was simply: which brownie recipe? After testing some of my favorites, my conclusion was to combine several of my favorite brownie recipes to come up with the following one, which I have decided to call "The Ultimate." You may dust the tops of these fudgy brownies with powdered sugar to dress them up a bit, but frosting is really not needed. If you want richness beyond belief, add 6 ounces of some very good semisweet chocolate chips.

        8 oz. good semisweet* chocolate, cut into small pieces
        1 stick (4 oz.) unsalted butter
        4 large eggs
        ½ tsp. salt
        2 cups sugar
        2 tsp. vanilla extract
        1 cup flour
        1 cup shelled pistachios or chopped pecans

- In a double boiler or heavy saucepan, melt the chocolate with the butter over moderate to low heat, stirring occasionally. Cool.
- In electric mixer, beat the eggs until frothy.
- Add salt to eggs.
- Gradually add sugar to eggs, beating constantly, until very light colored and thick—8-10 minutes.
- Add the cooled chocolate mixture and vanilla and mix well.
- Gently fold in the flour and nuts.
- Generously grease a jelly-roll pan.
- Line with parchment or waxed paper and grease the paper.
- Spoon in the batter.
- Bake in the center of a preheated 375-degree oven for 30-35 minutes.
- Cool on a rack.
- Invert and remove paper while still warm.
- Cool completely or chill in the refrigerator before cutting into squares.
- Makes 4 dozen small brownies.

*For a truly "ultimate" brownie, buy some premium-quality semisweet baking chocolate. You may need to go to a specialty store to find it.

Make-Ahead Meals

This is another topic inspired by my cooking classes. So many of my loyal students who came to many classes over the course of a number of years were people with extremely busy lives. A lot of them have full-time careers and lead active social lives as well. One of the reasons they kept coming back to the cooking school was because they loved having new material for entertaining. I knew that they were always happy to learn about a menu with which they could do most of the preparation ahead of time. Some of the preparation for all of these menus could start a couple of days prior to the dinner, with most of the remaining preparation easily whipped together the day before, leaving a minimum amount of work for that usual last-minute rush. Whether you are on a tight schedule and need some help in planning dinners that require very little last-minute work, or you are just in the mood to cook up some tasty food, I hope you will find some of the following useful.

**A CREOLE
FAVORITE MENU**

Crab-Stuffed Mushrooms

**Shrimp and Chicken
Creole Supreme**

Parsley Rice Pilaf

Creole French Dressing

Mardi Gras Bread

Marilyn's Pecan Pie

Café au lait

Choose mushrooms that are firm and free of discolored spots. Make sure that the cap closes tightly around the stem. An open underside indicates age. Mushrooms could be used at this stage in soups or sauces, but never to sauté or stuff.

I really did not realize that I would have so many Creole recipes in this book. When I started looking through my files to plan what should go into it, I kept pulling out favorites from my days in New Orleans, which have become an integral part of my culinary repertoire. I always enjoy making them for guests or for a class. By the way: you don't need to tell your guests how easy this meal is to prepare. Just relax and enjoy the compliments.

Crab-Stuffed Mushrooms

The Crab-Stuffed Mushrooms are an elegant first course or appetizer. Crabmeat was one of the staples of my existence when I lived in New Orleans, and some of my recipes called for as much as three pounds of lump crabmeat. After moving to Cincinnati, I soon found that I'd have to take out a second mortgage to afford that much crabmeat. So I've had to adapt some of my recipes, substituting more readily available (and affordable) foods. But crabmeat is still my choice, along with caviar, when I want something really special. Make this delicate stuffing several hours ahead, stuff the mushrooms, place them in their baking dish, cover tightly, and chill. They are ready to pop into the oven just before serving time.

> **12 large fresh mushrooms**
> **4 tbsp. unsalted butter or margarine**
> **½ cup chopped onion**
> **1 large clove garlic, minced**
> **3 tbsp. dry sherry**
> **1 cup fresh bread crumbs**
> **1 cup fresh or frozen crabmeat, or a 7-oz. can**
> **¼ tsp. dry marjoram leaves**
> **¼ cup chopped parsley**
> **Salt and freshly ground pepper, to taste**

- Clean mushrooms and remove stems.
- Chop stems.
- Melt 2 tablespoons of the butter in a skillet and sauté onion until tender.
- Add mushroom stems and garlic and cook for 2 minutes, stirring.
- Add sherry and turn to high for a minute or two to reduce by one-half.
- Stir in crumbs, crabmeat, marjoram, and parsley.
- Season to taste with salt and pepper.

- Melt remaining butter and brush some on mushroom caps.
- Fill mushroom caps, brush with remaining butter, and bake in a preheated 425-degree oven for 12-15 minutes or until golden brown.
- Serve hot as an appetizer.
- Makes 12.

Shrimp and Chicken Creole Supreme

Creole simply means a dish with a Creole sauce. The sauce can be cooked separately and spooned over the other ingredients. I developed this recipe from one that called for only shrimp. The addition of the chicken makes it a more economical dish without interfering with its elegance. It is pleasing to a wide variety of tastes and thus very successful for large dinner parties. The ingredients typify the traditional Creole flavors, although I have modernized it a bit and made it even more colorful by using three different types of peppers. This dish looks best when made just a few hours before it is to be served, but all of the chopping, boning, slicing, etc., can easily be done ahead. As far as flavor is concerned, it is delicious made ahead and reheated.

> 1 lb. medium, raw, peeled,
>   and deveined shrimp
> 3 whole chicken breasts, boned
> Salt and freshly ground pepper
> Flour
> 3 tbsp. vegetable oil
> 3 tbsp. butter
> 2 medium yellow onions
> 6 large ripe tomatoes
> 1 green bell pepper
> 1 red bell pepper
> 1 yellow bell pepper
> 3 large cloves garlic
> 1 tsp. dry thyme leaves
> 1 bay leaf
> ¼ cup chopped parsley
> 1 cup good chicken stock
> ½ cup dry white wine
> ¼ tsp. hot pepper sauce
> Parsley for garnish

The best lump crabmeat is often available in the refrigerated case in the seafood section. If not, shelf-stable canned crabmeat is perfectly fine for this recipe. When purchasing the canned variety, it is worth the extra money to buy a better grade, like lump crabmeat. If the claw crabmeat is the only kind available, be sure to spread it out on a plate and pick out any shell or cartilage before using it in a recipe.

Use only fresh garlic! Garlic is easy to peel by placing it flat side down on a cutting board; place the wide end of a chef's knife directly on top of the garlic clove and give it a sound smack with the heel of your hand. That loosens its skin and the peeled clove pops right out. You may then mince it with the same chef's knife or chop it in the food processor. I learned a good food processor trick from the Cuisinart people: turn the machine on with the steel blade in place and with a clean and dry bowl. Remove center of the feed tube and toss the garlic into the turning blade. It chops without getting caught under the blade. I find this to be a good time-saver if several cloves of garlic are needed at once.

- Wash and pat dry the shrimp.
- Cut the chicken breasts into 1-inch strips across the grain.
- Season both shrimp and chicken with salt and pepper.
- Dredge both shrimp and chicken in flour to lightly coat.
- Heat oil and butter in a large, heavy skillet.
- Sauté shrimp for 3-4 minutes, or just until cooked through. Remove to side dish and sauté the chicken for 4-5 minutes. Remove.
- Slice the onions and add to pan. Cook until translucent.
- Peel, halve, seed, and cut tomatoes into small strips. (Reserve juice to return to sauce.)
- Core the peppers, cut into small strips, and add tomatoes and peppers to skillet.
- Finely mince and add garlic and cook, stirring often, for about 10 minutes.
- Add thyme, bay leaf, and the chopped parsley.
- Stir in the stock, wine, and reserved tomato juice and cook, uncovered, for 10 minutes longer.
- Return shrimp and chicken to pan and reheat.
- Season to taste with salt and hot pepper sauce.
- Garnish with small parsley sprigs.
- Serve with Parsley Rice Pilaf.
- Serves 8.

Peeling and seeding tomatoes: choose ripe tomatoes! Pierce them with a cooking fork and lower into a pot of rapidly boiling water. Leave for 30 seconds to 1 minute. Remove and refresh under cold water. Core with a small paring knife. The peeling should be easily removed with your fingers. Cut in half crosswise so that all of the seed "chambers" are revealed. Hold over a sieve placed over a bowl if the juice is to be saved. Holding the tomato upside down in the palm of your hand, lightly squeeze to expel the seeds. Yes, it is important to seed tomatoes that are to go into a cooked dish. The seeds detract from the smooth texture of a sauce and also tend to lend a bitter taste when cooked.

Parsley Rice Pilaf

A proper rice pilaf should have each rice grain tender, but firm and not sticking together. Too much stirring is not good. When cooked undisturbed, the indication for doneness is the presence of "fish eyes" or tiny holes that form on the smooth surface of the cooked rice. The resting time allows the surface starch of each little grain to subside and creates a fluffier rice. The mixture of butter and sautéed onion, garlic, and rice can be put into the pan well ahead of dinnertime with the liquid ready to add in for cooking. Store the fresh chopped parsley in the refrigerator until it is time to toss it in. Though one cup full of parsley seems like a bit much, it is intended to add a lot of flavor as well as color to this dish. Parsley Rice Pilaf can be successfully reheated in the microwave. (Take care not to overcook.)

4 tbsp. butter or margarine
½ cup chopped onion
1 large clove garlic, minced
2 cups raw long-grain rice
½ cup dry white wine
3½ cups chicken stock
¼ tsp. hot pepper sauce
1 cup chopped parsley

- In a heavy medium saucepan, melt the butter.
- Sauté the onion, stirring, for 5 minutes or until translucent.
- Stir in the garlic and cook a minute more.
- Add the rice and stir until coated with the butter.
- Add wine, stock, and hot pepper sauce.
- Bring to boil, stirring only once or twice.
- Cover tightly, reduce to simmer, and cook for 20-25 minutes or until all liquid is absorbed.
- Let rest for 15 minutes.
- Toss in the parsley.
- Serve hot.
- Serves 8.

Always use fresh chopped parsley. Parsley is an herb that does not keep its original fresh flavor when dried. It is also easy to follow this rule, since parsley is the one herb that is available in the supermarket for a nominal price year 'round.

Parsley should go directly from the grocery bag (or your garden) into a large sink of lukewarm water. Let it sit for a while to allow the grit to sink. Lift out and spin dry in a salad spinner (a bulky, but handy gadget to have around) or spread on a soft dish towel or soft paper towels and dry well. Place in a plastic bag. Add a plain white soft paper towel to absorb extra moisture and place in crisper drawer of the refrigerator. You will have crisp, dry parsley, which is what you need for chopping, for several days.

Creole French Dressing

Lots of creations go by the name of "French dressing," including those bottles of orange gunk in the grocery store. The traditional French dressing is a vinaigrette, seasoned with salt and pepper and perhaps with Dijon mustard. This Creole version has added tomato sauce, herbs, and some brown sugar. It is very flavorful and is a great dressing to make ahead. Keep it in a tightly sealed container in the refrigerator and it will retain its fresh taste for a good week.

1 tsp. horseradish mustard
2 tbsp. fresh parsley leaves
½ tsp. salt, or to taste
1 tbsp. fresh tarragon leaves (or 1 tsp. dried)
½ tsp. cayenne pepper
2 tbsp. dark brown sugar
2 tbsp. coarsely chopped scallions
¼ cup tomato sauce
2 tbsp. white wine vinegar
½ cup vegetable oil

- Place all ingredients, except oil, in the food processor or blender. Process until smooth.
- With machine running, pour in oil in a slow, steady stream until all oil is incorporated.
- Makes about 1 cup.
- Toss just enough to coat a mixture of chilled and crisp romaine, bibb, and red-tipped leaf lettuce.
- Garnish salad with tomato wedges or cherry tomatoes.

Always toss the dressing with the salad greens to delicately coat each leaf or vegetable. Overdressing the salad is always a mistake.

When using cherry tomatoes in a salad, cut them in half. They taste better, look more attractive, and the salad is much easier to eat.

When salad greens are unpacked from the grocery store or brought in fresh from your own garden, submerge them immediately in a large basin of lukewarm water. Let sit so that the soil goes to the bottom. (Slightly warm water washes off the grit more efficiently!) Lift out and dry well by spinning in a salad spinner or with cloth or paper towels. Place in plastic bags. Add a plain white paper towel to absorb excess moisture and place in the crisper drawer of the refrigerator. You will have fresh and crisp salad greens for several days.

Mardi Gras Bread

New Orleanians, like their French ancestors, buy French bread daily and stress the importance of serving it fresh. This leads to many recipes for day-old French bread. The following is one of my favorites. It is very effective for slightly stale bread because the melted warm butter soaks in and it comes out like a wonderfully crisp crouton.

> **1 loaf French bread**
> **1 stick unsalted butter or margarine**
> **2 cloves garlic, minced**
> **Parmesan cheese**
> **Finely chopped parsley**
> **Paprika**

- Cut the loaf in half lengthwise.
- Melt butter and add garlic. Let bubble, without browning.
- Turn off and let sit for at least 15 minutes.
- Brush butter onto surface of bread.
- Sprinkle liberally with cheese. Add enough parsley and paprika for good color.
- Place on a baking sheet and bake in a preheated 450-degree oven for 8-10 minutes, or until hot through and lightly browned.
- Cut into pieces crosswise and serve warm.

Note: it is worth it when you want a lot of flavor to purchase imported Italian Parmesan cheese.

If you have a food processor or other good sturdy grater, always buy Parmesan and Romano in whole pieces. Keep it tightly wrapped in plastic in the refrigerator and shred or grate as needed. The original flavor will be maintained much longer.

Marilyn's Pecan Pie

A restaurant in town served this pie with great success after I had done some consulting work for them, and I actually had the temerity to serve it to Albert Roux when he came to my house for dinner. He said he liked it. I do, too, and so I have attached my name to it. Having grown up in the South, I have tasted more than my share of pecan pies and have experimented with many recipes over the years. This is my favorite. My first attempt at making a pecan pie was instructive, if a bit embarrassing. In graduate school I was trying to impress my husband-to-be, who loved pecan pies. I pierced the pastry as I was accustomed to do for "icebox" pies, put the pecan

For best flavor in all of your baked goodies, always buy pure and natural vanilla extract . . . never the vanilla with artificial flavor.

filling in, and baked it. The final product was very strange: the liquid filling ran through the crust. There was filling on the bottom, crust in the middle, and pecans on top. He married me anyway but the moral is: never pierce the pastry for a liquid filling pie. This pie has both light and dark corn syrup for just the right balance of flavor and four large eggs to yield a lighter custard rather than one with a heavy, sticky texture. The pastry is a derivation of a *pâte brisée*, which is used in French tarts. Since it takes this dense mixture so long to cool, it is far better to make this pie several hours ahead.

4 tbsp. unsalted, softened butter
1 cup sugar
1 tbsp. flour
1 cup light corn syrup
½ cup dark corn syrup
Pinch salt
4 large eggs
1¼ cups pecan halves
1 tsp. vanilla extract
9-in. unbaked pastry shell (see below)

- In electric mixer, cream butter.
- Add sugar and flour and cream until fluffy.
- Add both syrups and the pinch of salt.
- Beat until smooth. Add eggs, one at a time, beating well after each addition.
- Fold in the pecans and vanilla.
- Pour into the pastry shell.
- Place in the bottom one-third of a preheated 350-degree oven for 1 hour and 10 minutes or until puffed and golden brown.
- Makes one 9-inch pie. Serves 8-10.

Pastry

1½ cups unbleached or pastry flour
½ tsp. salt
1 large egg yolk
1 stick (4 oz.) very cold unsalted butter
5 tbsp. ice water

- In food processor with steel blade, place the flour, salt, and egg yolk.
- Cut the butter into 8 or 9 pieces and add.

To avoid a soggy bottom crust, bake all pies and tarts in the bottom one-third of the oven.

- Blend until mixture resembles coarse meal.
- Add ice water and blend until a dough forms.
- Remove and knead on a lightly floured surface with the heel of your hand until a smooth ball of dough forms.
- Press into a disc.
- Place in a plastic bag and chill for at least 2 hours.
- Let sit at room temperature for about 20 minutes, or until pliable enough to roll easily.
- Using a pastry rolling pin, roll out on a lightly floured surface to about ⅛ inch thick.
- Place the rolling pin on one edge of the pastry and quickly roll the pastry onto the pin.
- Unroll over top of the pie pan. Gently press into the pan. Trim and crimp the top edges.

If a food processor is not available, place the dry ingredients in a shallow mixing bowl. Add cold butter and cut in with two table knives with serrated edges, cutting in an *X* fashion. Beat egg yolk into the ice water. Make a well in center of the dry mixture and pour in the liquid. Blend quickly with fingertips and proceed as directed above.

Chilling pastry accomplishes several things. It allows the pastry to "rest" so that the gluten in the flour relaxes, which makes it easier to roll and less likely to shrink when placed in a hot oven. Chilling also causes the little flakes of butter to set and result in a flakier baked pastry. And, last but not least, the chilled pastry is easier to handle while rolling and placing in the pan.

Café au lait

Although it couldn't be easier to make, café au lait is a gracious finale to a fine Creole meal. I prefer traditional dark-roast New Orleans coffee, rather than the chicory type. Simultaneously pour boiled milk from one pitcher and coffee from another, ending up with a half-cup of each. The pouring is the heart of the recipe—it mixes the brew and becomes a special ceremony. Café au lait, with plenty of sugar in it, is the perfect ending for this dinner.

> **4 cups very hot, freshly brewed, strong, dark-roast coffee**
> **4 cups boiling whole milk**
> **Sugar, to taste (optional)**

- Into a coffee cup, pour together the hot coffee and milk (½ cup of each).
- Serve hot.

**A SOUTH OF THE
BORDER MENU**

Mexican Corn Soup

Pork Fajitas

Pinto Bean Salad

Chocolate Flan

Instead of devoting an entire chapter to Mexican- or Southwestern-style cooking, I chose to sprinkle my collection of tried and true favorites throughout the book. This batch of recipes seemed to go together nicely to form an entire meal that would just fit the bill for this chapter on make-ahead meals. The robust flavors in this colorful cuisine are what has won over many a devoted Mexican-food fan. These complex flavors often need time to develop fully, which means that a lot of these dishes are greatly enhanced when made several hours before they are to be served. This is good news for the host and hostess who hate being harassed by lots of last-minute kitchen chores and perhaps even better news for the hungry guests whose palates will come alive with the range of delicious tastes offered in this meal.

Mexican Corn Soup

I think it is nice to have a recipe that is not only quick and easy, but light enough to serve as a first course before a Mexican meal (or any meal, for that matter). This one also looks very attractive. Try it, if possible, with some freshly cut corn. I think you will find the contrast of the spicy soup and the smooth mild cream to be interesting. If the soup is not spicy enough, add more hot pepper sauce. Make it ahead except for adding the cream. It reheats beautifully. Whip the cream as long as three hours ahead and keep refrigerated.

> 1 tbsp. unsalted butter
> 1 tbsp. olive oil
> 1 tsp. chili powder
> 1 cup chopped mild green chile pepper
> 2 tbsp. chopped fresh jalapeño pepper
> 3 ears yellow corn, kernels cut off of cob
>   (or 1 10-oz. pkg. frozen kernels)
> ¼-½ tsp. hot pepper sauce
> 6 cups flavorful chicken stock
> 1 cup whipping cream
> Pinch salt
> ¼ cup chopped cilantro

- Heat the butter and oil in a large heavy pot.
- Stir in the chili powder and cook, stirring over medium heat for 2 minutes.
- Stir in both peppers and cook, stirring, for 3-4 minutes.
- Stir in the corn, hot pepper sauce, and chicken stock.
- Bring to a boil.
- Simmer for 5 minutes, uncovered.
- Whip the cream with the pinch of salt until very stiff.
- Serve the soup piping hot topped with a large dollop of the cream and a sprinkling of the chopped cilantro.
- Serves 8-10.

Pork Fajitas

Pork tenderloin is as versatile as boneless chicken breasts. Like the chicken breasts, it is a very tender cut and, when very well trimmed, is low in fat. Of course, it does not need to be marinated to make it tender, but this marinade infuses it with a wonderful flavor and helps to make it very moist and succulent. You can, by the way, substitute boneless chicken breasts in this recipe. (But please note that the cooking time would be cut in half, at least, depending on the size of the chicken breasts.)

> **2 lb. pork tenderloin**
> **½ cup fresh lime juice**
> **¼ cup golden tequila**
> **1 large onion, coarsely chopped**
> **5 large cloves garlic, crushed**
> **¼ cup olive oil**
> **1 tsp. crushed dried red pepper**
> **1 tsp. cumin**
> **1 tsp. chili powder**
> **½ tsp. salt**
> **2 tbsp. chopped fresh cilantro**

- Trim the tenderloins of all fat and remove the silver skin.
- Mix together the remaining ingredients in a heavy-duty gallon-sized plastic bag.
- Add the tenderloin and marinate at least 3 hours, or as long as overnight, in the refrigerator.
- Remove from marinade and place on a rack in a roasting pan.
- Roast in a pre-heated 450 F. oven for 20-25 minutes.
- Let rest for about 10 minutes before slicing into thin slices. May also be cooked on a hot grill.
- Internal temperature should be 160 degrees when removed from grill.*

*It is no longer necessary to cook pork to the high temperatures which were previously recommended. It is also important to remember that the internal temperature will continue to rise after the meat is removed from the grill or oven.

To Serve

12 large flour tortillas
2 cups sour cream (regular or reduced fat)
2-3 avocados, peeled and thinly sliced
1 recipe Salsa Verde (see below)
2 limes, cut into wedges
Cilantro sprigs

- Warm the tortillas by sealing them in a package of heavy-duty foil and placing in a 325-degree oven for 10-15 minutes.
- Place 3 or 4 thin slices of the pork in the center of a warm tortilla; top with a dollop of sour cream, a couple of slices of the avocado, and a large spoonful of the Salsa Verde.
- Serve garnished with lime wedges and a sprig of cilantro.
- Pass the extra Salsa Verde.

Salsa Verde

1 lb. tomatillos, husked and washed
1 large yellow onion, chopped
3 large cloves garlic, minced
2 tbsp. extravirgin olive oil
2 mild green chiles, roasted and chopped
3-4 medium jalapeño peppers
½ cup chopped fresh cilantro
Salt, to taste
1 tbsp. fresh lime juice

- Place tomatillos in a medium saucepan; cover with water and bring to boil.
- Cook for 5 minutes, drain well, and purée in the food processor.
- Sauté the onion and garlic in the olive oil until the onion is tender.
- Remove and cool. Stir together all ingredients.
- Chill for at least 2 hours to blend the flavors.
- Makes about 3 cups.

Note: the flavor is best when it's made the day before it is served.

Onions with a yellow skin are generally milder and sweeter than the white ones. They are preferable in a recipe with delicate flavors.

Pinto Bean Salad

An inexpensive source of protein, beans have long been considered peasant food in many cultures. The tasty little pinto, which has played an important role in Mexican cuisine for a very long time, has gained great popularity in this country. Because beans are such a good source of protein, without adding any fat or cholesterol to our diet, they are popping up on the menus of some very fancy and trend-setting restaurants. The pinto is the bean usually used to make the Mexican staple "refried" beans, but it makes a delicious salad, too. This salad is also delectable made with black-eyed peas or kidney beans. With its vinaigrette dressing, its flavor improves when made as long as 24 hours before it is served. (Save the *pepitas* to sprinkle on just before serving.)

2 1-lb. cans pinto beans, drained and rinsed
1 large red Spanish onion, halved and thinly sliced
1 large sweet red pepper, cored and chopped
3 pickled jalapeño peppers, seeded and finely chopped
1 medium jicama,* peeled and diced
Romaine lettuce leaves
½ cup toasted and salted pumpkin seeds**

- Toss together the beans with the onion, peppers, and jicama.
- Toss in the dressing (see below).
- Chill for at least 1 hour to blend the flavors.
- Serve piled onto crisp romaine leaves with the pumpkin seeds sprinkled on top.
- Serves 8 as a side salad.

*Jicama is a large, round vegetable with a brown peel that slightly resembles a potato in appearance. Its wonderful crunchy texture resembles that of a water chestnut. Peel it with a vegetable peeler or small paring knife in the same way you would peel a potato. Not only does it add great crunch to a salad, but it is good cut into strips to be used as a dipping vegetable. Some people simply like to sprinkle it with fresh lime juice and eat it.

**Toasted and salted pumpkin seeds can be found in the nut section of specialty or gourmet stores. The Mexicans call them "pepitas."

The Dressing

¼ cup red wine vinegar
½ cup extravirgin olive oil
½ tsp. salt
1 tsp. hot pepper sauce
1 tsp. sugar

- Whisk together just until well mixed.
- Stir just before tossing into the salad.
- Makes ¾ cup.

Chocolate Flan

Flan originated in the Spanish kitchen and is a very important part of many Mexican menus. This beloved dessert is the perfect cool, creamy, and elegant ending to any meal, but especially one that left some hot pepper on the tongue. The traditional Mexican flan is a vanilla custard baked with the caramelized sugar. It is also very delicious, but there is something even more special about ending a wonderful meal with some chocolate. Since it should be served well chilled, I always make the flan the day before.

> ¾ cup sugar
> 4 oz. good semisweet chocolate
> 2 cups light cream, scalded
> 6 large eggs
> 2 egg yolks
> 1 tbsp. pure vanilla extract
> 1 cup sugar

- Pour the ¾ cup of sugar into a heavy skillet. (Cast iron is preferable.)
- Heat over medium heat, shaking the pan occasionally, until sugar is melted and turns a dark amber color.
- Pour the caramelized sugar into a 9-inch round ungreased cake pan. Carefully revolve the pan to coat the bottom as evenly as possible.
- Melt the chocolate in a double boiler over hot, not boiling, water.
- In a large mixing bowl, whisk together the cream, eggs, egg yolks, vanilla, and 1 cup of sugar.
- Strain the egg mixture.
- Whisk in the chocolate.
- Pour custard into the sugar-coated pan.
- Add enough water to a large shallow baking pan so that, when the pan filled with the custard is placed in it, the water comes halfway up the sides of the cake pan.
- Place the pan of water in the center of a preheated 350-degree oven and gently place the flan in it.
- Bake the flan in the water bath for about 40 minutes or until it is puffed and set.
- Remove from oven and carefully remove the pan from the hot water.
- Cool on a rack and then chill overnight.
- To serve: invert onto a large serving platter.
- Cut into wedges and serve.
- Serves 8-10.

Sugar caramelizes at a very high temperature. Take care not to burn yourself when pouring it from one pan to another. The pans will also be very hot.

COZY COLD WEATHER DINNERS

Roquefort Triangles

Pork Medallions Juniper
or Curried Lamb Stew

Avocado-Fruit Salad
with Sherry Vinaigrette

Almond Cheesecake

Roquefort Triangles

I have talked about the virtues of frozen phyllo dough in the cocktail party chapter. Here is another easy, make-ahead recipe, which uses this versatile convenience product. This recipe can be done weeks ahead and frozen, or prepared just hours ahead and chilled until ready to pop into the oven. If you don't have the genuine "Roquefort," use another blue cheese. These tasty little golden triangles can also change places and be served at the end of a meal as the "cheese course." Add some fresh pear wedges and it is as elegant an ending as a beginning.

> **8 oz. cream cheese, softened**
> **4 oz. Roquefort cheese**
> **1 large clove garlic, minced**
> **⅛ tsp. cayenne pepper**
> **1 tbsp. Cognac**
> **1 egg**
> **¼ cup lightly toasted chopped walnuts**
> **16 sheets phyllo pastry**
> **1 stick unsalted butter or margarine, melted**

- In the food processor with steel blade, blend together the cheeses, garlic, cayenne, Cognac, and egg until smooth.
- Gently fold in the nuts.
- Using a soft-bristle pastry brush, brush a sheet of pastry lightly with the butter or margarine.
- Keep remaining pastry leaves covered with a slightly dampened towel to prevent drying.
- Top the pastry with a second sheet and repeat with buttering.
- Cut the sheet into 4 lengthwise strips.
- Place about 1 teaspoon of the filling on the end of a strip, leaving a 1-inch margin on the end. Fold over one edge to form a triangle shape.
- Continue to fold upwards as though you were folding a flag.
- Seal the edges with butter.
- Place on a parchment-paper-lined baking sheet.

- If desired, cover the baking sheet and chill until ready to bake and serve. Bake in a preheated 375-degree oven for 12-15 minutes or until golden brown.
- Serve hot.
- Makes 32.

Note: any leftover filling may be frozen for later use.

Pork Medallions Juniper

When these very lean and tender pieces of pork tenderloin are pounded into delicate medallions, they are on the way to becoming an extremely elegant pork dish. The end result is not only fit for the fanciest guest, but has a most intriguing flavor. Do all of this preparation ahead, including dicing the potatoes. (Cover them with ice water until ready to cook; dry very well before cooking.) After the dish is finished, it is happy to wait for an hour or two until dinner. Reheat very gently.

> 2 pork tenderloins, about 1½ lb. each
> Salt and freshly ground pepper
> Flour
> ½ cup extravirgin olive oil
> ½ cup thinly sliced scallions
> 2 large cloves garlic, minced
> 12 juniper berries, finely crushed
> 1 cup dry white wine
> 2 tbsp. gin
> ¼ cup finely chopped parsley
> 1 cup cream
> 4 cups peeled and diced red-skinned potatoes
> Parsley, for garnish

- Trim the fat and white skin from the tenderloins and cut them, across the grain, into ½-inch pieces.
- Place the pieces of meat between two sheets of plastic wrap, cut side up, and pound with a veal pounder to ⅛-inch thickness.

- Season with salt and pepper.
- Dredge the pork in the flour, coating well.
- Heat 4 tablespoons of the oil in a large, heavy skillet until very hot, but not smoking.
- Sauté the pork medallions for 2-3 minutes on each side, or until golden brown and cooked through.
- Remove to a side dish.
- Add the scallions, and sauté, stirring, for 2-3 minutes.
- Add the garlic, juniper berries, wine, gin, and half of the chopped parsley.
- Cook over high heat, stirring occasionally, until liquid is reduced to about ¼ cup.
- Whisk in the cream; cook until reduced by half.
- Taste the sauce and correct the seasoning.
- Return the medallions to the sauce.
- Reheat at serving time.

To Cook the Potatoes

- Heat the remaining oil (4 tablespoons) in a large nonstick skillet.
- Roll the diced potatoes in a thick dish towel to remove the surface moisture.
- Add potatoes and remaining chopped parsley to oil.
- Cook over high heat, turning with a spatula, for 15-20 minutes or until potatoes are golden and tender. Season with salt and pepper to taste.
- To serve, arrange pork medallions on top of a bed of potatoes, spoon over the sauce, and garnish with more parsley.
- Serves 8.

The pork medallions may be sliced and pounded flat several hours ahead of time. Refrigerate them encased between the two sheets of plastic in which they are pounded. It is, however, important to wait until time to cook the meat before dredging it in the flour. Otherwise the flour becomes sticky on the surface and the meat will not brown as nicely.

Curried Lamb Stew

This dish had to be a part of this chapter. Its sweet and spicy flavor is much fuller when made the day before. However, like most dishes enriched with cream, wait to add the cream until after the prepared dish is reheated, shortly before serving time. I can safely say, from much experience, that even folks who thought they did not like lamb will enjoy this dish.

½ cup white raisins
½ cup boiling water
3 tbsp. extravirgin olive oil (or vegetable oil)
2 lb. cubed lamb*
Salt and cayenne pepper
Flour
2 large yellow onions, sliced
2 Yellow Delicious apples, peeled and diced
3 ribs celery, thinly sliced
3 large cloves garlic, minced
2 tbsp. Madras curry powder
2 cups dry white wine
Juice of 1 lemon
1 cup heavy cream**
Chopped parsley, for garnish
1 recipe Parsley Rice Pilaf (see index)

Condiments

Mango chutney or Cranberry Chutney (see index)
Lightly toasted slivered almonds
Thinly sliced peeled and seeded cucumber that has been
    soaked in ice water for 30 minutes and patted dry
Peeled, seeded, and chopped tomatoes
Slivered candied ginger
Lightly toasted shredded unsweetened coconut

- Place the raisins in a small bowl and pour over the boiling water.
- Let sit for 30 minutes.
- Drain and reserve.
- Heat the oil in a large heavy pot.
- Season the lamb with salt and cayenne.
- Dredge the lamb in the flour to coat lightly.
- Brown the lamb in the hot oil. Remove to a side dish with slotted spoon.
- Add the onions to the pot and sauté, stirring, for 3-4 minutes. (Add a bit more oil if needed.)
- Stir in the apples, celery, garlic, and curry powder.
- Cook, stirring, for 8-10 minutes.
- Add the wine, scraping the bottom of the pan with a wooden spoon to deglaze the pan.
- Return the lamb.
- Bring to a boil, partially cover the pot, and simmer for 1 hour, or until lamb is fork tender.
- Taste and correct seasonings.
- Add lemon juice and drained raisins; cook, uncovered, for a few minutes more.
- Stir in the cream and cook until slightly thickened.
- Sprinkle with the chopped parsley.
- Serve over the Parsley Rice Pilaf or plain white rice.
- Pass small bowls of some or all of the suggested condiments to be spooned over the top.

*Best with lamb from the leg, but shoulder may be used. All fat should be trimmed from the lamb cubes.

**For a lighter stew, the cream may be omitted and ½ cup of water or chicken stock added when the wine is added.

Avocado-Fruit Salad
with Sherry Vinaigrette

I thought that a menu designed for cold winter weather should have a salad which features ingredients easily obtained during that season. This could be named "Winter Fruit Salad" since it features favorite winter fruits. If the avocados and pears are peeled and sliced ahead, you will need some lemon juice to sprinkle on them to prevent darkening.

> **2 ripe avocados, sliced**
> **2 medium pink grapefruit, peeled and sectioned**
> **3 navel oranges, peeled and sectioned**
> **2 ripe pears, peeled and sliced**
> **Crisp lettuce leaves (Bibb or leaf)**
> **1 recipe Sherry Vinaigrette**
> **Watercress sprigs**

- Arrange the avocados and fruit on the lettuce leaves.
- Drizzle over the dressing, coating the avocados and fruit lightly.
- Garnish with the watercress.
- Serve immediately.
- Serves 8.

> **Sherry Vinaigrette**
>
> **½ cup vegetable oil**
> **3 tbsp. sherry vinegar**
> **1 tbsp. cream sherry**
> **¼ tsp. salt**
> **1 tbsp. honey**
> **Dash hot pepper sauce**

- Whisk together until smooth and well mixed.
- Stir or shake just before using.

Almond Cheesecake

Often students or radio listeners ask me for an "easy" cheesecake recipe. (It's renewed proof that America does love a good cheesecake.) I usually go to the files to pull this one for them. With no crust to make, there is no question about the ease, and the taste and creamy texture make it an exceptional dessert. A beautiful and generous friend, Vicky Semler, shared it with me years ago when we worked together in a restaurant kitchen. It was her grandmother's recipe. Vicky agrees that it belongs in a chapter on "make-ahead" foods. She used to make enough in one afternoon of baking frenzy to feed a lot of people for several days.

4 large eggs
1 lb. cream cheese, softened
¾ cup sugar
½ tsp. natural almond extract
1 cup natural sour cream
3 tbsp. sugar
1 tsp. pure vanilla extract
16 whole lightly toasted blanched almonds

- In electric mixer, beat eggs until very fluffy, about 5 minutes.
- Cut the cheese into cubes and add.
- Beat until smooth.
- Add the ¾ cup of sugar and almond extract and beat until well mixed.
- Butter a 9-inch round pie pan.
- Pour the mixture into the pan.
- Place in the center of a preheated 350-degree oven and bake for 25 minutes or until slightly puffed.
- Gently stir together the sour cream, sugar, and vanilla just until mixed.
- Remove the baked cake from the oven and place on a rack.
- Spread the sour cream topping mixture on the hot cake and return to oven.
- Bake 10 minutes longer.
- Cool on a rack.
- Place the almonds around the outside edge.
- Chill for at least 3 hours.
- Cut into wedges and serve cold.
- Serves 8-10.

Since these dishes are most likely to be cooked and served in the warm-weather months when lighter menus are favored, I decided not to include an appetizer or soup in this menu. Also, the occasion that calls for such a grilled dinner is usually a casual affair and should be fun and easy. But if you are planning a big summer party and want to offer a light appetizer course, I suggest a Vegetable Basket with at least one Dipping Sauce (see index). Zippy Gazpacho (see index), served in chilled mugs, could also be just the right start for a "cookout dinner."

This is, by the way, the perfect menu for a picnic-type meal, which you might want to pack up and grill "on location" on your boat, at the beach, or in the park. The steak as well as the vegetable melange can be packed into zip-top bags and allowed to marinate as they are transported. (Pack them in ice in a cooler to maintain a cool temperature.)

SUMMER GRILL MEAL

Bourbon-Marinated Flank Steak

Skewered Vegetable Melange
with Lemon-Pepper Marinade

Grill-Roasted Potatoes

Summer Strawberry Pie

Bourbon-Marinated Flank Steak

I have already addressed the issue of beefsteak and expressed my preference for the lean and tasty flank steak. Since I do tend to serve it more often than any other cut of beef, I keep experimenting with various marinades that not only infuse the steak with marvelous flavors, but serve as a natural tenderizer as well. This is one of my recent attempts, which became a favorite as soon as I tasted the first sizzling bite right off of the grill. You don't have to grill this steak on an outdoor grill. It has a great flavor when broiled under a very hot, preheated broiler. The time would be approximately the same as the grilling time.

> 1 large flank steak (approximately 2 lb.)
> ½ cup light soy sauce
> 3 tbsp. vegetable oil
> 2 medium onions, sliced
> 3 large cloves garlic, chopped
> 2 tbsp. minced fresh gingerroot
> 2 tbsp. dark brown sugar
> ¼ tsp. hot pepper sauce
> ½ cup bourbon

- Trim all visible fat from the flank steak.
- In a heavy-duty, gallon-sized plastic bag with a zip top, mix together all of the marinade ingredients. Add steak.
- Refrigerate for at least 8 hours or as long as 24 hours.
- Cook on a hot grill for 8 minutes on the first side and 5 minutes on the second side for a medium-rare steak. Increase the cooking time if a more well done steak is desired.
- To serve, cut across the grain into 1-inch-wide strips.
- Serves 4-6.

Skewered Vegetable Melange
with Lemon-Pepper Marinade

Not only a tasty vegetable side dish that can accompany almost any grilled meat, poultry, or fish dish, this colorful kabob adds a decorative touch to an otherwise plain plate. It also makes a very easy addition to a casual grilled meal. Since the artichoke hearts are precooked and the mushrooms and peppers need only be heated through, a very short last-minute cooking time is all that is necessary.

Grilling the vegetables along with the meat course makes life easier for the chef since most of the meal is being cooked in one place. Do pay attention to the timing when grilling these vegetables. It is important not to overcook them. They should be cooked just long enough to develop the flavor but maintain a good firm texture.

24 large firm fresh mushrooms
1 red bell pepper
1 green bell pepper
1 large can artichoke hearts, rinsed and drained
**   (approximately 8-10 whole artichoke hearts)**
8 6-8-in. bamboo skewers
1 recipe Lemon-Pepper Marinade

- Clean the mushrooms and remove the stems. (Stems may be saved for flavoring stock or soup.)
- Wash, core, and stem the peppers. Cut each in half lengthwise and then into fourths. Cut the strips into squares and then halve the squares to make a triangle shape.
- Cut the artichoke hearts in half lengthwise (unless the very small artichoke hearts are used, in which case you will need twice as many and leave them whole).
- Soak the bamboo skewers in warm water for an hour. (Don't forget this step or your skewers may be flambéed on the grill.)
- Thread the vegetables onto the skewers in an alternating, attractive pattern.
- Place in the marinade and marinate for at least 3 hours in the refrigerator.
- Remove from marinade and place on a hot grill—about 6 inches from heat source. Grill, turning often, for about 5 minutes or until hot. (Do not allow the mushrooms to become overcooked and soft.)

Lemon Pepper Marinade

½ cup olive oil
3 tbsp. fresh lemon juice
1 tsp. finely chopped lemon zest
1 large clove garlic, minced
¼ cup chopped parsley
½ tsp. dried oregano leaves
2 tsp. coarsely ground black pepper
1 tsp. salt, or to taste

- Whisk together the oil, lemon juice and zest, and garlic until well mixed.
- Stir in the remaining ingredients.
- Makes about ¾ cup marinade.

Grill-Roasted Potatoes

This is definitely a "do-ahead," but remember not to do it too far ahead because the potatoes will darken. They will be fine if done an hour or so ahead.

8 Idaho baking potatoes, well scrubbed
1½ sticks (6 oz.) unsalted butter or margarine
Salt and freshly ground pepper

• Cut ½-inch crosswise slices about three-quarters through the potatoes.
• Place a slice of butter between each slice of potato. Season with salt and pepper.
• Wrap in heavy-duty foil.
• Place on a hot grill.
• Cover and roast for about 1 hour or until potato is tender.
• Serves 8.

Note: an alternative method for cooking potatoes on the grill is to slice well-scrubbed Idaho potatoes into approximately 1-inch crosswise slices, season with salt and freshly ground pepper, and brush liberally with some good olive oil. Place directly on the grill rack, about 6-8 inches from the heat. Grill, turning often with tongs and basting often with the olive oil. Grill until golden brown and crisp on the outside and fork-tender on the inside.

Summer Strawberry Pie

This is perhaps my favorite summer strawberry pie. The white chocolate negates the need for extra sugar and contributes to the creaminess of the cheese filling at the same time. This crust can be made days (or even weeks) ahead and stored in the freezer. All fresh strawberry desserts are best when served on the same day as they are made. This one goes together very quickly, and leftovers are seldom a problem.

4 oz. white chocolate
6 oz. cream cheese, softened
4 oz. natural sour cream
1 Chocolate Cookie Crust
1 qt. fresh strawberries
⅔ cup currant jelly

- Cut the white chocolate into pieces and melt in a double boiler over hot, not boiling, water.
- Whisk together the cheese, melted chocolate, and sour cream just until mixture is smooth and creamy.
- Spread the cheese mixture in the bottom of the prepared crust.
- Wash the strawberries (either in water or wine).
- Drain well.
- Cut off the caps, making the bottoms flat.
- Place the strawberries, cut side down, on the filling.
- Melt the jelly over gentle heat in a small heavy saucepan.
- Using a soft-bristle pastry brush, glaze the strawberries with the jelly. Chill until ready to serve.
- Makes one 9-inch pie.
- Serves 8-10.

Best made on the same day it is to be served.

Chocolate Cookie Crust

2 cups chocolate cookie crumbs
1 stick (4 oz.) butter or margarine, melted

- Stir together the crumbs and butter.
- Press into the bottom and sides of a 9-inch pie pan.
- Place in the freezer for at least 1 hour before filling.

Students' Favorites

Eggs au Gratin

Caponata-Cheese
Brunch Muffins

Cinnamon-Butter
Brunch Cake

Cauliflower Soup

Mushroom Soup

Marilyn's Antipasto
Pasta Salad

Ted's Pesto Sauce

Summer Potato Salad

Yen's Sweet and Sour
Shrimp

Pepper and Ginger
Salmon

Marilyn's Special
Grilled Lamb

Chicken Breasts
with Artichoke Hearts

Pork Tenderloin
with Bing Cherry Sauce

Mexican Chili Burritos

Zucchini Casserole Deluxe

Grilled Vegetables
with Goat Cheese

Carol's Pizza Pie

Sunday Supper
Chicken and Rice

Walnut-Oatmeal Bread

Green Peppercorn Bread

Zitronencreme
(Lemon Bavarian Cream)

Strawberries and Cream
with Orange Glaze

Being a cooking teacher differs somewhat from being a chef. Both need basic knowledge of techniques and an understanding of the chemistry of foods. A creative approach to flavors and appearance is certainly important for any successful cook. When a chef can capture all of these things and present it in the form of a magnificent plate of food, his quest is ended. But a teacher has another step in the creative process. For me, that is the most interesting step of all—communicating the skills to other people. A good cooking teacher always strives to impart an understanding of each and every detail of a recipe so that it will taste and look just the same when the students make it in their own kitchens.

I am always happy when students tell me that they have incorporated one of the recipes from my classes into their regular repertoires. It's nice to hear that they have changed a recipe to suit their own tastes or to please the palate of someone in their family. In my opinion, a good recipe is one that lives a long life and evolves as it goes along.

As I have said before in these pages, this book would never have happened had it not been for my cooking students who harassed and chastised me until I sat down and got busy. It seemed only fair to ask some of those people to take more than a passive interest in this endeavor. The recipes that follow were submitted by a few of my students and friends.

In this chapter I have departed from the planned format of presenting the recipes in menu form. I hope that you will find it an interesting potpourri sort of chapter. There are many good things to cook and eat and many of the dishes could be worked into the menus in earlier chapters as substitutions or additions.

Eggs au Gratin

Pam Shearer is one of those dear friends who started out as a cooking student. I cannot remember how many years Pam regularly attended my classes. In the last couple of years when she was coming to my classes in downtown Cincinnati, she had quite a drive from her lovely home in the Kentucky countryside. Sometimes we would receive a hurried call saying, "Start without me, I'll be there." But she often lingered a bit after class so we could chat about some of our favorite subjects such as shopping. Pam enjoys cooking for her husband, David, and their two sons. They tend to favor hearty, "real" foods, so I was not surprised when Pam sent this one as a favorite from her house. Pam says, "This wonderful scrambled egg dish with shallots and mushrooms is absolutely delicious. Let the cheese just barely melt into the eggs for unbelievably creamy scrambled eggs. I serve it with sausage and a bowl of fresh fruit."

> **1 stick unsalted butter**
> **2 shallots, minced**
> **½ lb. mushrooms, thinly sliced**
> **12 eggs**
> **½ cup light cream**
> **Pinch thyme**
> **Salt and pepper**
> **½ cup chopped parsley**
> **2 cups grated Cheddar cheese**

- Melt butter in a large heavy skillet; sauté shallots and mushrooms.
- Beat eggs until light and fluffy with cream, thyme, salt, and pepper.
- Pour eggs into skillet and stir until partially cooked.
- Sprinkle over parsley and cheese and finish cooking, stirring.
- Serves 6-8.

Note: any flavorful, natural cheese works well in this egg dish. For a full cheese flavor, try Gruyère or Emmenthaler. For a milder flavor, as well as a lower fat content, substitute a part-skim mozzarella.

Caponata-Cheese Brunch Muffins

Margaret Graham is actually representing a group of students with her presence in this book. It was a group of 8 or 9 people who met in my classes and grew to be good friends. They were regulars at the "Matching Food and Wine Seminars," which I team-taught with my friend and wine expert Marj Valvano. They were a great group. Margaret attended many other classes as well and is one of those students who became a good friend. I had already included Margaret's favorite Caponata Deluxe in this book, but she suggested that I also give you this version from a brunch class I taught several years ago. I thought this would be a good place to share it with you.

> **1 recipe Caponata Deluxe (see index)**
> **Butter**
> **8 English muffins**
> **16 slices Swiss cheese**
> **Parsley sprigs**

- Make the caponata (it will be tastier if made at least 24 hours ahead).
- Butter the muffin halves and toast.
- Just before serving time, spoon a generous amount of heated caponata on the toasted muffins and top each with a medium-thick slice of Swiss cheese.
- Place under broiler until cheese is melted.
- Garnish with parsley and serve warm.
- Serves 8.

Cinnamon-Butter Brunch Cake

Every bit the successful businesswoman who always looks the part, that's Marilyn Schott. But, I am happy to say, she is also a devoted cook and one of my longtime, loyal students. When I asked Marilyn to submit a recipe for this chapter, I received a very nice letter from her along with her favorite brunch recipe. She wrote: "I hope you realize how difficult a task this was since I've been an avid student of yours since 1974. Would you believe that I used to travel almost forty miles round trip to attend your classes and sometimes two and three times per week? Nevertheless, I have collected a volume of gourmet recipes to select from and wonderful memories as I serve these dishes with confidence." Thank you, Marilyn. This, by the way, is an easy-to-make and delicious brunch or breakfast cake.

> **2 sticks sweet butter, softened**
> **1¼ cups sugar**
> **½ tsp. cinnamon**
> **2 eggs**
> **2½ cups all-purpose flour**
> **4 tsp. baking powder**
> **½ tsp. salt**
> **1¼ cups milk**

- Cut the butter into pieces and cream together with the sugar and cinnamon. Mixture should be very light.
- Beat in the eggs.
- Sift together the flour, baking powder, and salt.
- Add the flour mixture alternately with the milk to the eggs and mix until batter is smooth.
- Pour into a buttered and floured 9-inch cake pan and bake in a 350-degree oven for 45 minutes or until browned.

Topping

> **⅓ cup sugar**
> **½ tsp. cinnamon**

- Mix topping ingredients and sprinkle on cake while it is hot.
- Serve cake warm.

Cauliflower Soup

One of the very first people to take my classes in Cincinnati was Lennie Fisher. She was just learning to cook in those days. She is now an accomplished hostess who enjoys cooking and entertaining with her husband, John. Do I deserve some of the credit? Well, why not? Lennie, in her typically generous fashion, not only sent me a recipe, but had some nice things to say. I couldn't resist printing this kind of flattering copy: "I started taking classes from Marilyn in about 1973 and she has become a part of my life. I use many of her recipes as part of my cooking repertory and her thoughts and opinions have become part of my thought processes. She has helped me evaluate and understand food and cooking and her sense of humor and personality led us to become friends." Lennie sent along a recipe for Cauliflower Soup, which she got from my class years ago. Here are her comments: "It is a fabulous soup—easy to make but tastes like a million. I especially like the consistency—smooth yet with some crunch from the puréed cauliflower. Even if you think you don't like cauliflower you will love this soup—the flavor is delicate and the seasonings make it truly an inspired dish."

1 large cauliflower
4 tbsp. butter or margarine
½ cup chopped onion
⅓ cup flour
4 cups chicken stock
1 tsp. salt, or to taste
Dash white pepper
Dash fresh grated nutmeg
1 egg yolk
2 cups light cream
Chopped parsley, for garnish

- Remove leaves and thick base of cauliflower.
- Wash, blanch 3-4 minutes, and refresh in cold water. Break into florets.
- Melt butter in large pan and sauté onions.
- Add flour and cook for 2 minutes.
- Add stock, beating with a whisk.
- Add cauliflower and seasonings.
- Cook for about 20 minutes or until cauliflower is very tender.
- Purée in food processor.
- Return to pan.
- Beat egg yolk into cream and whisk into mixture.
- Do not boil.
- Serve with chopped fresh parsley as garnish.

Mushroom Soup

She was a student of mine several years ago and then she moved away. One day I looked out into the audience and there she sat. Gail Thompson was back! And I don't think the moving van was fully unloaded before she showed up in class. Truly a loyal student and one of the liveliest ladies I know, Gail had this to say along with her favorite soup recipe, which she asked to have included in the book: "I have served this Mushroom Soup recipe to almost every person who has eaten at my table. I serve it for lunch as well as a starter for the main dinner course. One thing that makes this soup so special is serving it with whipped cream on the side. As the guests are seated, I usually say: 'This is mushroom soup.' Then, as I drop a dollop of whipped cream into the soup I add, 'Now this is cream of mushroom soup.' And their reactions are equally fun. 'I've never eaten soup like this before,' they tell me. Later I hear, 'That's the best mushroom soup I've ever eaten.'"

> 1 lb. mushrooms
> 2 medium onions, chopped
> 3 tbsp. butter
> 3 tbsp. flour
> 5 cups chicken stock, heated
> Salt and pepper
> 1 bay leaf
> ¼ cup sherry
> Chopped parsley
> 1 cup whipping cream, whipped with a pinch salt

- Wash and dry mushrooms, remove stems; chop stems and thinly slice caps.
- Sauté onions in butter.
- Add mushrooms—sweat in pan with tightly fitting lid for 5 minutes. Remove lid and stir in flour; cook 2 minutes without browning.
- Add warm stock and seasonings.
- Cover and simmer 20 minutes.
- Add sherry.
- Sprinkle chopped parsley on the soup.
- Pass whipped cream.
- Serves 8.

Marilyn's Antipasto Pasta Salad

A cheerful member "in good standing" of what I have come to think of as my cooking-student family, Jane Ellen Bowling asked me to be sure to put in her favorite pasta salad recipe. Jane added the following note: "I have attended Marilyn's cooking classes since the early 1970s. Her classes, which emphasize quality ingredients and proper technique, are also spiced with a dash of culinary history. Whether it's an elegant picnic, dinner party, or cocktail buffet, Marilyn is always my source for that special menu. She is a marvelously creative cook with a charming personality, enthusiasm for good food, and a never-ending repertoire of fresh ideas. The following recipe is one of my favorites—a gorgeous summer one-dish meal."

1 lb. fusilli pasta, cooked "al dente" and drained
2 tbsp. extravirgin olive oil
½ lb. prosciutto, cut into julienne strips (2" x ¼")
½ lb. fontina cheese, cut into julienne strips
2 small tender zucchini, julienned
1 red bell pepper, julienned
1 cup halved cherry tomatoes
½ cup black Italian olives
1 medium red Spanish salad onion, halved and thinly sliced
½ cup toasted pine nuts
1 recipe Basil Vinaigrette (see below)
1 head romaine, coarsely shredded
Olives, tomatoes, and parsley or basil, for garnish

- When the hot pasta is well drained, toss immediately with olive oil. Let sit until room temperature.
- Toss in the ham, cheese, zucchini, bell pepper, tomatoes, olives, onion, and pine nuts. Toss in the Basil Vinaigrette.
- Make a bed of romaine on a large platter and pile the pasta salad on it. Garnish.
- Cover and chill until serving time. Serve chilled or at room temperature.
- Serves 8.

Basil Vinaigrette

⅔ cup extravirgin olive oil
⅓ cup good white wine vinegar
1 clove garlic, minced
1 tbsp. Dijon mustard
½ tsp. salt
¼ tsp. freshly ground black pepper
¼ cup coarsely chopped fresh basil leaves
¼ cup chopped parsley

• Blend together until well mixed.

Note: other cheeses like provolone or Swiss may be substituted in this recipe.

Ted's Pesto Sauce

One day I was busy preparing for a class in the Fourth Street Market cooking school, which sat right in the focal point of the traffic pattern of a downtown department store, when a male voice demanded to know what I was doing. I might add that it was not an unusual occurrence to be asked that question since I did spend a lot of time cooking right there where half the world passed by each day. But as I looked up to get my first glimpse of Ted Bowden, I somehow knew that a simple answer was not going to satisfy his most active curiosity. An hour later we were deep in discussion about food and culinary matters and he was late for an appointment. He announced that, although he lived in Manhattan, he would be back to attend some of my classes. And back he came, for several classes. He is also a great correspondent who keeps me supplied with clippings from the New York food scene. A while back he shared his Pesto Sauce recipe with me in a very original manner, framed and beautifully illustrated by a New York artist. It is a great recipe for this traditional Italian sauce and tastes fantastic when tossed with some freshly cooked pasta.

2 cups fresh basil leaves
2 cloves garlic, crushed
2 tbsp. grated Romano (Pecorino) cheese
½ cup grated Parmesan cheese
2 tbsp. pignoli nuts, crushed
½ cup extravirgin olive oil
Pinch coarse salt

- Combine the basil, garlic, cheeses, and nuts in a food processor.
- Process to mix.
- With the machine running, slowly add the olive oil.
- Season to taste with coarse salt and process to a smooth paste.
- Let stand for at least 5 minutes before serving.

Summer Potato Salad

Loren Sheffield is one of our foremost local wine experts. He is also an excellent cook and we have spent many hours together deep in discourse about food and wine. Loren has tried enough of my recipes to write a book of his own and was in a dilemma deciding which one to include in this chapter. He decided on the following potato salad, which he claims to have improved with the addition of Vidalia onion and black olives. My original version was just an herbed potato salad with a vinaigrette dressing.

2½ lb. small "new" red potatoes
6 cups chicken stock
¼ cup white wine vinegar
1 medium Vidalia onion, finely chopped
½ cup chopped fresh parsley
¼ cup chopped fresh dill
2 tbsp. chopped fresh basil
Salt and freshly ground pepper
½ cup sliced black olives
½ cup extravirgin olive oil

Use Ted's Pesto Sauce to flavor mayonnaise and/or sour cream for tasty salad dressings or dips for crisp vegetables. For a quick and easy appetizer or vegetable side dish, spoon some pesto into a fresh mushroom cap and broil until hot and bubbly.

- Scrub the potatoes thoroughly.
- Slice into ¼-inch slices.
- Place in a pot with the chicken stock.
- Bring to a boil and simmer, partially covered, for about 15 minutes or until fork-tender—but not falling apart. Drain.
- Place in a bowl and pour over the vinegar. Toss lightly. Let sit until cooled to room temperature.
- Toss in the onion, herbs, salt and pepper, olives, and oil.
- Serve chilled or at room temperature.
- Serves 8.

Note: cooking the potatoes in chicken stock instead of water adds another dimension of flavor to this dish. Canned broth or reconstituted chicken-stock base (the refrigerated "paste" type) may be used. Little if any extra salt will be needed if these products are used.

Yen's Sweet and Sour Shrimp

She's one of the most talented of my food professional friends and a most creative cook. Her physician husband, Ron, has rescued me from a dire ailment or two. Yen Hsieh and I once had a grand time walloping up the food for a friend's wedding reception together. This is her version of a classic Chinese recipe. It is a super blend of flavors, and the spicy accents she has added make it a really special recipe.

> 3 tbsp. corn or peanut oil
> 2 cloves garlic, chopped
> 1 thin slice ginger
> 1 lb. shrimp (preferably fresh), peeled and deveined
> 2 tbsp. corn or peanut oil
> 1 Serrano chile pepper, deveined and chopped fine, or ¼ tsp. crushed hot red pepper
> ½ red bell pepper, cubed
> ¼ green bell pepper, cubed
> ½ yellow bell pepper, cubed

Sauce

6 tbsp. catsup
4 tbsp. vinegar (preferably rice vinegar)
5 tbsp. brown sugar
1 tbsp. lime or lemon juice
½ tsp. salt (optional)
3 tbsp. sherry or dry white wine
2 tsp. horseradish
2 scallions, chopped
¼ cup chopped cilantro

- Pat shrimp dry with paper towel; set aside.
- Heat 3 tablespoons oil in pan until hot, add garlic and ginger, fry for 20 seconds, add shrimp, and stir fry until shrimp curl.
- Remove from pan immediately.
- Do not overcook. If pan is smaller than 10 inches, fry shrimp in two batches.
- Add 2 tablespoons oil to pan. Add the Serrano chile or crushed red pepper, then the remaining peppers. Stir fry for 1 minute.
- Pour in the sauce ingredients, except the scallions and cilantro. Let it come to a boil; simmer for 1 minute.
- Add shrimp, scallions, and cilantro. Toss it quickly. Remove from heat. Serve immediately.

Note: if fresh shrimp are not available, the best type of frozen shrimp to buy are those that have grayish shells. The shrimp with reddish shells tend to have a tough texture.

Pepper and Ginger Salmon

Clara Jacobs is a very close friend who has shared cooking-class experiences, as well as many other experiences, with me both at home and abroad. She and her wonderful husband, Jake, are warm and friendly types who are natural-born host and hostess. Clara comes from a large Italian family where good food was an important part of daily life. She loves to cook for large groups. In fact, it is a good idea to gather together a large group when she cooks because she doesn't seem to be able to go into the kitchen without creating an enormous feast. Clara adapted this recipe from one of my classes and suggested it be included in the book.

> 4 6-oz. fresh salmon filets or steaks
> 2½ tbsp. gingerroot, finely minced
> 1 tbsp. fresh coarsely ground black pepper
> Salt, to taste
> 2 tbsp. unsalted butter, melted

- Pat fish dry with paper towel.
- Sprinkle with ginger, pepper, and salt to taste.
- Brush with butter.
- Broil under preheated broiler or on a hot grill until salmon just becomes opaque in center—10 minutes for each inch thickness.

Ginger Cream Sauce

> ¼ cup minced shallots
> 2 tbsp. minced scallions
> 1 medium tomato, peeled, seeded,
>   and finely chopped
> 1 tbsp. fresh gingerroot, minced
> 1 cup dry white wine
> 1 cup heavy cream
> 2 tbsp. unsalted butter or margarine
> 1 lime, sliced
> Parsley sprigs

- Combine in a large skillet the shallots, scallions, tomatoes, ginger, and wine. Cook over high heat until reduced to ⅓ cup.
- Add cream and reduce by one-half. Remove from heat and gently whisk in butter. Strain. Reheat strained sauce over gentle heat.
- Spoon sauce over bottom of four slightly warm serving plates and top with fish. Garnish with slices of fresh lime and sprigs of parsley. Serve immediately.
- Serves 4.

Marilyn's Special Grilled Lamb

Janet Forbes also comes from a household where good food is greatly appreciated. She, with her sparkling smile, has graced the middle of the second row during all the years that she has attended my classes and I appreciate her contribution to this chapter. Her family enjoys grilled foods and they grill all year. Her "boys" (all grown men) never liked the taste of lamb until she followed my advice to remove all fat. It is the lamb fat that imparts a strong flavor, which many people find objectionable. Actually the lean muscle is very mildly flavored.

> **1 leg of lamb (5-6 lb.), butterflied**
> **Several sprigs fresh sage**
> **Several sprigs fresh rosemary**
> **Several sprigs fresh thyme**
> **1 tbsp. peppercorns**
> **Salt, to taste**
> **½ cup extravirgin olive oil**
> **3 cloves garlic, peeled and thinly sliced**
> **Wedges of lemon or lime**
> **Herbs for garnish**

- Remove all of the excess fat from the boned leg of lamb. Place in a shallow large baking dish.
- Arrange the sprigs of fresh herbs over it. Sprinkle over the peppercorns and salt to taste.
- Brush generously with the oil, coating all of the lamb and the herbs. Add the garlic.
- Cover loosely with a tent of foil and let sit at room temperature for 1 hour.
- Place on a hot grill with the herbs and peppercorns still on the lamb. (The herbs should dry and char to give flavor as the lamb cooks.)
- Cook 45-50 minutes for medium-rare; longer according to preference. Remove peppercorns and dried herbs.
- Garnish with lemon wedges and fresh herbs to serve.
- Serve warm or at room temperature. Slice across the grain into thin slices.
- Serves 8-10.

Chicken Breasts
with Artichoke Hearts

This recipe also came from Janet Forbes with the following comments: "Marilyn's recipe called for fresh artichokes, but I use canned or frozen artichokes as well. I often add more stock and wine since my family likes the sauce so well." She added that she uses this recipe frequently for guests; once the breasts are boned and pounded ahead of time, the assembly and cooking goes quickly. I was most pleased to hear that it has been requested by repeat houseguests.

> **4 whole chicken breasts, cut in half,**
>   **skinned and boned**
> **Salt and freshly ground pepper**
> **6 tbsp. unsalted butter**
> **Flour**
> **3 tbsp. unsalted butter**
> **¼ cup thinly sliced scallions**
> **2 tbsp. flour**
> **¾ cup chicken stock**
> **½ cup dry white wine**
> **8 artichokes**
> **1 tbsp. fresh green peppercorns (canned in brine)**
> **Chopped parsley**

- Place chicken breasts between two sheets of plastic wrap and pound to an even thickness.
- Season with salt and pepper
- Melt 6 tablespoons butter in skillet.
- Dredge chicken in flour.
- Brown 3 minutes on each side.
- Transfer to a baking dish and keep warm in oven.
- Add 3 tablespoons butter to pan drippings.
- Sauté scallions, stirring.
- Add the 2 tablespoons of flour and cook 3 minutes, stirring constantly.
- Add chicken stock and white wine; whisk until smooth and thickened.
- Add artichokes and peppercorns.
- Heat and pour over chicken.
- Garnish with chopped parsley.

Pork Tenderloin
with Bing Cherry Sauce

I first met Glenn Rinsky, who should now be properly referred to as Chef Rinsky, when he was about 16 years old and came to see me to ask if he could teach a class in my cooking school. Though a bit dubious at the outset, I was soon convinced of his qualifications as a cook and abilities as a teacher. I will say that for someone who had no previous experience teaching he taught a pretty good class. Since then, Glenn has gone on to graduate from the Culinary Institute of America and is a full-fledged chef with some great experience. While a student at the Culinary Institute, Glenn would call from time to time to "check in" with me. Once he called with a touch of panic in his voice and said, "Marilyn, I need help." He had entered a cooking contest for the student chefs sponsored by the Michigan Cherry Council with a whopping $500 prize. He had thought of a recipe that seemed creative enough but he couldn't quite get it to work out or taste right. So . . . over the phone, we dissected, discussed, and amended that recipe. He went away and made it again, called back, and reported that it was a tasty dish indeed. He won. We thought the recipe should appear in this book.

1 pork tenderloin, trimmed of all fat,
    cut into 2-in. medallions, and pounded slightly
    with the back of a chef's knife
Salt and white pepper, to taste
1 tbsp. butter
1 tbsp. olive oil
¼ cup good brandy
½ cup chicken broth, de-fatted
1 tbsp. green peppercorns (packed in brine)
Zest of 1 orange
Juice of 1 orange
¼ cup heavy cream
1½ cups either canned red Michigan cherries
    or fresh cherries that have been pitted
Fresh mint, for garnish

- Season medallions of pork with salt and white pepper.
- In heavy-bottomed pan,* heat butter and oil over medium-high heat.
- Add medallions into pan, being sure not to overcrowd the pan.
- Sauté on one side for 1 to 2 minutes, then turn over and sauté briefly or until meat springs back when touched.
- Place cooked medallions on oven-proof tray, or on individual plates, and place in warm oven while sauce is made.
- Pour remaining oil out of pan and add brandy, ignite with match, flame, and let flame subside.
- Add chicken broth, green peppercorns, orange zest, and juice of orange. Let this reduce to one-third its original volume.
- Add the cream and reduce until thick enough to coat a wooden spoon—this should take a total of 3 to 5 minutes.
- Drain cherries and add to sauce.
- Heat through and spoon over warm medallions.
- Garnish with mint and serve.
- Serves 3 to 4.

*Glenn says do not use a nonstick pan in this recipe because the good flavor of the sauce depends on some of the browned particles from the sautéed meat remaining in the pan. This does not happen on a nonstick surface.

Mexican Chili Burritos

Jane Garfinkel and her husband, Lou Solomine, are two more interesting and sweet people who came into my circle of friends through cooking classes. Jane manages to be attorney, mother, and wife and still finds time to enjoy cooking. She always found time to attend a lot of my classes and has built quite a file of recipes from them. She said that she found it a difficult task choosing a contribution for the book. She settled on the following excellent recipe for chili Mexican style wrapped in whole-wheat flour tortillas because she has amended it to her taste since taking it home from class and that makes it a joint effort on the part of both teacher and student.

2 lb. lean pork, cubed
3 tbsp. extravirgin olive oil
2 cups canned Italian plum tomatoes,
   coarsely chopped
1 large yellow onion, chopped
3 cloves garlic, minced
3 poblano chiles, peeled, seeded, and chopped
3 Anaheim chiles, peeled, seeded, and chopped
2-3 jalapeño chiles, seeded and minced
1 tsp. chili powder
1 tsp. cumin
½ tsp. oregano
Salt, to taste
8 whole-wheat flour tortillas
Melted butter
1 lb. Sonoma Jack cheese
2 cups sour cream

- Brown the pork in the oil.
- Add tomatoes, onions, and garlic and cook, covered, for 30 minutes. Stir in the chiles and seasonings and cook 30 minutes longer, uncovered, stirring often.
- Cook until pork is tender enough to shred into large strips before filling into the tortillas.
- Brush 8 whole-wheat flour tortillas with melted butter.
- Heat wrapped tightly in heavy-duty foil for 10 minutes at 350 degrees.
- Place a tortilla on a plate. Sprinkle with cheese.
- Add a large spoonful of the meat mixture and top with some sour cream.
- Fold "burrito style" to encase the filling in the tortilla. Serve with lots of Marilyn's Salsa (see index).
- Serves 8.

Zucchini Casserole Deluxe

A fellow Southerner, Frances Hutcherson, who came to our part of the world a number of years ago to marry her charming husband, Bill, is proof that Southern women are truly gracious hostesses. She loves cooking and entertaining in her beautifully appointed home with its large, friendly kitchen. This zucchini recipe is one that she adapted from a class I taught on vegetable dishes. It is a most versatile vegetable casserole that can be an everyday supper dish or that can grace the company table. Make it ahead and it is ready to pop into the oven a half-hour before mealtime.

> **2 tbsp. extravirgin olive oil**
> **4 small zucchini, washed, trimmed, and shredded**
> **1 medium onion, finely chopped**
> **1 tbsp. cornstarch**
> **2 eggs**
> **1 cup light cream (Half & Half)**
> **¼ tsp. hot pepper sauce**
> **Dash freshly grated nutmeg**
> **1 tsp. salt**
> **4 oz. Gruyère cheese, shredded**

- Heat oil in skillet and sauté zucchini and onion for 5 minutes, stirring.
- Sprinkle cornstarch over and cook 1 minute longer.
- Remove from heat.
- Beat together eggs, cream, hot pepper sauce, nutmeg, and salt. Stir into cooked vegetables.
- Pour into well-buttered, shallow baking dish and sprinkle with cheese.
- Bake in a preheated 400-degree oven for 25-30 minutes or until hot through and lightly browned.
- Serve immediately
- Serves 8.

Grilled Vegetables
with Goat Cheese

Jane Garfinkel shares this recipe with us. This is one from her own files that she thought I should try. It is truly a taste treat as well as a most attractive vegetable dish. It would be great to accompany almost any grilled meat, fish, or poultry.

Salt, to taste
1 medium eggplant, halved
2 zucchini, halved
2 yellow squash, halved
1 Vidalia or Walla-Walla onion, thinly sliced
1 red pepper, halved
1 green pepper, halved
Extravirgin olive oil
1 tbsp. each freshly chopped basil, thyme,
   rosemary, and dill
2 cloves garlic, very finely minced
Salt, pepper, and dash of cinnamon
6 oz. mild goat cheese

- Salt eggplant and let stand ½ hour.
- Pat dry with paper towels.
- Brush all the vegetables with some of the olive oil and place them, cut side down, on grill.
- Grill 6 minutes per side, turning sooner if necessary to avoid burning.
- While vegetables are grilling, in a large heatproof bowl place herbs, garlic, ⅓ cup olive oil, seasonings, and crumbled goat cheese.
- Remove vegetables from grill and cut into large dice.
- Add to goat-cheese mixture in bowl and stir gently.
- Serve immediately or keep in a 200-degree oven for up to 15 minutes.

Carol's Pizza Pie

During the years when Carol Stockwell lived next door to me, we did a lot of cooking and laughing together. She was all of the things one can expect a good neighbor to be. And, although she now lives 100 miles away, I still think of her as a neighbor at a distance. Often I answer the phone to hear Carol on the other end all ready to discuss a recipe she is about to prepare, just as though she were still next door. Carol and Rex often have a house full of company and they enjoy feeding them good food. Many of those guests are hungry friends of their teen-age children. Her "Pizza Pie"—we know the title is redundant but read the recipe and you'll understand—is often requested and is packed with good flavors.

> **Pastry for double-crust 10-in. pie**
> **5 eggs**
> **1 lb. ricotta cheese**
> **2 tbsp. chopped onion**
> **1½ tbsp. chopped parsley**
> **1 cup grated Parmesan cheese**
> **Salt and fresh ground pepper, to taste**
> **2 tbsp. olive oil**
> **2 cloves garlic**
> **¾ tsp. basil**
> **½ tsp. oregano**
> **10 oz. tomato purée**
> **4 oz. tomato paste**
> **⅔ cup sliced ripe olives**
> **1 large green pepper**
> **½ lb. mozzarella cheese, thinly sliced**

- Prepare piecrust, line 10-inch pie pan, and reserve top crust.
- Beat eggs. Stir in ricotta cheese, onion, parsley, Parmesan cheese, and season with salt and fresh ground pepper. Set aside.

- Heat olive oil in small saucepan. Crush garlic into it and add herbs.
- Sauté until garlic is clear and golden. Stir in the tomato purée, paste, olives, and season with salt and fresh ground pepper. Set aside. Slice green pepper thinly.

To Assemble

- Spread half the ricotta cheese mixture in the prepared pie shell. Arrange half the mozzarella slices over it.
- Cover with half the tomato sauce and spread half the green peppers on top.
- Repeat all layers and cover with top crust.
- Bake in a preheated 425-degree oven for 35-40 minutes. Let stand for 30 minutes before serving.

Note: can be prepared early in the day and baked at dinnertime.

Sunday Supper Chicken and Rice

Vera Jung, who sat right in the middle of the front row, is a student who never hesitates to speak her opinion. I was most flattered when she had the following to say when she sent her recipe: "Marilyn Harris's cooking classes were always great—not just for the delicious food she prepared, but I could prepare the same recipe and it would taste just as good. She is a wonderful gourmet cook and teacher." Thanks, Vera, and thanks too for this recipe from one of my "One-Dish Meal" classes. This recipe also fits nicely into the "comfort food" category. Vera also points out: "For a do-ahead supper for family or company, this is a flavorful chicken dish that can be prepared ahead. And, unlike most chicken dishes, the chicken does not have to be precooked."

6 tbsp. extravirgin olive oil
4 lb. chicken pieces (meaty pieces; breasts are best)
2 large onions, chopped
½ lb. mushrooms, thickly sliced
2 cloves garlic, minced
½ lb. country ham (smoked), diced
1 green pepper, julienned
½ cup chopped parsley
2 bay leaves
3 cups long-grain converted rice
28-oz. can plum tomatoes, chopped
3 cups chicken stock
2 cups beer
1 cup chopped green olives
½ cup julienned pimiento
Salt, to taste
1 tsp. freshly ground pepper
Chopped parsley, for garnish

- In a large skillet, heat oil and brown the chicken, skin down first.
- Transfer to a casserole dish.
- Sauté the onions and mushrooms in the oil. Stir in the garlic (do not brown), ham, and green pepper. Cook a few minutes, stirring.
- Spoon over chicken.
- Sprinkle with the ½ cup parsley and add bay leaves.
- Add rice to skillet and stir until coated with the remaining oil (add a bit more if necessary).
- Spoon over the chicken and pour in the tomatoes, stock, beer, olives, and pimientos. Stir just to combine and season with salt and pepper.
- Cover with a tight lid (or a triple layer of heavy-duty foil).
- Bake in the center of a 375-degree oven for ½ hour.
- Uncover and let sit in turned-off oven 10-15 minutes.
- Garnish with more chopped parsley.

Walnut-Oatmeal Bread

Jill Bentgen is actually a good friend and neighbor and not a student—that is, unless you count the fact that she has observed me teach a couple of private classes. Jill, who is a talented food professional, is very creative in the kitchen. She especially loves to bake. Since I have often eaten wonderful freshly baked bread at her house, I thought it would be appropriate for her to share some of her great bread recipes with us for this book. She has generously sent two recipes. After tasting them both, it was impossible to choose one. I had the luxury of eating the black walnut version of Jill's Walnut-Oatmeal Bread. If you can find black walnuts, do try it with them. The English walnuts also give good flavor to this firm, moist bread. Great for breakfast!

> **1 cup whole milk**
> **1 cup water**
> **1 cup rolled oats, either quick or old fashioned**
> **2 tbsp. sweet butter**
> **¼ cup light molasses**
> **¼ cup honey**
> **1 tbsp. dry yeast**
> **½ cup warm water (less than 115 degrees)**
> **½ tsp. sugar**
> **Approximately 6 cups bread flour**
> **¾ cup English walnuts or black walnuts,**
>   **coarsely chopped**
> **2 tbsp. salt**
> **1 tbsp. cider vinegar**
> **Melted butter**

- In a saucepan, scald the milk with the water.
- Pour over the oats in a bowl and stir in the butter, molasses, and honey. Let this cool to lukewarm (less than 115 degrees).
- In a large mixing bowl, dissolve the yeast in the ½ cup of warm water with the sugar. Let sit for 10 minutes.

Kneading bread is important in order to achieve the proper texture of the finished product. It is also important to knead long enough and vigorously enough. There are traditional bread makers who believe that the best loaf is achieved only when it has been hand kneaded. It can be a fun activity and can serve to provide some tension-releasing exercise. If kneading is done by hand, do not be timid about manipulating the bread dough. Pick up that dough and slam it down on the bread board (or counter top). Using both hands, pull it toward you and, using the heels of your hands, energetically push away. You will be able to feel the texture of the bread dough changing as you work. Continue these motions until the dough is satiny smooth to the touch.

- Add the cooled oat mixture and 2½ cups of the flour. Beat with an electric mixer at least 2 minutes or at least 200 strokes by hand.
- Add 2 more cups of flour and beat an additional 2 minutes or 200 strokes.
- Mix in the nuts, salt, and vinegar.
- Gradually add more flour, as much as it takes to produce a dough that clings together and leaves the sides of the bowl.
- Turn the dough out onto a floured board and knead until smooth and elastic. Do not add too much flour to the board.
- The dough should be slightly tacky because of the oats. Put the dough into a buttered bowl and turn all around to coat or brush the top with melted butter.
- Cover with lightly dampened towel. Let rise until doubled in bulk.
- Punch the dough down, turn out onto a lightly floured board, knead a few times to press out air bubbles, cut in half, cover, and let rest about 10 minutes.
- Shape the dough into smooth oblongs and place in two buttered, medium loaf pans.
- Brush the tops with melted butter.
- Cover with damp towel and let rise until almost doubled.
- Preheat oven to 350 degrees.
- Place the bread pans in the middle of the oven and bake for 45 minutes, or until the bottoms sound hollow when tapped.
- Remove from pans and cool on a rack.
- Makes two loaves.

Variations: substitute raisins for part of the nuts or try different nut combinations. Substitute 2 cups of whole-wheat flour for 2 cups of bread flour.

Kneading time is cut in half when a heavy-duty electric mixer fitted with one or more dough hooks is used. A heavy-duty food processor cuts the time to a mere minute or two.

Green Peppercorn Bread

This spicy bread, which is studded with green peppercorns, tastes wonderful served warm with some butter or margarine spread on it. Try it the second day toasted to make a fantastic roast beef or chicken sandwich. *Magnifique!*

> 1¾ tsp. active dry yeast
> 1 cup warm water (less than 115 degrees)
> 2 tsp. olive oil
> 2¾ cups bread flour
> 1 tsp. salt
> 1¼ to 1½ tbsp. green peppercorns (packed in brine), well drained
> 1½ tsp. balsamic vinegar

- Stir the yeast into the water in a small bowl; let stand until frothy, about 10 minutes.
- Stir in the oil.
- Place the flour, salt, and peppercorns in a food processor fitted with the steel blade and process with 2 or 3 pulses to chop the peppercorns lightly.
- With the machine running, pour the yeast mixture through the feed tube as quickly as the flour can absorb it.
- Immediately add the vinegar.
- Process 45 seconds longer to knead.
- Add more flour if the dough does not pull from the sides of the bowl to form a ball.
- Finish kneading briefly by hand on a lightly floured board.
- Place the dough in a lightly oiled bowl, cover with plastic wrap, and let rise until doubled, about 1½ hours.
- Punch the dough down on a lightly floured surface and knead it briefly.
- Shape the dough into a long thin or a round loaf.
- Place the dough on a lightly oiled baking sheet.
- Cover with a damp towel and let rise until almost doubled.

Any addition of steam in a hot oven while baking bread will yield a loaf of bread with a thicker and crunchy crust.

It is important to make sure yeast dough does not become dry while it is rising. A dry crust that forms on the top from exposure to the air will result in hard or discolored spots in the finished bread. To prevent any drying out, I like to seal the dough in a large plastic bag. (Press out as much air as possible before sealing the bag.) Or place it in a greased bowl and cover with lightly oiled plastic wrap with the oiled side down toward the bread. Seal the plastic tightly around the edge of the bowl. If a damp towel is used, be sure it remains damp during the entire rising time.

Yeast is not a mystery substance. It is a living organism that reacts to moisture and temperature. Its action accelerates in warm temperatures and slows in cold ones. When the temperature is very cold, the growing process ceases entirely. When the temperature is too hot, the yeast cells are actually destroyed and its effectiveness as a leavening agent is diminished. It also has a readily determinable life-span, which is the reason you should pay careful attention to the dated packages.

- Flatten the bread slightly by pressing down firmly with the palm of your hand.
- Using a sharp knife, make three deep, parallel slashes across the top of the loaf.
- Preheat the oven to 500 degrees.
- Place the loaf in the oven and spray the oven with water.
- Immediately reduce the heat to 400 degrees.
- Bake 35 minutes, spraying the oven 3 times with water in the first 10 minutes.
- Cool completely on a rack.
- Makes one loaf.

Zitronencreme
(Lemon Bavarian Cream)

Renate Drexl Glenn has certainly been in enough of my classes to be called a "cooking student." However, Renate has been so much a part of my life for so many years, it would be difficult to come up with any one label for her. We have eaten a lot of food in one another's kitchens. When I asked Renate to contribute to this book, I decided that it should be her "Lemon Bavarian Cream." I have eaten this dish in Germany, but it always tastes best when Renate makes it. It is the perfect dessert to follow a hearty meal since its elegant lemon flavor satisfies one's sweet tooth without creating that overstuffed feeling.

> 1 envelope unflavored gelatin
> ¼ cup cold water
> 3 egg yolks
> ½ cup + 3 tbsp. sugar
> ¼ cup fresh lemon juice
> 2 tsp. finely grated lemon peel
> 1 cup whipping cream
> 3 egg whites
> 1 lemon, cut lengthwise in paper-thin slices
>   for garnish

- In a heatproof bowl, sprinkle gelatin over ¼ cup cold water.
- Soften gelatin 2-3 minutes, put into double boiler over simmering water, and stir until gelatin dissolves completely.
- Take double boiler from heat, but leave pot with gelatin in the water.
- With a beater, beat egg yolks with ½ cup sugar until yolks are pale yellow and thick enough to fall back in a ribbon when the batter is lifted from the bowl.
- Stir in gelatin, lemon juice, and lemon peel.
- Whip cream in chilled bowl until it holds its shape firmly. With rubber spatula fold the cream into egg and lemon mixture.
- Beat egg whites until frothy.
- Sprinkle in 3 tablespoons of sugar and beat until whites are stiff.
- Gently fold egg whites into lemon mixture.
- Cover tightly and refrigerate at least 3 hours.
- Serve in clear glass bowl or in individual parfait glasses, garnished with lemon slices.

Strawberries and Cream
with Orange Glaze

We started this chapter with a recipe from Pam Shearer so it is fitting that we conclude with one from her as well. She says of this dish, "I like to serve it in summertime. It's refreshing and pretty but a relatively simple dessert."

> 2 egg whites, at room temperature
> ¼ tsp. cream of tartar
> 6 tbsp. sugar
> 1 cup whipping cream
> 1 tsp. vanilla
> 1 qt. strawberries, washed and hulled
> 6 tbsp. strawberry preserves
> 3 tbsp. kirsch
> 3 tbsp. Triple Sec or Cointreau

When it is necessary to beat both egg whites and whipped cream for the same dish, always beat the egg whites first. Egg whites will not whip properly unless the bowl is clean, dry, and free from any fat. The cream, on the other hand, can be quite successfully whipped in the same mixer bowl following the egg whites without even washing the bowl. If the kitchen is very warm, the bowl may need to be chilled in order to obtain the maximum volume from the cream.

• Beat egg whites with cream of tartar; gradually add sugar and beat until stiff, but not dry.
• Whip the cream until stiff. Add the vanilla.
• Gently fold together the egg-white mixture and whipped cream until well blended.
• Spread mixture over bottom and sides of shallow serving dish.
• Arrange strawberries, pointed side up, over meringue.
• Thin the preserves with liqueurs and carefully pour over strawberries, taking care to glaze each strawberry.
• Chill before serving.
• Serves 6 to 8.

Note: this dessert can be made 2-3 hours before it is to be served and refrigerated immediately. If made too far in advance, the cream and meringue begin to break up and become watery. Always serve directly from the refrigerator.

Marilyn's Favorites

Spicy Vegetable Soup

Creamy Onion Soup

Chicken Pâté
with Hot and Sweet
Mustard Sauce

Filled Cucumber Cups
with Red Pepper Mousse

Zwiebelkuchen
(Onion Tart)

Bob's Pasta Spinach Rolls

**Marilyn's Thanksgiving
Salad**
with Lemon-Walnut Dressing

**Three-Green Salad
with Pears**

Herring Salad

Christmas Wreath Salad

Shrimp Veracruzana

Scallops in Wine Sauce

Chicken Breasts
in Apple-Orange Sauce

Wild Rice Mushroom Pilaf

Cranberry Chutney

Pastry Tulip Cups
with Caramelized
Apple Filling

Pears Helene
with Hot Fudge Sauce

Chocolate-Orange Mousse

Chocolate-Orange Torte

**Mother's Chocolate
Cream Pie**

It seems an amazing thing to me finally to reach the last chapter in this book. When we started with this business of creating a cookbook, my organized academic husband encouraged me to make an outline and then try to adhere to it. My initial approach was to sit for hours sifting through files of recipes that represented many years of taking classes, teaching, and generally collecting favorite recipes. I probably don't need to tell you that I was soon overcome by stacks of paper that quickly got out of control.

So . . . I sat myself down to work on the outline and to start thinking in a more organized fashion about the actual contents of a potential book. Gradually it began to become clear what fit together and what would go into each chapter. I will admit here that I initially thought of this last chapter as being "Holiday Favorites." Then one day all of the other chapters were completed and I realized that I had some recipes left over that, although they did not have a logical place in the menus, just had to go into the book.

These recipes are, after all, not just holiday favorites, but some of my genuine all-time favorites. That is when the title suddenly changed to *Marilyn's Favorites*. To try to make some sense out of this collection, I have organized the recipes in the chapter in roughly the same order as the foods would appear in a meal. There are some dishes that do not have a definitive place in this scheme. For example, the Onion Tart could be a first course for dinner, a party food, or the main course for a lunch, brunch, or supper.

But I really hadn't intended to get so involved in trying to explain all of this. My wish is that you will look upon this last batch of recipes as some great things to eat and fun things to cook. It would be very nice if you find that some of the following get to be your favorites too.

Spicy Vegetable Soup

Anyone who has taken a cooking class or two from me has discovered my "spicy tooth." It is true that I always travel with a bottle of Tabasco® in my handbag. No, I don't sprinkle it on everything. I simply feel that one faces a lot of bland dishes in places like airports and hotel coffee shops, which can be greatly improved with a dash or so of that wonderful, piquant sauce. So, I guess that explains why one of my all-time favorite comforting supper dishes is my version of a cream of vegetable soup. The carrots give it a very pleasing color, and the creamy texture along with the delicious flavors make it a real joy to look forward to on a cold evening. If your palate does not favor spicy foods, add only one jalapeño. That is not enough to make it spicy, but the acid in the pepper serves to enhance the other flavors.

Red-skinned potatoes make a lighter-textured and creamier potato soup. They are also my preference for mashed potatoes. The brown (or yellow) skin Idaho potatoes are always used for roasting or baking.

They are also best for recipes where the potatoes are grated, like potato pancakes or hash browns.

3-4 fresh jalapeño peppers
4 tbsp. butter
1 lb. carrots, peeled and sliced
1 large yellow onion, chopped
1 large clove garlic, minced
Dash hot pepper sauce
1 bouquet garni composed of:
   2 sprigs fresh thyme
   2 sprigs parsley and a bay leaf
5 cups chicken stock
2 large red potatoes, peeled and cubed
1 cup heavy cream
Salt, to taste
3 tbsp. chopped cilantro or parsley

- Wash peppers and remove the stems and seeds. Mince finely.
- Melt the butter in a heavy pot.
- Add the carrots and jalapeños.
- Sauté, stirring over medium heat, for 2-3 minutes.
- Add onions and garlic.
- Sauté for 2 minutes more, stirring.
- Add the hot pepper sauce, bouquet garni, chicken stock, and potatoes.
- Bring to boil, partially covered.
- Reduce heat to low and cook, stirring occasionally, until carrots are very tender, about 25-30 minutes. Remove bouquet garni.
- Purée in the blender and return to clean pot.
- Stir in the cream and salt to taste.
- Serve hot, topped with the chopped cilantro or parsley.
- Serves 8-10.

Note: for a lighter soup, light cream may be substituted for the heavy cream.

Creamy Onion Soup

I find that people have very definite opinions about onion soup. Because it has such a prominent flavor, they either like it a lot or they simply don't care if they never eat it. That, of course, is in reference to the traditional clear onion soup, which is served with croutons and grated cheese. I have often surprised people in my classes with this far milder and most attractive version of onion soup. It has an especially inviting taste when made in the early fall when the new crop of yellow onions has just landed in the market. You will find it to be a faithful standby to use as a company soup for dinner parties. It always draws raves at my house and from my students.

When making cream soups ahead of time, finish the soup up to the addition of the cream. It can then be cooled, covered, and refrigerated. At serving time, reheat the soup to serving temperature and then add the cream and heat just long enough to heat the cream. Most cream soups will curdle when brought to the boiling point. Therefore, waiting to add the cream takes the risk out of the reheating process. It also tends to give the soup a fresher taste.

4 tbsp. unsalted butter or margarine
5 medium yellow onions, thinly sliced
1 tsp. salt
White pepper, to taste
3 tbsp. flour
5 cups chicken stock, warmed
1 cup heavy cream
1 egg yolk
1 carrot
2 sticks celery
4 green onions
2 tbsp. parsley, for garnish

- Melt butter and sauté onions until tender; cover and cook over low heat for 10 minutes.
- Season with salt and white pepper.
- Add flour and cook over medium heat for 2 minutes—do not brown.
- Whisk in stock and simmer 15 minutes.
- Purée in the blender or food processor.
- Whisk together cream and yolk and whisk in; do not boil.
- For garnish: cut vegetables into very thin julienne strips (1" x ⅛"), and blanch for 2-3 minutes in a small amount of boiling water.
- Refresh in ice water and drain. Add to soup just before serving.
- Before serving, sprinkle with some parsley.
- Serve hot.
- Makes 8 servings.

Chicken Pâté

This recipe is a far cry from the traditional French pâtés that I have learned to make over the years in assorted cooking classes on French cuisine. One of the basic ingredients in a traditional French pâté is the proper percentage of pork fat. So, from that perspective, this is not a proper pâté at all, but it is an attractive and elegant-flavored dish that can be served as a first course at a seated dinner or cut into small slices and served with its mustard sauce on thin slices of party rye bread as finger food. Though not low in calories with its cream content, it is much lighter textured and lower in fat than most pâtés. The food processor allows one to create a most impressive finished product with a minimum amount of time and effort. It can be made a couple of days before the party and stored well wrapped in the refrigerator. If you are in a very creative mode, a simple design of blanched parsley leaves could be arranged on top and coated with a layer of aspic. The aspic also protects against drying out when made ahead.

2 cups heavy cream
3 sprigs thyme
2 bay leaves
3 sprigs parsley
¼ tsp. freshly grated nutmeg
1 medium onion, peeled and quartered
1 tsp. whole black peppercorns
1½ lb. boneless and skinless chicken breasts
1 tsp. salt
¼ tsp. hot pepper sauce, or to taste
2 egg whites
¾ cup chopped parsley
1 tbsp. chopped fresh tarragon (or 1 tsp. dried)

- In a small, heavy, nonreactive saucepan, mix together the cream, thyme, bay leaves, parsley sprigs, nutmeg, onion, and peppercorns. Heat until bubbles form around the edges—do not allow to boil.
- Remove from heat and let steep for 10 minutes.
- Strain and chill until very cold.
- When cream is cold, cut chicken breasts into pieces and place in food processor bowl with steel blade. Add salt and hot pepper sauce and process until finely chopped.
- Continuing to process, pour cream through feed tube slowly, so that all cream is taken up by chicken.
- Add egg whites and process until light and fluffy.

When making the mixture for a pâté or terrine, the quality of the final product is greatly affected by the temperature of the ingredients. The meat (or poultry) should be very cold when it goes into the processor to be chopped. Leave the cream in the refrigerator until it is ready to be added.

- Add parsley and tarragon and pulse on and off (or use spatula) just to blend.
- Poach a spoonful in a small amount of simmering water and taste; correct seasonings.
- Butter a 6-cup loaf pan or pâté mold generously.
- Spoon in the chicken mixture and tap on counter top to remove air bubbles. Top with a piece of buttered parchment paper that has been cut to fit the top of the pan.
- Cover tightly with a double layer of heavy-duty foil, sealing well around edges.
- Place in a pan of hot water, with water coming halfway up on the pâté pan.
- Bake in a preheated 325-degree oven for 1 hour.
- Remove from water bath and weight by placing another pan on top and filling with pie weights or other heavy objects.* Chill for at least 2 hours.
- Slice to serve and serve with Hot and Sweet Mustard Sauce.
- Serves 8-10.

    Note: may be made 2-3 days ahead.

*I use a brick wrapped in aluminum foil.

Hot and Sweet Mustard Sauce

½ cup hot and sweet mustard
¾ cup mayonnaise
¼ cup sour cream
1 tbsp. fresh lemon or lime juice
Dash hot pepper sauce
Salt, to taste

- Stir together until smooth and thoroughly mixed and chill until serving time.
- Makes about 1¼ cups.

Filled Cucumber Cups
with Red Pepper Mousse

Sharon Shipley of Sunnyvale, California, is too busy directing her marvelous catering business, not to mention looking after the cooking school, her husband, and three charming children, to write a cookbook. At least, that is what she uses as an excuse. We like to share recipes with one another. So, I am sharing them with you. This is one that she makes in huge quantities for her catering clients. She sent it to me with instructions for me to "try it." I did just that and also took the liberty of making a couple of small changes. But the beautiful color and marvelous flavor are not altered. This is certainly what I think of as a "California recipe" and one of those fun things to set out on your party table.

> **6 medium cucumbers**
> **Salt**

- To make cucumber cups, score cucumbers lengthwise with a fork. Slice thick segments crosswise.
- Use a melon baller or a serrated spoon to scoop out the cucumber flesh, leaving shells about ¼ inch thick. Salt the cups.
- Invert them on a rack to drain briefly.
- Add the filling.

> **Filling**
>
> **1 large red pepper, roasted, peeled, and seeded**
> **8 oz. cream cheese, cut into small cubes**
> **1 tsp. finely grated onion**
> **Salt and white pepper**
> **¾ cup chicken stock, heated to boiling**
> **1 tbsp. gelatin softened in 3 tbsp. cold water**
> **2 tbsp. white wine vinegar**
> **1 tbsp. sugar**
> **½ cup whipping cream, lightly whipped**
> **Watercress leaves**

- Pulse red pepper in processor.
- Mix the cheese with onion, salt, and pepper.
- Pour boiling stock onto softened gelatin; stir until dissolved then add it to the cheese (be sure that the stock is only warm before adding to cheese).

- Cover with plastic wrap and chill.
- Mix together vinegar and sugar; add the red pepper.
- When the cheese mixture is quite cold, fold in the pepper mixture and the lightly whipped cream.
- Spoon into a large pastry bag fitted with a 7-8-mm star tip.
- Pipe onto the drained cucumber cups and garnish with watercress leaves.
- Makes about 3 dozen.

Zwiebelkuchen
(Onion Tart)

I had just returned from one of my trips to Germany when my good friend, the late Bert Greene, called to ask for a couple of recipes to go into a column he was writing about me. I had enjoyed eating this wonderful tart in Freiburg, which, of course, is located in the part of Germany that borders on Alsace-Lorraine, the area of France where the quiche was created. One can enjoy a tantalizing array of similar tarts and other pastries in this beautiful part of the world, and this one is a first cousin to the "Quiche Lorraine." In the region of Baden, where some of the best German wines are made, it is customary to serve onion tart with the new vintage. Like a lot of traditional dishes, there are numerous versions of this tart. Try this one for a simple supper or to serve as the first course for a more complex dinner party. I have also served it at brunch, where it garnered good reviews.

> **1 recipe pâte brisée prebaked in a 13-in.
>   removable-bottom tart pan**
> **6 slices bacon, diced**
> **4 tbsp. unsalted butter**
> **1 lb. yellow onions, chopped**
> **½ tsp. salt**
> **1½ tsp. caraway seeds**
> **2 tbsp. flour**
> **1½ cups light cream**
> **5 large eggs, beaten**

- Cook the bacon, stirring often, in a heavy skillet until crisp and golden brown.
- Remove with a slotted spoon to drain on paper towels.

- Pour off the bacon grease, but do not wash the skillet.
- Melt the butter in the skillet and cook the onions over low heat until they are softened and golden—about 10 minutes.
- Add salt and caraway seeds; stir in flour. Remove from heat.
- Whisk in the cream and then the eggs. Mix well.
- Pour into precooked pastry-lined pan and bake in the bottom one-third of a preheated 375-degree oven for 30-35 minutes or until puffed and golden.
- Serve as first course or as a light lunch or brunch dish.
- Serves 8-10.

Pastry: Pâte Brisée (Savory Pie/Tart Pastry)

2 cups unbleached flour
½ tsp. salt
3 tbsp. vegetable shortening (Crisco)
1 stick (4 oz.) chilled unsalted butter, cut into 8 pieces
4-5 tbsp. ice water

- Place the flour and salt in the food processor or mixing bowl.
- With steel blade in food processor or using two table knives, cut the shortening and butter in until the mixture resembles coarse meal.
- Add water gradually until a ball of dough forms.
- Pat into a smooth disc.
- Wrap in plastic and chill for at least 2 hours.
- Roll out to ⅛-inch thickness and place in an 11-inch removable-bottom tart pan.
- Line dough with foil or parchment paper.
- Fill pan with pie weights (or dried beans).
- Bake in bottom one-third of a preheated 400-degree oven for 10 minutes.
- Remove paper and weights and bake 1-2 minutes longer or just until pastry is set. Cool on a rack.
- Fill with filling.

Note: this pastry dough may be made ahead, wrapped air-tight, and frozen for as long as several months. As a time-saver, it is a good idea to have some on hand. Thaw overnight in the refrigerator and then let sit at room temperature just until pliable enough to roll.

Prebaking, which is often called "blind baking," is an important step for pastries like pies, tarts, and quiches. When an uncooked liquid filling, like quiche filling, is poured into an unbaked pastry the pastry will remain uncooked and will have a soggy texture and raw flour taste.

If the pastry rim on a pie or tart begins to brown too much before the filling has finished cooking, stop the browning by gently pressing a long strip of aluminum foil over the pastry rim. Carefully remove the foil just a few minutes before the entire pie has finished baking.

Bob's Pasta Spinach Rolls

Bob and Marj Valvano are unofficial family. Marj has been one of my major sources of knowledge concerning wines and Bob and I have spent many hours cooking in one another's kitchens. Together we've all shared some wonderful meals accompanied by some truly great wines. Bob is not only of Italian heritage, but spent many years working as a consulting engineer in northern Italy. He is without question the best pasta maker I know and I am not the only friend who requests these wonderful spinach rolls when Bob decides to cook for us. When I asked him to share the recipe for this book, the only version he could supply was one scrawled in Italian from his friend who had given it to him several years back. We managed to get it into the proper form for the book. It is not the easiest recipe you will read in this book, but I will tell you that it is worth some effort to experience the marvelous end result. As Bob would say, it is *delicioso*!

Bob included his tips for successful homemade pasta:

1. When making pasta with semolina flour, always follow this proportion: one-third semolina to two-thirds white flour.

2. For the best texture always use bread flour for the white flour.

The Pasta

3 cups unbleached flour
3 large eggs
Approximately 3 tbsp. cold water (more as required)

- Place the flour, eggs, and 3 tablespoons of water in the food processor with steel blade or heavy-duty mixer fitted with a dough hook.
- Process until mixed, adding more water, a teaspoon at a time, if necessary, to make a ball of dough that holds together.
- Knead pasta dough by processing until dough is smooth.
- Wrap in plastic to prevent drying and set aside until ready to roll out and assemble the spinach roll.

The Filling

2 lb. fresh spinach, washed and cooked until wilted,
or 3 10-oz. pkg. frozen chopped spinach, thawed
1 cup Béchamel Sauce (see index)
1 lb. ricotta cheese
1 cup freshly grated imported Parmesan cheese
1 large egg, lightly beaten
1½ tsp. salt, or to taste
½ tsp. freshly grated nutmeg
4 tbsp. melted unsalted butter
Extra freshly grated Parmesan

- Squeeze all of the excess liquid from the spinach and pulse it in the food processor. Scrape into a mixing bowl.
- Stir the Béchamel into the spinach.
- Crumble the ricotta cheese and stir into the spinach mixture along with the Parmesan cheese.
- Stir in the egg and seasonings.
- Cover and chill until ready to use.

To Assemble

- With a hand-operated or electric pasta machine, roll out the pasta into one continuous wide sheet.
- Cut the strip in half to make two strips.
- Spread a strip with half of the spinach filling, leaving ½-inch margins on the edges.
- Roll, jelly-roll fashion, taking care not to press too hard so that the filling comes out on the sides.
- Place the roll on a large piece of cheesecloth that is long enough to encase it twice and wide enough to tie at each end.
- Roll the pasta roll tightly into the cheesecloth.
- Tie the ends in the same way a sausage is tied into the casing. Repeat process with other pasta strip.
- Simmer in a large pan of water for 1 hour.
- Do not allow to come to a rolling boil.
- Unwrap and cut into ½-inch slices.
- Allow 2-3 slices per person as a pasta course.
- Drizzle some warm melted butter over each slice and sprinkle with some Parmesan cheese.
- Makes 2 rolls.
- Each roll serves 6 people.

Marilyn's Thanksgiving Salad

This crunchy, colorful salad is so named because for years I have made a version of it to serve with that annual feast. It works very nicely as the appetizer salad course or can be served after the main course, where it does double duty as the fruit and cheese course in European fashion. I think that you will find the combination of flavors and textures to be just what one expects in a salad for this season. It is indeed best in these autumn months when the Red Delicious apples are at their peak. It is necessary to acidulate the apples in the lemon juice just as soon as they are cut up so they will not turn an unattractive shade of brown.

> **2 large heads Belgian endive**
> **3 large Red Delicious apples, cored and halved**
> **2 tbsp. fresh lemon juice**
> **4 large ribs celery, strings removed**
> **1 cup walnut halves**
> **½ cup white raisins**
> **1 recipe Lemon-Walnut Dressing (see below)**
> **1 medium head romaine, washed, dried, and chilled**
> **4 oz. fresh goat cheese**
> **Watercress sprigs**

- Wash the endive, separate it into individual leaves, wrap in paper towels, place in a plastic bag, and chill for at least 1 hour.
- Slice the apple halves into thin slices. Toss gently in the lemon juice. Slice the celery into thin slices.
- Toss together the apples, celery, walnuts and raisins with the dressing.
- Shred the romaine.
- Arrange 3 or 4 endive leaves on an individual salad plate.
- Make a bed of the shredded romaine in the center of the leaves.
- Top with a large spoonful of the apple mixture.
- Crumble the goat cheese and sprinkle some on the top of each salad.
- Garnish with a watercress sprig.
- Serve immediately.
- Serves 8.

Lemon-Walnut Dressing

½ cup walnut oil
2 tbsp. fresh lemon juice
1 tsp. finely chopped lemon zest
2 tsp. honey
Pinch salt

- Blend together until well mixed.
- Makes about ¾ cup.

Three-Green Salad with Pears

And once again a Sharon Shipley recipe. This one reminds me of California cooking with all of its innovative ideas and fresh ingredients, and appropriately so, since that is its origin. This makes a great late autumn salad when the summer salad ingredients have long since faded and the pears are at their best.

3 large ripe pears
1 cup brandy
1 head Boston lettuce
2 bunches watercress, large stems removed
3 heads Belgian endive
6 tbsp. olive oil
2 tbsp. walnut oil
1 tbsp. fresh lemon juice
2 tbsp. sherry vinegar
2 tbsp. chopped fresh mint leaves (or 2 tsp. dried)
1 tsp. salt
1 tsp. pepper

- Peel and core the pears. Cut them into fine julienne strips.
- Pour brandy over pears and simmer on top of stove for about 20 minutes. Cool and set aside.
- Arrange the Boston lettuce leaves around the side and bottom of a salad bowl and mound the watercress in the center.
- Trim the stem ends off each endive and cut the leaves into ½-inch pieces.
- Sprinkle over the watercress.
- Whisk together the olive and walnut oils.
- One at a time, add the lemon juice, vinegar, mint, salt, and pepper, whisking to blend thoroughly.
- Drain the pears thoroughly and dry with white paper towels.
- Arrange them in a fan shape over the greens.
- Immediately before serving, pour the dressing over the salad and toss.

Herring Salad

You may think this a somewhat unlikely mixture of foods to have all gathered in one bowl. Unless you are a herring hater, I hope you will actually taste it before forming your final opinion. (In my opinion, the herring in wine sauce does not have an extremely strong "fishy" taste.) I first tasted it in Berlin when we were living there as students. In many German families, it is traditional to serve this on Christmas Eve. It is important to serve such an easy, make-ahead dish since the entire household is involved with decorating the Christmas tree on that evening. I have also known many German families who wouldn't think of starting the new year without eating Herring Salad on either New Year's Eve or New Year's Day. Once, I talked about it during the holiday season on my radio show and a whole string of callers confirmed my suspicions that there are numerous versions of this dish. I've tried several and have settled on what has become my own version and my definitive favorite.

1 1-lb. can or jar pickled beets,
   cut into julienne strips
2 large, crisp apples, washed, cored, and cubed
3 tbsp. chopped sweet Spanish onion
   (or other sweet salad onion)
1 cup coarsely chopped celery
1 cup walnuts
1 8-oz. jar herring filets packed in wine sauce,
   drained and cut into small pieces
1 cup mayonnaise
1 tbsp. fresh lemon juice
Freshly ground pepper, to taste
Pinch salt
Crisp lettuce leaves

- Toss together the beets, apples, onion, celery, walnuts, and herring.
- Mix together the mayonnaise and lemon juice.
- Stir into salad and season to taste.
- Chill, covered, for at least 2 hours.
- Pile onto lettuce leaves to serve.
- Serve with crusty French bread.
- Serves 8-10.

Christmas Wreath Salad

It seems to be especially important during the holiday season to create dishes that look festive and appealing. I've done this vegetable salad for holiday classes for a number of years. You can always count on getting pretty cauliflower and broccoli in the wintertime and even the cherry tomatoes, unlike their larger counterparts, usually have good flavor then. It really resembles a Christmas wreath without requiring too much time fussing over it and it has plenty of decorative value whether on a buffet table or at a more traditional seated dinner. The "wreath" can be totally assembled several hours ahead, covered, and refrigerated. It is important not to pour over the dressing until the last minute. The vinegar and lemon juice will destroy the beautiful emerald-green color of the broccoli.

> **2 medium heads broccoli**
> **1 large head cauliflower**
> **5 cherry tomatoes, cut in half**
> **½ cup extravirgin olive oil**
> **2 tbsp. white wine vinegar**
> **1 tbsp. fresh lemon juice**
> **½ tsp. Dijon mustard**
> **Salt and white pepper, to taste**
> **Pinch sugar**

- Wash broccoli and cauliflower and trim into florets.
- Steam each separately for 2-3 minutes.
- Refresh in ice water for a few minutes; drain well and pat with paper towels.
- On a large round platter, arrange the broccoli and cauliflower alternately in a wreath shape.
- Place the cherry tomato halves on the "wreath."
- Cover and chill until serving time.
- With the remaining ingredients, make the dressing in the food processor or blender or whisk together.
- Just before serving, drizzle over just enough of the dressing to coat the vegetables lightly.
- Serves 8-10.

Shrimp Veracruzana

I have consulted on menu planning and recipe development in several local restaurants. This recipe comes from one that no longer exists, "Amanda." It was one of the first restaurants around here to offer Southwestern cuisine and I suspect that the audience for such a dish as this was not nearly as great in those days as it might be today. It is a super dinner-party recipe, easily made ahead and reheated. Add a tossed green salad with some avocado slices and some warm, buttered flour tortillas to round out the meal.

1 clove fresh garlic, minced
1 large onion, sliced
3 tbsp. extravirgin olive oil
1 large red sweet pepper, cut into strips
1 large green pepper, cut into strips
2 large ripe tomatoes, peeled, seeded, and chopped
1 cup canned tomato purée
1 tsp. sugar
2 jalapeño peppers, chopped
1 tbsp. capers
2 tbsp. red wine vinegar
2 tbsp. dry sherry
½ tsp. dried leaf oregano
¼ tsp. each ground cinnamon and cloves
¼ cup chopped fresh cilantro
Salt, to taste
1½ lb. medium-sized raw shrimp, peeled and deveined
10 each black and green pitted olives

- Sauté fresh garlic and onion in oil; add pepper strips and sauté for 3 minutes, stirring. Set aside.
- Simmer together for 20 minutes all ingredients down to shrimp.
- Stir in shrimp and olives and cook for 3 to 4 minutes.
- Add the onion mixture and cook 2 minutes more.
- Top with parsley and more olives, if desired.
- Serve over rice.
- Serves 6.

Scallops in Wine Sauce

I had initially planned for this dish to go into the chapter on "Make-Ahead Meals," but in all of the shuffling of recipes, it did not end up that way. However, I just couldn't bring myself to leave it out completely since it is so handy to have in your "quick and easy" repertoire. My hardworking students who attended so many of my lunch-hour classes were always anxious for any recipe they could have ready to pop in the oven in a jiffy on Friday night. This was always a hit. For my taste, it is at its best made with plump fresh sea scallops, but the small bay scallops can be used. I have also made it with filets of firm fresh fish like halibut. The sauce may look overly thick and rich to you, but remember that the natural fish juices will thin it as the cooking process takes place. The recommended Parsley Rice Pilaf makes an elegant combination, but it also goes very nicely with boiled new potatoes that have been tossed with some fresh parsley. Some crisp steamed broccoli napped with fresh lemon juice or stir-fried fresh spinach leaves would round out the plate with both good flavor and color.

1 stick (4 oz.) butter or margarine
1 tsp. sweet paprika
3 tbsp. flour
⅔ cup dry white wine
1 cup cream, heavy or light
1 tbsp. Cognac
1 tsp. salt, or to taste
¼ tsp. white pepper
1 lb. sea scallops
Chopped parsley

- Melt butter, stir in paprika and flour, and cook 2 minutes.
- Add wine and stir until mixture is smooth.
- Gradually add cream, which has been heated, and stir until smooth and thickened.
- Cook for 3 minutes, adding Cognac, salt, and pepper.
- Place scallops in a shallow greased baking dish and pour over the sauce.
- Bake, uncovered, in 375-degree oven for 20 to 25 minutes.
- Sprinkle with parsley.
- Serve with Parsley Rice Pilaf (see index).
- Serves 6.

Chicken Breasts
in Apple-Orange Sauce

My editor husband said when he saw me adding this recipe, "Are you sure you want to add another chicken breast recipe to the book?" I didn't have to think long before answering in the affirmative. My question could then be, "Can one have too many chicken breast recipes?" I doubt it. The chicken breast, especially in the form the French call a "Suprême"—that is, with skin, fat, and bones removed—could hardly be more versatile. It has no cholesterol, is very low in calories, has a mild flavor that lends itself to all sorts of sauces, and cooks in under 10 minutes. There must be a reason why so many chicken breast recipes have collected in my teaching files over the years. Perhaps it's because I have never heard a complaint from a student when presented with yet one more tasty chicken dish. In fact, my classes featuring only chicken dishes were always filled. So, here's one more chicken dish. Try this one for a cold-weather dinner party. The oranges are at their best in the winter months and apples are fresh and tasty too. The contrast of the tangy fruit with the rich, smooth cream makes a sauce that will cause your guests to ask for a second piece of French bread for sopping the last drop of it from their plates.

> **4 whole chicken breasts, halved, boned, and skinned**
> **6 tbsp. unsalted butter or margarine**
> **2 navel oranges, zested and juiced**
> **1 cup peeled and minced Granny Smith apple**
> **¼ cup Grand Marnier**
> **½ cup chicken stock**
> **1 cup heavy cream**
> **Extra orange slices, for garnish**
> **Parsley or watercress**

- Flatten the chicken slightly between two sheets of waxed paper.
- In a heavy skillet, melt butter over high heat and sauté chicken breasts just until opaque, about 3 minutes on each side.
- Remove to a side dish, cover, and keep warm.
- Add orange juice and zest to the pan. Cook over high heat for 2 minutes, stirring.
- Stir in apple and cook, stirring, over high heat for 3-4 minutes.
- Add the Grand Marnier and cook until reduced to 2 tablespoons.
- Add the chicken stock and the cream and cook over moderate heat, stirring until sauce is reduced by one-half.
- Return chicken and baste it in the sauce over low heat for a few minutes, or until thoroughly reheated.
- Garnish with thin orange slices and parsley or watercress.
- Serves 8.

Wild Rice Mushroom Pilaf

This is my favorite choice as a side dish for an autumn or mid-winter dinner that features beef. With the addition of a green vegetable, one has a traditional dinner that guests always seem to savor. I have also used dried morels instead of the porcini (also called "cèpes") with delicious results. Make it an hour or two ahead and keep it warm in a heavy casserole dish on a warm oven setting.

> 1½ cups long-grain wild rice
> 4 cups boiling water
> 1 oz. dried porcini mushrooms
> 1 cup hot water
> 3 large shallots, minced
> 4 tbsp. unsalted butter or margarine
> 12 oz. fresh white button mushrooms,
>   washed, dried, and thickly sliced
> ¼ cup Cognac
> 1 cup dry wine
> 1 tsp. salt, or to taste
> ¼ tsp. freshly ground black pepper
> ½ cup chopped fresh parsley

- Place the rice in a sieve and wash by holding under a stream of running water. Drain. Place in a bowl and pour over the boiling water. Let sit for at least 2 hours (or as long as 4-5 hours).
- Place the porcini in a small bowl and pour over the hot water. Let sit for at least 30 minutes. Lift out the mushrooms and wash well under a stream of running water. Drain and chop.
- Strain the mushroom water through a layer of strong white paper towel. Reserve liquid.
- In a heavy saucepan, sauté the shallots in the butter over high heat for 2 minutes, stirring.
- Add the sliced fresh mushrooms and the chopped porcini and cook, stirring, for 3-4 minutes.
- Pour in the Cognac and reduce over high heat to 2 tablespoons.
- Drain the water from the rice and add to the pan. Stir to mix with other ingredients. Add the reserved water from the porcini and the wine. Bring to boil, cover, and cook over low heat for 45-50 minutes.
- If all liquid is not absorbed, remove lid and raise heat to medium; cook until liquid is gone.
- Toss in the salt and pepper and parsley.
- Taste and correct seasonings. Serve hot.
- Serves 8.

Cranberry Chutney

Another holiday favorite of mine is this intriguing blend of sweet, sour, and spicy. It just wouldn't be an official holiday dinner without cranberries in some form. I had always made the whole-berry homemade cranberry sauce until someone shared the idea of cranberry chutney with me. That was a number of years ago and I have since, in the holiday spirit, shared it with more people than I could count. I have a couple of friends who make it every Christmas and put it into attractive little jars or crocks to give to friends and neighbors as Christmas gifts. It is not a difficult or time-consuming recipe and is easily made in large batches.

Dried wild mushrooms infuse a dish with a wonderfully pungent flavor, but they must be carefully washed. They will contain a large amount of grit because they are almost always dried just after they are picked and not previously washed. After soaking in hot water to reconstitute them (at least 30 minutes), lift out the mushrooms and rinse them thoroughly under a steady stream of warm running water. When possible, the soaking liquid should be reserved to use in the recipe as well, since it contains so much flavor. Strain the liquid through a strong white paper towel before adding to a dish.

1¾ cups each sugar and water
1 lb. fresh cranberries
1 cup golden raisins
½ cup red wine
1½ tsp. curry powder
2 tbsp. molasses
2 tbsp. freshly grated gingerroot
1 tbsp. Worcestershire sauce
1 tsp. salt
½ tsp. hot pepper sauce

- In a medium saucepan, bring sugar and water to a boil; simmer for 5 minutes.
- Add cranberries and cook just until skins pop—about 5 minutes.
- Stir in remaining ingredients; simmer uncovered for 15 minutes or until thickened, stirring occasionally.
- Cool and refrigerate until ready to serve.
- Makes about 3 cups.

Pastry Tulip Cups
with Caramelized Apple Filling

Mastering the art of working with frozen phyllo pastry is a fun activity. It is rather amazing how many different ways it can be used. Probably most popular as a dough for encasing bits of food for appetizers, it can be very effectively utilized to create quick and easy desserts that are most impressive in appearance and taste. (No need to tell your awed guests how easy it was!) Easily made hours ahead, this apple filling can be reheated in the microwave or in a heavy pan over gentle heat. If you don't have the apple brandy, Calvados, substitute some good Cognac.

**6 large tart cooking apples, peeled, cored,
   and diced
6 tbsp. unsalted butter
6 tbsp. sugar
½ of a vanilla bean, split lengthwise
¼ cup Calvados
1 tbsp. fresh lemon juice
1 cup whipping cream
2 tbsp. confectioners' sugar**

- In a large skillet, stir the apples with butter and sugar over medium heat until butter melts. Add the vanilla bean to the mixture.
- Increase heat to medium-high and cook, stirring frequently, until apples are brown and caramelized—about 30 minutes.
- Remove the vanilla bean.
- Pour off any excess butter and add the Calvados.
- Cook for 1 minute more over high heat, scraping up any caramel from bottom of the pan. Stir in the lemon juice.
- Whip the cream until thickened; add the confectioners' sugar gradually and continue to whip until very stiff.
- While still slightly warm, spoon the apple mixture into Pastry Tulip Cups and top each with a large dollop of the freshly whipped cream.
- Makes 6 servings.

Pastry Tulip Cups

**4 sheets phyllo
Melted unsalted butter**

- Stack phyllo with butter brushed between the sheets.
- Cut into 4-inch squares.
- Press each square into a buttered muffin tin, pressing the bottom flat and folding excess dough to create a petal effect on the sides.
- Bake in the bottom third of a 375-degree oven for 10-12 minutes or until golden.
- Remove from muffin tins and cool on a rack.

Pears Helene

Poached pears always bring smiles at dessert time. They are also so easy to do. They can be poached in the early hours of the day or even as long ahead as the night before and they can sit in the poaching liquid all day. For best results, choose firm eating pears that are not quite ripe enough to eat raw. They should be very tender when the poaching process is finished, but not falling apart. The vanilla bean infuses the pears with a wonderful flavor. A teaspoon of pure vanilla extract may be substituted for the vanilla bean. It is worth the extra money and effort to obtain the best semisweet chocolate available to you to make the fudge sauce. Your taste buds will be grateful.

4 ripe but firm pears (Anjou, Bartlett, Bosc, etc.)
⅔ cup sugar
2 cups water
1 2-in. piece of vanilla bean, split lengthwise
8 scoops vanilla ice cream
1 recipe Hot Fudge Sauce
Fresh mint leaves (or crystallized mint leaves)

- Peel, core, and halve pears.
- Combine sugar and water and boil until sugar is dissolved. Add pears.
- Simmer, covered, until pears are tender—about 30 minutes, turning them once.
- Add vanilla bean and let the pears cool completely in syrup.
- To serve, drain pears, place round side up on top of a scoop of ice cream, and top with Hot Fudge Sauce.
- Garnish with mint leaves.
- Serves 8.

Hot Fudge Sauce
12 oz. good semisweet chocolate, cut into pieces
1 cup heavy whipping cream
¼ cup rum or Cognac

- Melt chocolate in double boiler over hot, but not boiling, water.
- Add cream and rum or Cognac.
- Whisk until smooth and creamy.
- Serve warm.
- Makes about 2 cups.

Chocolate-Orange Mousse

My students have often heard me say that my favorite flavor combination for dessert is chocolate and orange. (I also like chocolate and lemon a lot.) I know that the world probably has enough chocolate mousse recipes, but don't say that until you try this one. This one has had many return engagements in my classes and at our dinner parties since I brought it back with me from an advanced cooking course in London. There are purists who say that a true "mousse" does not contain gelatin, but the relatively small amount in this dessert just assures its good creamy and smooth texture.

6 oz. semisweet chocolate
5 tbsp. water
3 whole eggs
2 egg yolks
Zest and juice of 1 orange
½ cup sugar
1 cup whipping cream, whipped to a soft whip
1 rounded tsp. gelatin
Extra cream for garnish, stiffly whipped
    and lightly sweetened
½ thin slice orange

- In a small heavy saucepan, melt the chocolate with the water; cool.
- Whisk eggs, yolks, zest, and sugar in a double boiler until mixture is light, fluffy, and lemon colored.* Remove from heat, place pan over ice water, and whisk until completely cooled.
- Fold in the melted chocolate and then the whipped cream.
- Soften the gelatin in the orange juice. Place over a gentle heat and shake the pan until all gelatin is dissolved.
- Cool and fold into the mousse. Spoon into a 1½-quart attractive serving dish.
- Place in the refrigerator; chill for at least 4 hours.
- To serve, garnish with whipped cream rosettes centered with a very thin and twisted half slice of fresh orange.
- Serves 8.

*Eggs cook at a low temperature. When cooking such a base that has eggs and egg yolks as the binding or thickening ingredient, do not allow the temperature to climb too high or the egg yolks will quickly become overcooked. When the mixture is thickened and feels very warm to one's fingertip, it is done.

Powdered gelatin should always be softened in a cool or room-temperature liquid before being dissolved in a boiling liquid. It is best not to stir it, but shake the pan gently as the gelatin dissolves.

Chocolate-Orange Torte

Here's a second dessert that has, in my mind, the all-time best marriage of flavors—orange and chocolate. This torte may not seem very large or impressive, but its intense flavor and texture cause it to be a dessert from which one can easily obtain 10 servings. (I usually count on 8 in case someone wants seconds.) Its very moist consistency allows it to be made a day or so ahead without any sacrifice of quality. It freezes beautifully. If you do freeze it, set it in the freezer uncovered for 1 hour to freeze the glaze. Before the glaze can soften, quickly wrap it in plastic or freezer paper. When it is removed from the freezer, unwrap in the frozen state and allow to thaw at room temperature. The result is a beautiful torte virtually unmarked from the wrapping and unwrapping process. Use this trick for all frosted cakes that you wish to preserve in the freezer.

> **4 oz. semisweet chocolate**
> **1 stick butter, softened**
> **⅔ cup granulated sugar**
> **3 eggs**
> **Zest of 1 orange**
> **1 cup ground almonds**
> **¼ cup very fine bread crumbs**
> **Whole blanched almonds, lightly toasted**

- Melt chocolate over hot, not boiling, water. Cool.
- Cream butter until fluffy and add sugar a bit at a time, beating constantly.
- Add eggs, one at a time, beating after each addition.
- Stir in chocolate, orange zest, ground almonds, and bread crumbs.
- Butter an 8-inch round pan and line bottom with buttered waxed paper.
- Pour batter in pan and bake in a 375-degree oven for 25 minutes.
- Cool 1 hour before turning out.
- Top with following glaze.
- Place the whole almonds around the outside edge as decoration.

The Glaze

2 oz. unsweetened chocolate
2 oz. semisweet chocolate
½ stick unsalted butter
2 tsp. honey

- Combine all ingredients together in double boiler and melt. Beat until cool and glossy.
- Spread onto completely cooled torte and place the almonds around the outside edge as decoration.
- Refrigerate about 30 minutes to set the glaze.
- Cut into small wedges to serve.
- Serves 8-10.

Mother's Chocolate Cream Pie

My mother is a very good Southern cook and I knew from the outset of this book endeavor that I would want to include one of her recipes. The decision of which one was not difficult. Every time we visit at her house, or have her visit us, our first request is that she make her old-fashioned chocolate pie. When I called her with the request for this recipe, she confessed that she had it in no written form, and, in fact, did not make use of standard measuring utensils when baking it. So, she dutifully made one shortly thereafter and took care to measure each ingredient before it was added. Thanks, Mother. It was worth your effort because it really is a pie worth sharing.

Filling

1 cup sugar
2½ tbsp. flour
2 tbsp. cornstarch
1 cup milk
2 egg yolks
2 oz. unsweetened chocolate, melted
1 tbsp. butter or margarine
1 tsp. pure vanilla extract

- In top of a double boiler off of the heat, stir together the sugar, flour, and cornstarch. Gradually whisk in the milk, whisking until well mixed. Place the pan over boiling water and cook, stirring until mixture is thickened.
- Beat the egg yolks until frothy. Whisk in quickly.
- Add melted chocolate and cook 1 minute.
- Remove from heat and add butter and vanilla.
- Cover top with a round of buttered waxed paper and let cool completely.
- Pour into baked pastry shell.
- Top with meringue, taking care to seal well around the edges.
- Place in upper one-third of a preheated 375-degree oven for 12-15 minutes or until meringue is golden brown. Cool on a rack.
- Makes 1 9-inch pie.

Pastry

1¼ cups all-purpose flour
¼ tsp. baking powder
6 tbsp. butter or margarine, cut into 6 pieces
3 tbsp. ice water

- Stir together the flour and baking powder.
- Cut in the butter until mixture resembles coarse meal.
- Add ice water and gather into a smooth ball.
- Roll out on a lightly floured board to ⅛-inch thickness.
- Place in a 9-inch pie pan.
- Prick approximately every ¼ inch with a fork.
- Place in the lower one-third of a preheated 375-degree oven and bake for 20-25 minutes or until golden brown.
- Cool completely before filling.

Meringue

3 large egg whites, at room temperature
6 tbsp. sugar
1 tsp. pure vanilla extract

- Beat the egg whites in a clean, dry mixing bowl until frothy.
- Add the sugar, 1 tablespoon at a time, beating continually.
- Add the vanilla.
- Beat until the mixture is stiff, but not dry. (Should be very shiny.)
- Spread onto pie, taking care to seal around the edges, and bake immediately.

Index

A

Almond Cheesecake, 182
Amanda's Chicken Taco
    Salad, 72
Angel Biscuits, 24
Appetizers: Asparagus in
    Phyllo, 60; Baked Seafood
    Cakettes, 44; Bleu Cheese-
    Walnut New Potatoes, 64;
    Breaded Mushrooms, 52;
    Caponata Deluxe, 38; Car-
    men's Canapé Bread, 55;
    Cheese-Filled Brussels
    Sprouts, 67; Cheesy Tostada,
    36; Chicken Liver Pâté
    Spread, 33; Chilled Peppered
    Tenderloin, 53; Cocktail Piz-
    zas, 41; Crab-Stuffed Mush-
    rooms, 163; Endive, 154;
    Herbed Pita Triangles, 40;
    Marilyn's Holiday Pâté, 34;
    Melon with Prosciutto, 90;
    Pecan Chicken, 50; Piquant
    Beef Triangles, 58; Piquant
    Pecans, 51; Pork and Pecan
    Stuffed Mushrooms, 61;
    Roquefort Triangles, 177;
    Savory Mushroom Tartlets,
    62; Shrimp Profiteroles, 56;
    Smoked Salmon Spread,
    68; Spicy Sweet-Potato
    Petite Pancakes, 57; Sun-
    Dried Tomato Spread on
    Zucchini Slices, 66; Vegetable
    Basket, 47
Apple Filling, Caramelized, 241

Apple-Orange Sauce, 238
Apricot Filling, Creamy, 82
Artichoke Salad, 94
Asparagus in Phyllo, 60
Asparagus, selecting, 134
Avocado, peeling, 71
Avocado, prevent darkening, 71
Avocado, Tomato-Stuffed, 157
Avocado-Fruit Salad, 182

B

Bacon, Pecan-Glazed, 20
Baking, blind, 228
Barbecue: Oven-Barbecued
    Chicken Breasts, 116
Basil Vinaigrette, 197
Bavarian Cream, Lemon, 215
Bavarian Tartar Sauce, 53
Beans: Easy Refried, 36; Pinto
    Bean Salad, 174; Red Beans
    and Rice, Zesty, 144;
    Vegetarian Black Bean
    Soup, 83
Béarnaise, Sauce, 64
Béchamel Sauce, 29
Beef: Bourbon-Marinated Flank
    Steak, 184; Chilled Peppered
    Tenderloin, 53; Piquant Beef
    Triangles, 58; Stuffed Flank
    Steak, 84
Berry: Melon-Berry Compote,
    27; Strawberry Mimosas, 28;
    washing, 28
Biscuits: Angel, 24; Deep South
    Sticky, 25
Bleu Cheesecake, 45

Bleu Cheese-Walnut New
    Potatoes, 64
Blind baking, 228
Bouquet garni, finding, 151
Bourbon Custard Sauce, 130
Bourbon-Marinated Flank
    Steak, 184
Bread, Carmen's Canapé, 55
Bread crumbs, 52
Breaded Mushrooms, 52
Breading tip, 51
Breads: Caponata Cheese
    Muffins, 192; crust, 214;
    Dainty Dinner Rolls, 79;
    Foolproof French, 87; Green
    Peppercorn, 214; kneading,
    213; Mardi Gras, 168; Pepper
    and Herb Flat, 158; rising
    dough, 214; Spicy Corn-
    Bread Muffins, 119; Walnut-
    Oatmeal, 212; yeast, 215
Brownie, The Ultimate, 160
Brussels Sprouts, Cheese-
    Filled, 67
Burritos, Breakfast, 19

C
Cabbage Soup, Hearty, 115
Café au lait, 170
Caponata-Cheese Brunch
    Muffins, 192
Caponata Deluxe, 38
Caramelized Apple Filling, 241
Carmen's Canapé Bread, 55
Carol's Pizza Pie, 209
Carrot-Walnut Soup, 105
Cauliflower Soup, 193
Celery-Seed Dressing, 127
Cheaty Chicken Stock, 135
Cheese Grits, Baked, 26
Cheese Filling (Manicotti), 92

Cheesecake, Almond, 182
Cheesecake, Bleu, 45
Chicken: Amanda's Chicken
    Taco Salad, 72; Chicken
    Breasts in Apple-Orange
    Sauce, 238; Chicken Breasts
    with Artichoke Hearts, 203;
    Chicken Florentine, 155;
    Chicken Supreme Poached in
    Fresh Tomato Sauce, 109;
    Grilled Lime Chicken, 102;
    Ham and Chicken Jambalaya,
    150; Oven-Barbecued
    Chicken Breasts, 116; Pecan
    Chicken Appetizers, 50;
    Shrimp and Chicken Creole
    Supreme, 164; Spanish
    Chicken, 140; Sunday Supper
    Chicken and Rice, 210
Chicken Liver Pâté Spread, 33
Chicken Salad Deluxe, 133
Chicken Stock: Cheaty, 135;
    Easy, 142
Chocolate Cookie Crust, 188
Chocolate Cream Pie,
    Mother's, 246
Chocolate Flan, 175
Chocolate Mousse, Instant, 104
Chocolate Mousse Torte, 88
Chocolate-Orange Mousse, 244
Chocolate-Orange Torte, 245
Christmas Wreath Salad, 234
Chutney: Cranberry, 241;
    Mayonnaise, 51
Cinnamon-Butter Brunch Cake,
    192
Coffee: brewing, 30; Café au
    lait, 170; Cinnamon, 30
Compote, Melon-Berry, 27
Compote, Orange-Pineapple, 27
Corn Soup, Mexican, 171

Corn-Bread Muffins, Spicy, 119
Corn-Bread Stuffing,
    Zesty, 124
Cornichons, 35
Crab-Stuffed Mushrooms, 163
Cranberry Chutney, 241
Cream Puffs Extraordinaire, 81
Creamy Lemon Dressing, 137
Creole French Dressing, 167
Creole Stuffed Eggplant, 143
Crudités, 47
Cucumbers: Filled Cucumber
    Cups, 226; Sautéed Dilled,
    106; seeding, 61
Curried Lamb Stew, 180

D
Dainty Dinner Rolls, 79
Desserts: Almond Cheesecake,
    182; Bleu Cheesecake, 46;
    Caramelized Apple Filling,
    241; Chocolate Flan, 175;
    Chocolate Mousse Torte, 88;
    Chocolate-Orange Mousse,
    244; Chocolate-Orange Torte,
    245; Cinnamon-Butter
    Brunch Cake, 192; Fresh
    Pineapple with Kirsch, 112;
    Golden Peach Strudel, 121;
    Hot Fudge Sauce, 243;
    Instant Chocolate Mousse,
    104; Lemon-Lime Tart, 95;
    Marilyn's Pecan Pie, 168;
    Mother's Chocolate Cream
    Pie, 246; Orange Flan, 75;
    Pastry Tulip Cups, 241;
    Pears Helene, 243; Praline
    Cheesecake Squares, 152;
    Strawberries and Cream,
    216; Strawberries with Black
    Pepper and Balsamic

Vinegar, 107; Summer
    Strawberry Pie, 187; The
    Ultimate Brownie, 160;
    Zitronencreme, 215
Dill-Cucumber Sauce, 60
Dressings: Basil Vinaigrette,
    197; Celery-Seed, 127;
    Creamy Lemon, 137;
    Creole French, 167; Fabulous
    Salad, 152; Lemon-Walnut,
    232; Picante, 73; Salad
    Niçoise, 78; Sherry Vinai-
    grette, 182; Tomato French,
    Fresh, 157

E
Eggplant, Creole Stuffed, 143
Eggs: beating egg whites, 217;
    Eggs au Gratin, 191; Ham
    and Eggs in Easy Pastry
    Cups, 17; Summer Egg
    Mousse, 29
Endive Appetizers, 154

F
Fajitas, Pork, 172
Filo. *See* Phyllo
Flan: Chocolate, 175; Orange, 75
Flank Steak, Stuffed, 84
Flat Bread, Pepper and
    Herb, 158
French Bread, Foolproof, 87
French Dressing, Creole, 167
French-Fried Sweet Potatoes,
    117

G
Garlic, peeling, 165
Gazpacho, Zippy, 101
Ginger Cream Sauce, 201
Gingerroot, storing, 102

Glaze, Orange, 216
Green Beans with Roasted Red
    Pepper Sauce, 106
Green Peppercorn Bread, 214
Green Peppercorn Sauce, 54
Grill-Roasted Potatoes, 187
Grilled Lime Chicken, 102
Grilled Vegetables with Goat
    Cheese, 208
Grits, Baked Cheese, 26
Guacamolé, 38
Guacamolé Soup, 71

H
Ham: and Chicken Jambalaya,
    150; and Eggs in Easy Pastry
    Cups, 17; Country, 23
Herbed Tomatoes, 86
Herbs, dried, 138
Herring Salad, 233
Hot Fudge Sauce, 243

I
Instant Chocolate Mousse, 104

J
Jambalaya, Ham and Chicken,
    150
Jicama, 175
Juniper, Pork Medallions, 178

L
Lamb: Curried Lamb Stew,
    180; Marilyn's Special
    Grilled, 202
Lemon Bavarian Cream, 215
Lemon Pepper Marinade, 186
Lemon-Lime Tart, 95
Lemon-Tarragon Wine Sauce,
    155
Lemon-Walnut Dressing, 232

M
Manicotti, Cheese-Filled
    Homemade, 90
Mardi Gras Bread, 168
Marilyn's Antipasto Pasta
    Salad, 196
Marilyn's Holiday Pâté, 34
Marilyn's Pecan Pie, 168
Marilyn's Special Grilled
    Lamb, 202
Marilyn's Thanksgiving
    Salad, 231
Marinade, Lemon Pepper, 186
Mayonnaise, Chutney, 51
Melon with Prosciutto, 90
Melon-Berry Compote, 27
Meringue, 248
Mexican Corn Soup, 171
Mexican. *See* Southwestern
Mimosas, 28
Mousse (dessert): Chocolate
    Mousse Torte, 88; Chocolate-
    Orange, 244; Instant
    Chocolate, 104
Mousse, Red Pepper, 226
Mousse, Summer Egg, 29
Muffins: Breakfast Muffins
    Deluxe, 20; Caponata-Cheese
    Brunch, 192; Pecan Bran, 15;
    Spicy Corn-Bread, 119
Mushrooms: Breaded, 52;
    cleaning, 17; Crab-Stuffed,
    163; Mushroom and Smoked
    Turkey Omelet, 16; Pork and
    Pecan Stuffed, 61; sautéing,
    17; Savory Mushroom
    Tartlets, 61; Soup, 195; Wild
    Rice Mushroom Pilaf, 239

O
Omelet, Individual Pan, 16

Onion: Creamy Onion Soup, 222; sweeter, 133; Tart, 227
Orange Flan, 75
Orange Glaze, 216
Orange-Pineapple Compote, 27

P

Pancakes, Spicy Sweet-Potato Petite, 57
Parsley: Rice Pilaf, 166; washing, 166
Pasta: Bob's Pasta Spinach Rolls, 229; Marilyn's Antipasto Pasta Salad, 196; Spaghetti with Fresh Tuna-Caper Sauce, 139; Summer-time Pasta Skillet, 137
Pastry: chilling, 170; Chocolate Cookie Crust, 188; Easy Pastry Cups, 18; Lemon-Lime Tart, 95; Pâte au Choux, 81; Pâte Brisée, 228; pie, 169; Savory Pie/Tart, 228; Tulip Cups, 241
Pâté: Chicken Liver Pâté Spread, 33; Marilyn's Holiday, 34; temperatures, 224
Peach Strudel, Golden, 121
Pears Helene, 243
Pecan: Chicken Appetizers, 50; -Glazed Bacon, 20; Marilyn's Pecan Pie, 168; Pecan Bran Muffins, 15; Piquant, 51; Pork and Pecan Stuffed Mushrooms, 61; Toasted Pecan Soufflé, 128
Pepitas, 175
Pepper and Ginger Salmon, 200
Pepper and Herb Flat Bread, 158

Pepper Sauce, Homemade, 145
Peppers, roasting, 38
Pesto Sauce, Ted's, 197
Phyllo: Asparagus in, 60; Easy Pastry Cups, 18; Golden Peach Strudel, 121; Pastry Tulip Cups, 242; Piquant Beef Triangles, 58; Roquefort Triangles, 177
Picante Dressing, 73
Picante Sauce, 74
Pie, Mother's Chocolate Cream, 246
Pilaf: Parsley Rice, 166; Wild Rice Mushroom, 239
Pinto Bean Salad, 174
Piquant Pecans, 51
Pita Triangles, Herbed, 40
Pizza: Carol's Pizza Pie, 209; Cocktail, 41; toppings, 43
Poaching Stock (chicken), 73
Pork and Pecan Stuffed Mushrooms, 61
Pork Chops, 124
Pork Fajitas, 172
Pork Medallions Juniper, 178
Pork Tenderloin with Bing Cherry Sauce, 204
Potatoes: Bleu Cheese-Walnut New, 64; Grill-Roasted, 187; New Potatoes in White Wine, 111; selecting, 221; Summer Potato Salad, 198
Praline Cheesecake Squares, 152
Profiteroles, Shrimp, 56

R

Red Beans and Rice, Zesty, 144
Red Pepper Mousse, 226
Refried Beans, Easy, 36

Remoulade Sauce, Skinny, 108
Remoulade, Shrimp, 149
Rice Pilaf, Parsley, 166
Roquefort Triangles, 177
Rutabaga Soup, 123

S

Salads: Amanda's Chicken
    Taco, 72; Avocado-Fruit, 182;
    Chicken Salad Deluxe, 133;
    Christmas Wreath, 234;
    cutting cherry tomatoes,
    167; Fresh Artichoke, 94;
    Herring, 233; Marilyn's
    Antipasto Pasta, 196;
    Marilyn's Thanksgiving, 231;
    Niçoise with Fresh Tuna
    Filet, 77; Pinto Bean, 174;
    Seashell Salmon, 136;
    Spinach-Orange, 127;
    Succotash, 118; Summer
    Potato, 198; Three-Bean
    Salad with Pears, 232;
    Tossed Salad Greens, 152;
    tossing, 167; washing
    greens, 167
Salmon: Baked Fresh Salmon
    Steaks, 105; Pepper and
    Ginger, 200; Seashell Salmon
    Salad, 136; Smoked Salmon
    Spread, 68
Salsa: Marilyn's, 37; Verde, 174
Sangria Blanc, 74
Sauces: Apple-Orange, 238;
    Barbecue, 116; Bavarian
    Tartar, 53; Béarnaise, 64;
    Béchamel, 29; Bing Cherry,
    204; Bourbon Custard, 130;
    Chili Pepper Dipping, 48;
    Dill-Cucumber, 60; Fresh

Herb Dipping, 49; Fresh
    Tomato, 92, 110; Ginger
    Cream, 201; Green Pepper-
    corn, 54; Homemade Pepper,
    145; Hot and Sweet Mustard,
    225; Hot Fudge, 243; Lemon-
    Tarragon Wine, 155;
    Marilyn's Salsa, 37; Picante,
    74; Pizza, 42; Salsa Verde,
    174; Skinny Remoulade, 108;
    Soy-Ginger, 85; Sweet and
    Sour, 200; Tartar, 45; Ted's
    Pesto, 197; Tuna-Caper, 139;
    Watercress Dipping, 49
Sausage, Homemade
    Spicy, 25
Savory Mushroom Tartlets, 61
Scallops in Wine Sauce, 237
Seafood Cakettes, Baked, 44
Seasoning an omelet pan, 16
Sherry Vinaigrette Dressing, 182
Shrimp: Boil, 150; and Chicken
    Creole Supreme, 164;
    Profiteroles, 56; Remoulade,
    149; Veracruzana, 236; Yen's
    Sweet and Sour, 199
Soufflé, Toasted Pecan, 128
Soups: Carrot-Walnut, 105;
    Cauliflower, 193; Creamy
    Onion, 222; Fresh Tomato
    Bisque, 76; Guacamolé, 71;
    Hearty Cabbage, 115;
    making cream soups, 223;
    Mexican Corn, 171; Mush-
    room, 195; Rutabaga, 123;
    Spicy Vegetable, 221;
    Vegetarian Black Bean, 83;
    Zippy Gazpacho, 101
Southwestern: Amanda's
    Chicken Taco Salad, 72;

Breakfast Burritos, 19; Chili Pepper Dipping Sauce, 48; Easy Refried Beans, 36; Guacamolé, 38; Guacamolé Soup, 71; Marilyn's Salsa, 37; Mexican Corn Soup, 171; Pork Fajitas, 172; Zippy Gazpacho, 101
Soy-Ginger Sauce, 85
Spaghetti with Fresh Tuna-Caper Sauce, 139
Spanish Chicken, 140
Spinach-Orange Salad, 127
Spreads: Caponata Deluxe, 38; Chicken Liver Pâté, 33; Smoked Salmon, 68; Sun-Dried Tomato, 66
Squash, Southern Summer, 126
Sticky Biscuits, 25
Stock: Cheaty Chicken, 135; Easy Chicken, 142; Poaching (chicken), 73
Strawberries: and Cream, 216; with Black Pepper and Balsamic Vinegar, 107; Summer Strawberry Pie, 187
Strudel, Golden Peach, 121
Stuffing, Zesty Corn-Bread, 124
Succotash Salad, 118
Summer Potato Salad, 198
Summer Squash, Southern, 126
Summer Strawberry Pie, 187
Sun-Dried Tomato Spread on Zucchini Slices, 66
Sunday Supper Chicken and Rice, 210
Sweet Potatoes: French-Fried, 117; Spicy Sweet-Potato Petite Pancakes, 57

T
Tartar Sauce: 45; Bavarian, 53
Ted's Pesto Sauce, 197
Tenderloin, Chilled Peppered, 53
Three-Bean Salad, 232
Toasted Pecan Soufflé, 128
Tomato(es): Fresh Tomato Bisque, 76; Fresh Tomato French Dressing, 157; Fresh Tomato Sauce, 92, 110; Herbed, 86; peeling and seeding, 165; -Stuffed Avocado, 157; Sun-Dried Tomato Spread on Zucchini Slices, 66
Tostada Appetizers, Cheesy, 36
Tuna: -Caper Sauce, 139; Salad Niçoise with Fresh Tuna Filet, 77
Turkey Omelet, Mushroom and Smoked, 16

U
Ultimate Brownie, The, 160

V
Vegetable: Basket, 47; Kabobs, Grilled Herbed, 103; Melange, Skewered, 185; Soup, Spicy, 221
Vegetarian Black Bean Soup, 83

W
Walnut-Oatmeal Bread, 212
Watercress Dipping Sauce, 49
Wild mushrooms, preparing, 240
Wild Rice Mushroom Pilaf, 239